EDUCATIONAL TELEVISION IN INDIA

About the author

Dr. Shahid Rasool is Director, Educational Multimedia Research Centre (EMRC), University of Kashmir. He also Heads the Media Education Research Centre at the University. A former U.S. Fulbright fellow in Communication technology, he has done M.A. Ph.D in Mass Communication and Journalism from University of Kashmir and M.S in Communications, with specialization in Radio, Television and Film, from the Syracuse University, New York, U.S.A. Dr. Shahid has been involved in teaching of mass communication at postgraduate level, production of educational television films/documentaries and research in educational media for over two decades. He is also engaged in production of educational multimedia for the last 5 years. Besides production of over 300 educational television films, including four national level award winning films, over 30 e-contents/multimedia, over 100 Learning Objects for the Learning Object (LOR) of Consortium for Educational Communication, he has authored several research papers/articles published in reputed journals.

A member on several national and State level committees/boards Dr. Shahid has attended over 30 international/national seminars, workshops and conferences. He has been a member of various core groups, constituted by CEC-UGC, for drafting policy documents for use of information and communication technology for higher education.

A widely travelled person, Dr. Shahid is passionate about use of television and new technologies for taking quality education to the doorsteps of students, irrespective of their geographical location. He believes technology can be a great help in equalizing educational opportunities for all across the globe.

EDUCATIONAL TELEVISION IN INDIA

Present Scenario and Future Prospects

Dr. Shahid Rasool

CONCEPT PUBLISHING COMPANY PVT. LTD.
NEW DELHI-110059

ISBN-13 : 978-81-8069-827-9

First Published 2012

Published and Printed by

Concept
Since 1974

Concept Publishing Company Pvt. Ltd.
Regd. Office :
A/15-16, Commercial Block, Mohan Garden
New Delhi-110059 (India)
Phones : 25351460, 25351794, *Fax* : 091-11-25357109
Email : publishing@conceptpub.com,
Website: www.conceptpub.com

Editorial Office :
H-13, Bali Nagar, New Delhi-110 015, India.

Cataloging in Publication Data--*Courtesy:* D.K. Agencies (P) Ltd. <docinfo@dkagencies.com>

Rasool, Shahid.
Educational television in India : present scenario and future prospects/ Shahid Rasool.
p. cm.
Includes bibliographical references (p.) and index.
ISBN 9788180698279

1. Television in education—India. 2. Educational television programs—India. 3. Television in higher education—India—Kashmir, Vale of. 4. Educational television programs—India—Kashmir, Vale of. 5. Educational technology—India. I. Title.

DDC 371.33580954 23

Preface

As far back as 1964, famous Canadian social scientist and media commentator Marshall McLuhan, realizing the importance of television in education, wrote in his famous book, *Understanding Media* :

> "When the three-year old sits watching the President's press conference with Dad and Grandad, that illustrates the serious educational role of TV. If we ask what is the relation of TV to the learning process, the answer is surely that the TV image, by its stress on participation, participation dialogue, and depth, has brought to America new demand of crash programming in education. Whether there ever will be TV in every classroom is a small matter. The revolution has taken place at home."
>
> (p. 362)[1]

He carries on the argument and concludes :

> "Mere classroom use could not extend its influence. Of course, in the classroom its role compels a reshuffling of subjects, and approaches to subjects. Merely to put the present classroom on TV would be like putting movies on TV. The result would be a hybrid that is neither. The right approach is to ask, "what can TV do that the classroom cannot do for French or for physics?" The answer is: "TV can illustrate the interplay of process and the growth of forms of all kinds as nothing else can."
>
> (pp. 362-363)[2]

More than four decades after, television is yet to make to the classrooms in a significant manner. Though it has remarkably affected our daily lives outside the classroom and is considered as the most versatile,

---

1. McLuhan, Marshall. *Understanding Media: the extension of man.*(London: Routledges and Kegan Paul, 1964), p. 362.
2. McLuhan, *ibid.*, pp. 362-363.

influential and persuasive medium, its role in formal education is yet to gain the serious attention of broadcasters and the acceptance of the academia. Television continues to be used the world over, more as a source of endless entertainment and information than for education. The case is no different in India. Prior to cable and satellite channels, television in India was represented only by Doordarshan. Even today Doordarshan, because of its terrestrial broadcast mode, is having the highest viewership in the country. Though being the leading public broadcaster, Doordarshan could not show any significant contribution in making use of the medium for formal education. In a country like India, due to the lack of enough resources, education, especially the higher education, has remained the province of a very small percentage of the population.

Television, owing to its versatile characteristics, could have been effectively utilized for the purpose of taking quality education to the doorsteps of students across the country. But that has not happened despite the tremendous growth registered by television. While Doordarshan, like other private channels, due to commercialization, has put the educational programmes on the back burner, teachers, students, parents, planners, broadcasters and academics are yet to understand the importance of the medium as a source of education. The perceptions of the academics and students about television vary. A sizable section of the people still presumes television as a "frivolous" and "non-serious medium", too ineffective for teaching and learning. Yet a vast majority believes that television has the potential to make a significant contribution in education, provided it is taken seriously by the broadcasters, teachers and students.

This is what necessitated the need for a serious study of educational television in India. The aim is to analyse the present scenario of educational television in India, its growth and contribution to higher education. The study is also aimed at measuring the potential and listing the implication of using television, together with the new communication technologies, for higher education. The idea is also to take the advantage of the digital revolution and the convergence of information and communication technologies, to prepare a new paradigm of educational television in India. The new paradigm shall help in making the quality education available to all irrespective of their geographical location.

The seed of this book sprouted from my numerous discussions, on the subject, with Prof. Richard Breyer and Prof. Michal Epstein, during my year-long stay as a Fulbright fellow at Syracuse University, USA, in 1998-99. While Prof. Breyer wanted me to figure out how television can be taken to the classroom in the existing academic scenario, and become a partner in teaching and learning process, Prof. Michal Epstein wondered how educational television can stand on its own and compete with the commercial television. The idea moved further with the encouragement and advice that I received from a famous American social scientist Prof. George Comstock. I had the honour to attend a course, "Television and the Society" at Syracuse University, taught by Prof. Comstock, the author of many books on the subject including, *Television and the American Child*, and *Television and the Human Behaviour*. Prof Comstock infused in me the importance of looking at the issue from the perspective of existing research, taught me the fine art of locating and interpreting the original sources of research. He advised me to study the television as tool for education in a complex social, economic and political order. Again Prof. Patricia Longstaff, an authority on economic and social implications of new communication technologies in USA, under whom I had an opportunity to study the latest trends in new communication technologies, asked me to examine and analyse the implications of using new technologies in conjunction with television. Her guidance helped me to finalize the topic for this study. All the four professors allowed me to use their personal libraries and often passed on to me the relevant reading and reference material on the subject. I am overwhelmed to record my heartfelt thanks to them.

The present book, divided into seven chapters, is a humble attempt to study and analyse the growth and development of educational television in India particularly with reference to its contribution to higher education, with a special reference to the valley of Kashmir. The study also analyses the challenges it faces, lists the failures and successes and explores the implications of using television for higher education. The study further attempts to offer a new paradigm of educational television for better utilization. The study also makes an attempt to examine the present scenario of educational television in the valley of Kashmir.

Chapter one provides a detailed account of history and growth of television as a medium in general and educational television in particular. The chapter provides a global perspective and discusses in detail the educational television in India.

Chapter two examines the extensive research at national and international level regarding television in general and use of television for education in particular. The chapter provides a detailed account of the research conducted on use of television for higher education particularly on University Grants Commission's (UGC) Countrywide Classroom on Doordarshan.

Chapter three presents a detailed profile of University Grants Commission's Countrywide Classroom project, from one hour telecast on Doordarshan in 1984 to the establishment of a 24-hour higher educational channel Vyas and the launch of virtual classrooms throughout the country. The chapter also analyses the establishment, growth, role and functioning of Consortium for Educational Communication (CEC) and their experience and significance of using television and new technologies for higher education in India.

Chapter four is a detailed study of the perceptions of people about television as a medium of education and the potential of television for education in India. The chapter is based on in-depth interviews with academics and broadcasters and makes various suggestions about how television and new technologies, along with the teacher, can make teaching and learning an enriching experience for students at large.

Chapter five provides a new paradigm for educational television. The new paradigm is based on convergence of technologies that has made it possible for teachers and students, irrespective of their location, to come together on the same platform and share their knowledge, ideas and resources with each other. The chapter explains in detail how a multi-pronged strategy, using educational television, new communication technologies and virtual classroom operations, can help make quality education available to all across the country, anywhere, any time.

Chapter six is a detailed account of the television and educational television in the valley of Kashmir. The chapter presents the present scenario of using television for education in the valley, lists the contribution of Educational Multimedia Research Centre in the field of using television and new technologies for higher education, explores the possibilities for the growth of educational television and examines the implications of using new technologies for higher education in the valley of Kashmir.

Chapter seven is the synthesis of the entire study. It concludes the discussion, summarises the conclusions and makes recommendations for effective use of TV and new communication technology for higher education.

Today when I write these lines I cannot forget the support and encouragement that I received from various persons and institutions in completing this book. But for their help I may not have been able to produce this study. It may not be possible for me to thank each one of them, individually, as the list is quite long, but I deeply thank all of them collectively for their kind cooperation, support and encouragement.

I am indebted to my supervisor Prof. G. R. Malik, a friend, philosopher and guide for helping me in organizing my ideas into the Ph.D. thesis that became the basis for this book. His constant affectionate encouragement, scholarly insight and critical examination of the various thoughts helped me shape the thesis and the book. Without him I may not have been able to complete the study in the present form. Words fail me to express my thanks and gratitude to Prof. Malik.

I am also highly grateful to Prof. Abdul Wahid, the former Vice Chancellor of the University of Kashmir for his fatherly affection and encouragement throughout my career and also for sanctioning the leave that enabled me to concentrate more on the subject. My thanks are also due to the present Vice Chancellor of the university, Prof. Riyaz Punjabi, for permitting me to proceed on leave and also for his encouragement to complete the research and publish the findings.

I am thankful to all the respondents who gave their valuable time during the collection of data. Their ideas, perceptions and the concern for using television for education form the core of my research. They have been wonderfully cooperative and candid during the in-depth interviews. Theirs has been a whole hearted support, which I will always remember.

I am also indebted to hundreds of scholars and researchers whose solid research work helped me to understand the dynamics of educational television in a complex social order and formulate my ideas for this work.

Prof M. Aslam, the then Head Media Education Research Centre took the pains of going through the draft of this book and made valuable suggestions at the right time. I am thankful to him for being supportive in completion of this research work.

I take pride in expressing my deep gratitude to Prof. Biswasjit Das, Director Centre for Culture, Media and Governance, Jamia Millia Islamia, New Delhi and Prof. Jaishri Jethwaney, from Indian Institute of Mass Communication, New Delhi, who reviewed my Ph.D. thesis as experts. The valuable comments of both the Professors encouraged the publication of the present book. Prof. Biswasjit Das, in his report on the thesis, while recommending the publication of the research work at the earliest commented that, *"this thesis will be first of its kind after Helen Paris's work on educational television in India. The work of Helen Paris explored prior to television in India. The present work is an answer to that."* He further noted that :

> ".....The candidate is well-exposed to the literature pertaining to educational role of television both in India and abroad. Besides the candidate has shown the analytical ability to weave the argument in the literature and followed through the next chapter.
> Along with scholarly literature, the candidate has blended well the historical presence of Indian Educational Television. It has followed closely the trajectory and growth of Educational Television initiative in India by the University Grants Commission.........The candidate has collected data and presented them well without disrupting the flow of the narrative in the chapters. The candidate's use of quantitative data and its use is commendable; further the contents of the programme are well illustrated."

Prof. Jaishri Jethwaney in her report while congratulating the author for having *"undertaken this study and done a marvellous job"*, rated the study as, *"an outstanding work, that deserves to be published."* Prof. Jethwaney in her detailed report noted :

> "Mr. Rasool's background as a Fulbright scholar and an academic has stood him in good stead in articulating the thought process in the entire thesis. Some of his recommendations are very apt, especially the recommended synergy among the channels and the world of Academia".

The comments by Prof. Biswasjit and Prof. Jethwaney motivated me to work further on the topic, and that led to the publication of the book, so I thank them for their encouraging words.

I appreciate the valuable help rendered to me by all my colleagues at Educational Multimedia Research Centre and thank them for their constant encouragement during the study. In particular I am thankful to Farooq A. Lone, Shafqut Habib, Aijaz-ul-Haq, Tariq Abdullah, Abdul Rashid, Akhter Rasool, Feroz Ahmad, Gulzar and Gowhar Hafiz for doing whatever they could in the completion of this work.

My parents, my mother-in-law and my other family members were very supportive and highly cooperative throughout my career. Mir Aijaz Hasan, my cousin, provided valuable support. Dr. Salima, my wife, apart from being an unfailing source of love and inspiration, critically evaluated each thought presented in this book. Her scholarly comments helped me formulate the thesis. My two little cute sons, Imad and Aetimad, had to bear my long separation. I thank them all for their cooperation.

I am also thankful to Concept Publishing Co. Pvt. Ltd., New Delhi for publishing this work in the form of the book.

Last but not the least, I thank Allah, the Benevolent and the Merciful, for all He has given me. He alone is besought for help and on Him alone wc depend.

Srinagar **Dr. Shahid Rasool**
October, 2010

Contents

List of Abbreviations

AIR	-	All India Radio
ATS	-	Advanced Television Satellite
AVRC	-	Audio Visual Research Centre
BBC	-	British Broadcasting Corporation
CD	-	Compact Disc
CEC	-	Consortium for Educational Communication
CEMCA	-	Commonwealth Educational Media Centre for Asia
CIET	-	Central Institute of Educational Technology
CNN	-	Cable News Network
COL	-	Commonwealth of Learning
CPB	-	Corporation for Public Broadcasting
CWCR	-	Countrywide Classroom
DD	-	Doordarshan
DECU	-	Developmental Educational Communication Unit
DTH	-	Direct to Home
DVD	-	Digital Video Disc
EESeC	-	Educational Effectiveness Standards of e-Content
EMMRC	-	Educational Multimedia Research Centre
EMRC	-	Educational Media Research Centre
ETV	-	Educational Television
GNP	-	Grand National Product
GPRS	-	General Packet Radio Service
ICT	-	Information and Communication Technology
IGNOU	-	Indira Gandhi National Open University
INFONET	-	Information Network
INSAT	-	Indian National Satellite
ISRO	-	Indian Space Research Organization
IT	-	Information Technology

IIM	-	Indian Institute of Management
IIT	-	Indian Institute of Technology
ITV	-	Instructional Television
LAN	-	Local Area Network
LOD	-	Lecture on Demand
LOR	-	Learning Object Repository
MIT	-	Massachusetts Institute of Technology
MOU	-	Memorandum of Understanding
MPATI	-	Midwest Programme of Airborne Television Instruction
NAAC	-	National Assessment and Accreditation Council
NASA	-	National Aeronautics and Space Application
NCERT	-	National Council of Educational Research and Technology
NET	-	National Educational Television
PBS	-	Public Broadcast System
SAC	-	Space Application Center
SCORM	-	Shareable Content Object Reference Model
SIET	-	Satellite Instructional Educational Television
SIET	-	State Institute of Educational Technology
SIT	-	Satellite Interactive Terminal
SLO	-	Short Learning Object
STD	-	Subscribers Trunk Dial
TAM	-	Television Audience Measurement
TDCC	-	Training and Development Communication Channel
TV	-	Television
UGC	-	University Grants Commission
UNDP	-	United Nations Development Programme
UNESCO	-	United Nations Educational, Scientific and Cultural Organization
USA	-	United States of America
USSR	-	Union of Soviet Socialist Republic
VAT	-	Value Added Tax
VOD	-	Video on Demand
WAN	-	Wide Area Network

List of Figures and Maps

Chapter - 1

Introduction

Growth of Television and Educational Television – Historical Perspective, Present Scenario, Problems and Prospects

The Global Overview

With the invention of television by John Baird in 1924, erstwhile Union of Soviet Socialist Republics (USSR) became the pioneers in television. The first telecast in USSR was made in 1931 and by 1938 two full-fledged television stations were operational telecasting programmes on regular basis (UNESCO : 1964).[1] The British Broadcasting Corporation (BBC) started the first public telecast on November 2nd 1936. Since then television has established itself, the world over, as a potent medium of information, education and entertainment. The first public broadcast of television in the United States of America (USA) was made in 1939 and the commercial broadcasting on regular basis started in that country in 1948. Since then the television industry in USA has come a long way and has become one of the major popular industries after the automobile industry. As far back as 1959, James Kinder reported, in his book, *Audio Visual Materials : Television,* that "television has literally captured" the whole of USA. He continues the argument and writes that, "its expansion has been much more dramatic than that of radio or the automobiles. It has become an important part of our way of life, so much so that it is difficult to say whether it is a luxury or a necessity" (Kinder : 1959).[2] The educational television in America, however, started only in 1953 with a television station at Houston that was licensed to University of Houston and the Houston Public School. In 1954, the National Educational Television (NET) in USA began to provide thousands of recorded programmes for use of instructional television stations. The telecast of programmes was designed to improve the standards of classroom education. Kinder (1959)[3], reported that, the teachers in the schools of Philadelphia in USA were able to report excellent outcomes from viewing of educational television programmes by the students. After seeing a science series called "science is fun" most of the students were seen "collecting insects, building small radios, conducting various experiments" and also carrying out certain activities similar to the activities shown in the programme. Another programme series titled, "Everyone is an artist" was an instant hit with the students and resulted in the development of many art projects by the students in the classroom.

The need for educational television in USA stemmed up from the dearth of good laboratories, libraries, and most important acute shortage of good teachers. In the absence of these primary requisites for education it became imperative to search for new ideas of teaching and learning. This led to making use of television for equalizing the educational opportunities in a cost effective manner. Therefore, by 1960, Pennsylvania State University offered 14 courses in liberal arts, air sciences and education through Close-Circuit Television and the University of Detroit made use of Open-Circuit Television to offer 15 semester-hours of freshman courses. Owing to the success of open-circuit educational television, by 1966 about 111 open-circuit ETV stations were on the air in USA and 42 were in the process of being constructed. "Until 1967, non-commercial television was known as educational television. Most of the programmes were instructional and were criticized for being dull" (Dominick :1996)[4].

Realizing the need and importance of educational television, FCC in 1951 reserved 267 channels for non-commercial and educational use, but only around 50 of them were on the air even by 1960. By the year 2000 about 600 channels were reserved for this purpose but there were very few takers, as only 363 were being used. The educators were finding it difficult to operate educational television channels as the TV was too demanding in terms of the initial costs and exorbitant operational expenses. By 1963, the role of television in education changed considerably. It assumed a prominent place in the American educational life. In 1964, more than 90 non-profit educational television stations were on the air in the United States (Ford Foundation : 1965)[5]. Much of the credit for this goes to Ford Foundation which played a prominent role in the development of educational television in U.S.A and pumped in a lot of money to finance construction of TV stations, research, experimentation on educational television, production of programmes, and creation of infrastructure in schools enabling students and teachers to benefit from the educational programmes.

Realizing the need and importance of non-commercial and educational television the Carnegie Corporation of New York sponsored, what came to be known as "Carnegie Commission on Educational Television". The committee submitted its report in 1967[6]; the report among various other things, strongly recommended a strong corporation for the development of educational television, which will mobilize and distribute funds for the creation of facilities for the production and dissemination of quality educational programmes. The commission urged the government at "federal, state, and local level" to patronize the use of television for education and provide financial support to educational television stations.

Following Carnegie Commission report, the US Congress created "Corporation for Public Broadcasting" (CPB). The primary purpose of CPB was to help in the development of public broadcasting and mobilising the funds for the projects which are supportive of public broadcasting. Going a step further CPB on November 3, 1969 created its own broadcasting service "Public Broadcasting Service" (PBS) (Wikipedia : 2008)[7]. Since then PBS has grown into a strong educational television service, not network. Some of the landmarks of PBS over the years include creation of a wide variety of educational television programmes that have been produced and telecast. These include the wonderful programme created by "Children's Television Workshop" the "Sesame Street". The programme for children was created in 1969 and is still very popular. Notwithstanding the criticism of "Sesame Street", then that "it widened the knowledge gap between the advantageous and the disadvantageous", the programme helped children in general, especially the pre-nursery school children, to learn substantially various traits in "Geometric forms; functions of parts of body; understanding of role of community members; matching by forms; naming letters; letter sounds; sight readings; recognizing numbers; counting; relational terms; classification and sorting" (Ball and Bogatz : 1970)[8]. The other equally important programmes telecast by PBS were "The Civil War", "The West", "Civilizations", "Vietnam: A Television History", "Masterpiece Theater", "Great Performances", " The Ascent of Man", "Nova" and a wide array of programmes on geography, nature, science, performing arts, besides children's programmes and news and information programmes like " The news hour with Jim Lehrer" (Engelman : 1996)[9].

Though PBS is not a network, but a programming service, it is interconnected with a number of stations all-over USA. This is done to pool the resources which are otherwise limited as compared to commercial networks. A major difference between PBS and other commercial networks is that while the commercial networks pay compensation to affiliates in various markets for carrying the network programmes, the PBS receives payments from the local stations for providing them the programmes. This helps PBS to defray some of the production costs and strengthen the service. PBS and the associated stations depend for funds on Federal, State, and Local governments, Foundations, Pledges, Auctions, Merchandising, Donations, and Under-Writings. The PBS stations are mostly owned by communities, universities or other educational institutions, local authorities, and several state agencies. Some of the key PBS stations include WGBH-Boston, WNET-New York, WETA-Washington, and KCET-Hollywood. Despite challenges from the popular commercial television networks and shortage of resources PBS is still growing stronger with every passing day. Today, "PBS is a media enterprise that serves 355 public non-commercial television stations and reaches nearly 73 million people each week through on-air and online content. Bringing diverse viewpoints to television and the internet, PBS provides high-quality documentary and dramatic entertainment, and consistently dominates the most prestigious award competitions. PBS is a leading provider of digital learning content for pre K-12 educators, and offers a broad array of other educational services. PBS 'premier kids' TV programming and website, PBS KIDS Online, continues to be parents' and teachers' most trusted learning environment for children" (PBS Website)[10].

A report from PBS in 1998 revealed a strong financial position of the service. The report showed "an increase of 23% at the end of the fiscal year 1998; crossing over the estimated target of $224 million by about $23 million." The sound financial base, which is akin to any successful programme, is attributed to the growth of PBS "Business Channel", PBS "Adult Learning Service and PBS "Home Videos."(Rasool : 2002)[11].

Additionally "Discovery" and "National Geographic" with mind-boggling programmes on nature, environment, animal kingdom, insect world, Science and technology, etc; "Disney" and "Nickelodeon" with excellent children's programming have added a variety and respectability to educational television in USA and all-over the world.

The success stories of educational television are not limited to the USA alone. Many countries around the world have been making use of television in training and teaching the students, at national level much more innovatively, quickly, economically and efficiently. Japan, for example, is the most advanced country where every school and educational institution is automatically linked and equipped with television receivers. As far back as 1965, Japan organized the first ever annual international educational television festival (Moir : 1967)[12]. The Japanese television is controlled by the government and educational television is a part of the national television system called NHK. The 70 per cent schedule of NHK is devoted to educational programming including both formal and informal education. By 1964; Japan's publicly owned educational television service had already covered around 42 per cent of the population. Around 100 relay stations, by 1967, were interconnected with key broadcast stations to provide the most complete educational television coverage in the world.

In most of the European countries, in sixties, educational television was extensively developed. But the density of television sets and number of hours for telecast of educational programmes were far less as compared to other western and developed countries like Canada, Australia and the United States. In France, during the same period, only sixty hours of telecast time per week was done and even Britain allowed the networks only 50 hours of telecast per week. But despite this more than 80 per cent of the population in the United Kingdom watched ETV programmes for about 9 hours per week. It is encouraging to note in some countries like Denmark, Italy, Germany, France and the United Kingdom, school television is being developed on the modern lines and made an integral part of teaching and training.

While Europe and the western countries were taking advantage of television for education, many developing and underdeveloped countries, due to lack of enough resources were not able to show much progress. As late as 1950, many countries in Africa, South America, Asia and Oceania had no television receivers at all. Masterman (1980)[13] reported that until 1962 the entire African continent remained almost untouched by television, with Morocco being the only exception where regular broadcast service began in 1956. Many countries in Asia, Africa and Oceana areas, which had the technology, were not able to meet the production cost of programmes, nor were they able to import quality programmes from other countries. As a result television, particularly Educational Television, was not able to register a positive impression on the audience and was not taken very seriously. In Asia apart from Japan, Lebanon was the only country with more than one television receiver per 100 persons. In China, the television sets were located at public meeting places and workers clubs and in Korea government installed 40,000 sets for community viewing. In some countries including, Iraq, Iran, Thailand, Philippines, Syria, Saudi Arabia, Singapore, etc. educational television programmes were being telecast for only a few hours a day. In Cambodia and Kuwait, it was used only on an experimental basis. But still there were some developing countries which made efforts to make use of television in much creative and imaginative way. The broadcasting corporation in Nigeria, for example, telecast three hours of quality educational programming, on a daily basis, to all the schools; which were an instant hit and very popular with the general public also.

Wittich and Schuller (1968)[14] reported in their book, *Audio-Visual Material : Their Nature and Use*, a unique educational television experiment conducted on the remote Islands of American Samoa, some 2300 miles south-west of Hawaii. A television studio and open broadcast facility, worth US $ 200,000, was constructed in Samoa Island. Educational Television programmes, aimed to cover the entire core of syllabi, rather than to supplement the classroom teaching, were produced with the help of American teachers who worked closely with the Samoan teachers. The programmes produced were telecast to all the schools in Samoa, for three hours a day. At school level the Samoan teachers guided the students for theory and practical work. They also steered students to find out what to watch and how to follow it up after the telecast was over. This was a unique and well coordinated effort by American and Samoan teachers to make the best use of television for education.

George Gordon (1970)[15] reported another exciting television experiment, Midwest Programme of Airborne Television Instruction (MPATI) in his book, *Classroom Television: New Frontiers in ITV*. MPATI experiment, funded by Ford Foundation and Private Industry began in 1959. A team of quality teachers, technical experts and production staff was put together to produce high quality educational television lessons, that were recorded on video tapes. The recorded video tapes were played from playback machines, and transmitter fitted aboard an aircraft flying at a very high altitude, and simultaneously covering an area of 78,000 square miles in the seven states adjacent to Purdue, benefiting over 6,000,000 students and 250,000 teachers. The MPATI experiment was so successful that only after one year it had become self-sufficient. Over 2000 schools participated in the programme, paying an enrolment fee of $2 per student per year. The MPATI also leased its educational video programmes to a number of broadcast stations and networks in USA.

There are numerous other examples all-over the world that have demonstrated the capability of television in the field of education at school and university level. Nonetheless educational television the world over is dominated by entertainment and mainstream television due to their more popular appeal and the ability to generate revenue with increasing commercialization.

Television in India

People in India saw television for the first time in the International Industries Fair in Delhi in 1955. At the conclusion of the fair All India Radio purchased the television equipment, on concessional rates, from Philips Company. With UNESCO providing some 70 television sets, the first experimental television service in India began on 15th September, 1959 in Delhi. Initially 66 teleclubs were set up for community viewing, some of them located in schools. Taking the advantage of teleclubs located in schools, AIR in January 1960, together with the Education Department of Delhi Administration, started the telecast of a weekly series of specially designed programmes for ninth class students. By the end of 1960 India, with assistance from Ford Foundation, procured the necessary television equipments for strengthening the television service in Delhi. This led to the launch of "Delhi School Television Project", for Delhi Schools in 1961. 360 television sets were installed in 150 schools in Delhi, benefiting around 20,000 students of secondary classes. By 1965, Delhi Doordarshan started its general service, the number of teleclubs by now had grown to 182 and the number of schools provided with TV sets to 255. The number of telecast hours also rose from 6 hours 20 minutes per week in 1961 to 17 hours 40 minutes in 1965. A special programme service for farmers and agricultural workers, KRISHIDARSHAN, was launched in 1966. The programme was designed to promote rural development and give a boost to agriculture, by introducing new and scientific methods of farming as also to impart social and adult education.

The second television station in India was established at Bombay in 1972. The Bombay station went on air on Gandhi Jayanti — 2nd October, 1972, with a documentary titled, "Gandhiji in Bombay". A year after its establishment, in 1973, the Bombay station also started transmission of educational television programmes in English and Science (Behra : 1991)[16]. A few months from the launch of Bombay TV station, the third station was also launched on 26th January, 1973, at Srinagar in the Kashmir valley. Doordarshan Srinagar also transmitted two weekly educational programmes on general science for the primary schools and one weekly enrichment type programme for the university students. Under community viewing scheme, 218 schools in and around Srinagar city were provided with television sets (Raina : 1997)[17]. This followed the launch of television station in Amritsar in September 1973; television relay station in Pune in October 1973; television stations at Calcutta, Madras and Lucknow in 1975. Though the growth and expansion of television stations in India, owing to lack of enough resources, was quite slow, but all the seven stations, launched between 1959 to 1975, televised educational programmes benefiting students in the urban schools where television sets were provided by the government.

Television broadcasting got a fillip in India after the country started the launching spree of broadcast satellites in the early 1980s. The launch of INSAT-1(A) made it possible to link all the Doordarshan stations in a national network and allowed people to get direct reception from satellite through specially designed antenna. This paved the way for the national telecast of programmes from Delhi Doordarshan from 15th August, 1982. The day also marked the beginning of colour television transmission. Though INSAT-1(A) did not last even for a month and developed snags only after 15 days of its launch and was abandoned in the first week of September 1982, it was followed by the launch of INSAT-1(B), almost a year later and with this India started launching of a series of geostationary satellites most of which are used for beaming radio, telephone, television signals besides monitoring weather forecasting and other meteorological observations. The satellites have also made remote sensing of earth possible for environment, geographical, geological and geophysical studies.

Prior to the launch of communication satellites, which connected various *Kendras* of Doordarshan across the country, educational programmes of varying nature and duration, were telecast from various stations of Doordarshan in an unorganized manner. The launch of satellites facilitated the telecast of educational programmes at national level or at least over a vast area for the benefit of a sizable chunk of population. Soon after the launch of INSAT-1(A) in 1982, INSAT educational television service was started for elementary schools of

Orissa and Andhra Pradesh. Two programmes of 20 minutes duration each, were telecast each day, for five day a week – from Monday through Friday, for two groups of students ageing 5-8 and 9-11 years. (Mohanty : 1984)[18]. On Saturdays a special 45-minute duration, programme was telecast for the elementary school teachers. The programmes were specially produced by Doordarshan in collaboration with Central Institute of Educational Technology (CIET) of National Council of Educational Research and Technology (NCERT). The programmes were telecast from Sambalpur and Hyderabad stations of Doordarshan and continued for over a year up to October 1983. The ETV programmes telecast with the help of INSAT-1(B) were received with a great success and brought about a marked change in the educational scenario of the area. This also left a good impact, in terms of qualitative and quantitative improvement, on the overall development of education.

For effective use of INSAT for education a study group was constituted by the Ministry of Education and Culture. The group for INSAT television utilization for education and development in its report (1981)[19] opined that :

> "the main thrust of the programme, to widen and enrich the child's horizons, could best be achieved through bringing about in him an awareness of the country as it is today, with emphasis on development and change taking place and also by making him understand the history and culture of the country at large and of his own immediate environment. Therefore, history and culture and modern India should also be included among the identified themes." (p. 157)

The group also recommended that the demonstrative quality, television should be exploited in imparting vocational training or developing and broadcasting television programmes for transferring different kinds of instructional skills relevant to the children in the rural areas. But despite over 2 decades of transmission of ETV programmes in the country, demonstrative capability of the television is yet to be tapped in a serious manner.

Television has now been around, in India, for about 5 decades. Today Doordarshan, the national television of India, is one of the largest terrestrial networks in the world and DD-1 operates through a network of 1,042 terrestrial transmitters of varying powers reaching over 87 per cent of the population. There are 65 additional transmitters giving terrestrial support to other channels of Doordarshan. Doordarshan uses a large number of transponders on the Indian National Satellites (INSAT) and other satellites to network its terrestrial transmitters and also to extend coverage. For production of programmes, Doordarshan has established production facilities with latest broadcast quality equipment in 49 cities across the country. Doordarshan's DD-2 Metro Entertainment Channel, is now available terrestrially in 62 cities. In other parts of the country, the programmes of this channel could be received through dish antennas or through cable operators. Doordarshan also has 11 regional language satellite channels. The programmes on these channels include the regional service, which is available terrestrially for an average of five hours daily in the concerned State and additionally round-the-clock on the satellite mode. Doordarshan also operates DD-News, telecasting news and news-based programmes round the clock, and DD-Sports, the only, free-to-air channel available in India devoted exclusively to sports programmes. DD Bharti an international channel of Doordarshan serves as a window on India for the outside world. Over the years Doordarshan's coverage increased phenomenally also increasing its viewership but now the DD channels are facing a stiff competition in viewership from private cable and satellite channels.

Since 1959, Indian television has come a long way and is today considered the most influential and potent medium of information and entertainment; though the educational potential of television is yet to be fully exploited. Usha Rani (2006) categorized the history of Indian Television in five distinct stages :

> "The stage First, from 1959 to 1975, covers the introduction, growth and development of television in the initial years.
>
> The second stage covers Satellite Instructional Television Experiment (SITE), considered the world's biggest ever Indian experiment with television.

> The third stage describes TV as a political weapon of the government during emergency; as a result of which the advantage of SITE could not be capitalized and policies for making use of television for education and development could not be formulated.
> The fourth stage, termed as Video Revolution hovers around nineteen eighties, when India moved from black and white to colour, cable and newer technologies, like video cassette recorders/players, arrived and live telecast of Asian games was done from Delhi with great success.
> The fifth stage, from 1991 onwards, includes the war from skies and the onslaught of satellite channels. While the live coverage of gulf war by CNN led to a revolution in broadcast journalism, the launch of Star TV in 1991 resulted in the spread of satellite television in Indian cities and towns. This stage also saw the spread of cable in cities, towns and even rural areas adjoining the suburbs."
> (Rani : 2006, pp. 2-11)[20]

Television today occupies the central space in every family and television programmes are talked about in every social gathering. Television, therefore, is the most wonderful and most powerful medium available today and can be effectively used for the purpose of education and information. Unfortunately, its potential as a medium of education and social uplift has not yet been fully tapped, as television is still considered as a medium for entertainment and to some extent as a source of information.

In rural India, where over eighty per cent of the population lives, good teachers, good libraries, laboratories and other basic requirements for schools and colleges are hard to imagine. The students of these areas are at a disadvantage as compared to their contemporaries in the cities. The students from remote, rural and border districts of India only can realize and experience what it means to study in a village, where even basic tools like blackboards and chalks are not available at times. The result is that a very small percentage of rural population is able to get proper education and majority of them drop out of the schools and those who reach colleges find it hard to compete with students from urban areas. Since television penetration in rural India now is quite satisfactory, it is possible to make use of the "idiot box" in taking quality education to the doorsteps of poor and needy in remote parts of India.

Television in India which till recently was completely under the direct control of government as DOORDARSHAN with multiple channels at the national level and some local channels in all the major States, has slightly grown out of the government shadow under Prasar Bharti. The stations are connected with the national network through satellite or microwave links. The national network through local stations and low power transmitters caters to "over 65% of the Indian landmass and over 87% of the Indian Population." (Rani : 2006)[21] During the past one decade, especially for the last five years, private satellite channels and cable networks have mushroomed in the urban areas reducing the viewership of Doordarshan in urban areas considerably. However, in rural areas, thanks to the non-availability of cable and still higher costs of DTH services, Doordarshan enjoys an almost absolute viewership. The cable channels have mushroomed in every city and scores of private Satellite TV channels have been launched. Thanks to the growth of Direct to Home (DTH) television many satellite foreign TV channels are also available to the audience across India. Despite invasion of cable and private satellite channels Doordarshan has retained more than 50 per cent of the viewership in urban areas and more than 90 per cent of the viewership in the rural areas in most of the States. (website indianetzone)[22]

According to the "Ministry of Information and Broadcasting", in 1995 India had 40 million television households and 250 million television viewers. The position has changed dramatically since then. In 2003, the television ownership had grown to 86 million of the 202 million homes, i.e., 42 per cent set penetration. In urban areas the set penetration was shown at 75 per cent and in rural areas it is 30 per cent (Phadnis : 2008)[23]. There has been a significant growth in set penetration during the last 5 years and the penetration in rural area can safely be estimated at 60% households. The government has also provided sets for community viewing in some villages, though most of these sets, by now are either out of order or remain underutilized due to non-availability of electricity. Doordarshan in 2007 reported that 375 million people can watch Doordarshan programmes in their homes. Besides people watch programmes on community television sets, offices and other public places. As per the report an estimated 500 million people watch DD programmes at least once a week (Indianetzone)[24].

Despite tremendous growth of television, both in government and private sector, the educational television in India could not show a significant growth and even today is somewhat unorganized and lacks the appropriate punch and appeal. This in spite of the fact that the history of educational television in India dates back to the very inception of television in India. Television was introduced in India as a medium of education and in the beginning hardcore educational programmes were telecast for the students in various schools of Delhi. In 1966, Doordarshan Delhi started an agriculture based programme, KRISHI DARSHAN, to promote agriculture and rural development by introducing new and scientific methods of farming, besides imparting social and adult education. These programmes were later extended to other stations of Doordarshan at Srinagar, Bombay, Jullander, Lucknow, Madras, etc. In 1973, a year after its establishment in October 1972, Bambay Doordarshan also started telecast of two programmes of 20 minutes duration each per week in English and Science. Srinagar station of Doordarshan followed by telecasting programmes for primary level students and the university students. A host of new programmes for children, women and adults were also introduced by each station. Special children's programmes were launched and continued for decades; some of them still continuing with little or no change in format and presentation. Some stations even started telecast of special educational programmes on science and mathematics for various age groups ranging from 2nd to 8th class. The programmes were devoid of any professional touch and lacked imaginative treatment. Besides, the telecast of such programmes always clashed with school timings and most of the schools had either no television sets or no electricity. Then there where some schools which had no space for viewing of these programmes. At places the television sets were either dumped in the stores or shifted by the teachers to their respective residence. The result was that the programmes did not serve any worthwhile purpose and were not even noticed.

With sporadic educational telecasts, without proper planning and very little or no serious effort by the programme producers, Doordarshan gradually drifted from its educational and social agenda to more lucrative entertainment programming. This relegated the telecast of educational programmes to inconvenient time slots.

A dedicated effort for educational television programming by Doordarshan remained a far cry. The first ever serious attempt towards educational television in India was taken up in 1975, by what came to be known as SITE (Satellite Instructional Television Experiment). The SITE experiment, regarded as the largest ever experiment in the field of mass communication using satellite television, was carried out from 1st August, 1975 to 31st July, 1976, with the help of NASA's Satellite ATS-6. The basic idea and the objectives behind SITE, as reported by Chander and Karnik (1976, p. 51)[25] were :

1. to gain experience in the development, testing and management of satellite based instructional television system particularly in rural areas and to determine optimal system parameters;
2. to demonstrate the potential value of satellite technology in the rapid development of effective mass communication in developing countries;
3. to demonstrate the potential value of satellite television broadcasts in the practical instruction for village inhabitants;
4. to stimulate national development in India, with important managerial, economic, technological and social implications.

To meet the above objectives and make the best use of the experiment for rural development and education, experts from various fields including education, media, agriculture, health, social science and communication were brought together to prepare a proper blueprint. The necessary equipment including Direct Reception Systems were set up in six States and television sets were installed for community viewing at various schools and village community centres. While selecting the clusters care was taken to include people from different, social, cultural, linguistic, and agricultural backgrounds.

This experiment was conducted in 2,330 villages, for one year, in six different States including Rajasthan, Karnataka, Madhya Pradesh, Bihar, Orissa and Andhra Pradesh. The selected villages prior to this experiment had no access to television. Specially designed programmes on health and hygiene, nutrition, agricultural practices, national integration, primary education, etc., were made and telecast in four different languages spoken in these States. For the programmes production three centres were set up at Delhi, Hyderabad and Cuttack which produced the majority of programmes. The science programmes, however, were produced by the Developmental Educational Communication Unit (DECU) at Space Application Centre (SAC), Ahmedabad. The viewers saw these programmes on community television sets on selected locations. (Aggarwal : 1981)[26]

The television programmes telecast during SITE were separately designed for the rural community in general and the students in particular. The programmes for the rural community covered areas like agriculture, health, hygiene, nutrition and family planning. Keeping in view the dearth of good teachers, lack of infrastructural facilities in the schools and a very high dropout rate in rural areas, special instructional programmes for children, in the age group of 5-12, were telecast in the morning. Special instructional programmes were also designed and telecast for in-service teachers for the teaching of science and to help them upgrade their skills to adopt new techniques of teaching. The idea was to supplement the classroom teaching and "to make the process of imparting education innovative, interesting, creative, purposeful and stimulating so as to improve the overall quality and reduce the incidence of wastage and stagnation". (Chander and Karnik : 1976)[27]

With SITE India became the first country, at least in the 'Third World', to have launched such a mega satellite instructional television experiment. Though the objectives set for the experiment mostly remained unaccomplished, the SITE provided an opportunity for Indian scientists to make serious efforts in making use of satellites for television broadcasting. The Indian scientists and engineers got an opportunity to work in close cooperation with NASA and gain the basic knowledge and skills in fine tuning the technology and practices to cater to the requirements of satellite broadcasting. At the same time programme planners and producers got a first hand experience to produce programmes specially designed to cater to the specific and general needs of audiences located in various linguistically, geographically, culturally, socially and economically heterogeneous backgrounds. The experiment also provided an opportunity to the social scientists to closely monitor and critically analyze the strengths and weaknesses of television as a tool for social and educational development.

The problems encountered during SITE were mostly at the receiving end. Either the sets were not properly maintained and functioning, owing to lack of power supply, low voltage, malfunctioning of battery or reluctance of the custodian to switch on the set on time or the lack of proper pre - and post-telecast discussions due to incompetence of the person monitoring the telecast at the receiving end. The lack of enough space for viewing at various places also made community viewing difficult. The students, due to various reasons, at many places also could not see most of the programmes meant for them (Doshi : 1986).[28] SITE on the whole was a wonderful and useful experiment which left a remarkably notable impact on the viewers. This also triggered a need for educational television programming in an organized manner for the overall development of the nation and benefit of the students particularly in rural areas, who face dearth of good teachers, classrooms, teaching aids, laboratories and libraries.

One of the major outcomes of the SITE was the launch of Kheda Communication Project. The project was launched in collaboration with milk cooperative, rural bank, health, education and other departments of Gujarat government. With the financial support of UNDP, a TV transmitter was installed at PIG village in Kheda district in Gujarat State. The low power transmitter was linked to a television studio and an earth station at Space Application Centre, Ahmedabad. Around 650 television sets were installed in various schools and village community centres, covering 400 villages in a radius of 35 kilometres. SAC Ahmedabad produced programmes, mostly in local language involving the local people, on agriculture, animal husbandry, poultry, rural development, sanitation, population control, health and hygiene, etc. The project was an instant success as the programmes telecast covered the problems faced by the people in their day-to-day life. Agrawal and Malik (1986)[29] concluded, "that TV programmes on agriculture, animal husbandry and poultry raised the viewers level of awareness, created a desire to do new things, and made them conscious of the availability of infrastructure, which they could use for their development." They also reported that, "health programmes achieved their objective as they could generate discussion among the viewers and also gave them the long and much needed information on subjects that they wanted to know." (Agrawal *et al.* : 1986)[30]

The Kheda project, which was successfully run for 10 years, demonstrated that television can be effectively used for developmental and educational communication. Supporting the above argument Usha Rani remarks that :

> "the establishment of Kheda station was a milestone in the history of Indian broadcasting, as it was the first full-fledged rural television station devoted exclusively for development and education." (Rani 2006, p. 22)[31]

The above experiments, SITE and Kheda, created a realization in India that television can be effectively used for the purpose of school and college education at national level. So with the rapid expansion of Doordarshan in early nineteen eighties, in terms of number of stations, transmitters, channels, hours of telecast, etc. education got another opportunity to get on the national flagship of Doordarshan. This was also primarily necessitated by the increasing demand for television programmes rather than, probably, the concern for educational television.

Taking a cue from SITE and Kheda experiments, and realizing the potential of television in dissemination of education, the University Grants Commission (UGC) of India in 1984 started what was known as "Countrywide Classroom"(CWCR) on Doordarshan National Network for undergraduate and post-graduate students across the country. For the production of educat ional television programmes, the University Grants Commission established "Media Centres" in various universities. Equipped with broadcast quality equipment and professional manpower these centres came to be known as Audio Visual Research Centres (AVRC) and Educational Media Research Centres (EMRC); conveniently called "Media Centres". By 1995, the number of these media centres rose to 17 and all of them were established in universities and educational institutions in 14 States. Today these centres are called Educational Multimedia Research Centres (EMMRC) and are located at University of Kashmir, Srinagar; Punjabi University, Patiala; Jamia Millia Islamia, New Delhi; J.N.V University, Jodhpur; Devi Ahilya Vishwa Vidyalaya, Indore; Gujarat University, Ahmedabad; Harisingh Gour Vishwa Vidyalaya, Sagar; University of Poona, Pune; Osmania Univerity, Hyderabad; English and Foreign Languages University, Hyderabad; University of Mysore, Mysore; Anna University, Chennai; Madurai Kamraj University, Madurai; University of Calicut, Calicut; St. Xaviers College, Kolkata; University of Manipur, Manipur; and Indian Institute of Technology, Roorkee.

One of the reasons, these production centres were located in the universities was to help them make the best use of the expertise of academics and scientists working in these institutes. The university teachers were involved in the production of programmes as subject experts and script writers. The programmes produced by the UGC media centres were telecast on Doordarshan. Initially, from August 1984 to January 1993, the programmes were telecast on DD1, six days a week between 13:00 hours to 14:00 hours with a repeat telecast at 16:00 to 17:00. The repeat telecast was made to enable the students watch programmes as per their convenience. Since 1994, the timings were repeatedly changed by the DD1 to accommodate commercially viable programmes. In 2008, the UGC programmes were telecast on DD1 between 05:30 hours to 06:00 hours five days a week and today in 2010 the programme slot has been completely withdrawn. Though some of the UGC ETV programmes are also shown on DD Bharti. With the launch of many local and regional channels by Doordarshan, some of the UGC centres, notably EMMRC Mysore, EMMRC Calcutta, EMMRC Pune and EMMRC Hyderabad started telecast of UGC programmes in regional languages. The UGC ETV programmes are now also shown in 4-hour time slots on GYANDARSHAN, a satellite channel of IGNOU, launched on 26th January, 2000, besides VYAS— the dedicated higher educational satellite television channel of UGC launched on 26th January, 2004.

It is an irony that the public broadcast system in India does not have any worthwhile time slot available for much needed educational programmes. The disinterest shown by DD towards educational programmes is rooted in growing commercialization of Doordarshan and the apathy of the authorities who refuse to see beyond the iron curtains of commercial television. Otherwise Doordarshan that covered "77.5% the land area and access to 87.6% population of India" (Rani : 2006)[32] in 2002 could have helped take education to people in remote areas of the country. During the financial year 2005-2006, it was reported to the Parliament that Doordarshan earned Rs. 946.96 crores through commercial advertisements. (outlookindia.com)[33]

For better co-ordination among the media centres and to take the educational television to newer heights UGC constituted the Consortium for Educational Communication (CEC). The role of CEC was to collect programmes from centres, conduct proper preview and technical check, make programme capsules of one hour or of a duration suiting the requirements of transmission, and send the programmes to Doordarshan for telecast at national network. The CEC also maintained a video tape library of the programmes produced by the media centres, by now the number of these programmes has crossed 17,000, with around 1,000 fresh programmes added every year. The CWCR programmes, till recently were more of enrichment type programmes, and not necessarily, based on syllabi. The programmes were meant to "broaden the mental horizons of students, whet their appetite to know more, and stimulate them." For the last few years the centres are concentrating more on lecture and discussion type programmes based on UGC model syllabi for the undergraduate students. Initially, the programmes were mostly produced in English language but of late programmes are made in Hindi and some regional languages also.

Various viewership surveys conducted by the media centres showed these programmes were being watched by a sizable population of students and teachers besides a very high percentage of housewives and retired persons and elderly. National Viewership Survey conducted by ADMAR services (P) Ltd., New Delhi in 1993 and 1997 also showed very encouraging results. As per the reports the overall viewership of UGC countrywide classroom in 1993 was 21.29 million with about 4 million captive viewers on an average day and around 2 million dedicated viewers, who were watching UGC programmes over 4 days a week (ADMAR : 1993)[34]. The report produced by ADMAR in 1997 showed viewership of countrywide classroom as stagnant at 12% of the total but with increase in the viewership base from 21.29 million to 22 million (ADMAR : 1997)[35]. Another survey done by "Center for Media Studies, New Delhi", a decade and a half back, reported that the CWCR enjoy a viewership of 12 million (Mishra : 1997)[36]. "At the peak of its popularity UGC countrywide classroom on Doordarshan enjoyed a viewership of 20 million people with a daily viewership of 4 million" (Rani 2006)[37]. It may be noted, however, that in a country of one billion people, this constitutes a very small percentage. Nonetheless by today's viewership standards, when each channel has a very small percentage of viewership owing to fragmentation, 20 million is not a small percentage in terms of commercial viability.

Alongside the UGC countrywide classroom in 1984 the National Council for Educational Research and Training (NCERT), with the establishment of Central Institute of Educational Technology (CIET) at New Delhi and State Institute of Educational Technology (SIET) in six States also launched broadcast of school education programmes on Doordarshan. The programmes produced by CIET, involving subject experts, faculty members, and teachers catering to the age group of 5-8 years and 9-11 years, were telecast at national network of Doordarshan at 0545 hours to 0600 hours, 7 days a week and 1000 hours to 1100 hours 5 days, Monday through Friday, a week. The programmes are now also shown in various time slots on GYANDARSHAN of IGNOU on regular basis. Besides VHS copies of the programmes are also made available to the students and teachers

Recognizing the importance of ETV in distance education, Indira Gandhi National Open University (IGNOU), with an enrolment of over 75,000 students across the country, in 1993 started producing educational television programmes for distance learners. The enrolment of IGNOU had grown to 3,16,574 students in various subjects across the country in 2003 (IGNOU : 2003)[38]. Finding the educational television programmes very effective for the distance learners, in 1995 IGNOU established a full-fledged studio, Electronic Media Production Centre (EMPC), at the *Sanchar Kendra* at the IGNOU campus. Born out of a collaboration of JICA Japan, EMPC is among the best facilities available in any university in the world. EMPC is also the centre from which Gyandarshan educational television channel of India is telecast.

EMPC was equipped with a huge infrastructure, a full-fledged television studio and state of art broadcast quality television/video production equipment, with financial support from Japan. The centre also made appointments of 'quality professional manpower' with experience in production of television programmes and immediately started production of ETV programmes involving faculty members from various IGNOU departments and academics from other institutions. The programmes were aimed at thousands of UG/PG students enrolled by IGNOU across the country besides targeting students of secondary and higher secondary classes. For dissemination of ETV programmes and interaction with the students across the country, IGNOU in 1995 also launched Training & Development Communication Channel (TDCC), a satellite based interactive training television channel. Students enrolled at various IGNOU regional/study centres would watch the ETV programmes and interact with the experts in the EMPC studio through telephone lines.

On January 26, 2000, IGNOU created history in educational television by launching a dedicated satellite based national educational channel GYANDARSHAN. Gyandarshan was launched using INSAT-2B with uplink facility at the Indira Gandhi National Open University (IGNOU) campus at New Delhi. The transmission was later shifted to INSAT-3C on C-Band. Termed as 'India's first truly educational channel' Gyandarshan was jointly launched by the

Ministry of Human Resources Development, Government of India and *Prasar Bharti* with IGNOU as the nodal agency. Starting with four hours of telecast, from 1700 hours to 2100 hours seven days a week, in January 2000, the channel gradually became a 24 hours educational television channel by November 2000. The free to air satellite channel is available to the students across the country through cable operators or is directly received by various institutions/homes through small dish antennas costing around Rs.4,000. Through cable Gyandarshan has potential access to "415 million viewers in 52 million cable homes in India" (Rani : 2006).[39] The ETV programmes produced by various agencies including Consortium of Educational Communication (CEC), New Delhi; UGC Media Centres, Educational Multimedia Research Centres (EMMRCs), located in various universities; National Council for Educational Research and Training (NCERT), New Delhi; Central Institute of Educational Technology (CIET), New Delhi and State Institutes of Educational Technology (SIET) located in various States. Gyandarshan in January 2003 became digital and this led to the launch of number of channels catering to the specialized needs of students from various categories.

While Gyandarshan primary channel, GD-1, retained its centrality and telecasts a mix of quality education programmes for various categories of students, pre-school kids, primary/secondary school children, college/university students, youth seeking career opportunities, housewives, adults and others, many specialized channels in Gyandarshan bouquet, catering to the specific needs of students in various categories, were launched in the last 6 years. Gyandarshan-2 (GD-2) is an interactive channel meant for distance education students enrolled with IGNOU. The viewers can directly access the experts in the studio across the country, during an ongoing programme, on a toll free number, express their views and get their doubts cleared. The feature of inbuilt interactivity has made educational television more interesting and useful.

On 26th January, 2003, Gyandarshan-3 (GD-3), a technology channel EKLAVYA, was launched in association with the Department of Technical Education of the Ministry for Human Resource Development and Indian Institutes of Technology (IITs) with IIT

Delhi as the nodal agency. Dedicated to technical education, EKLAVYA telecasts programmes produced by various IITs. The aim is to take technical education to thousands of engineering students in various engineering colleges of the country making the best use of the expertise and resources available at various IITs. On weekdays, the channel carries hardcore syllabus based television programmes, most of them in video lecture format, and on Sundays special interest programmes in science and technology are telecast. A good number of quality ETV programmes on technical subjects, imported from various production agencies across the globe are also telecast on EKLAVYA besides GD-1. This offers viewers, particularly students, a much needed window to the world and helps them know what is happening in the field of science and technology across the globe.

Gyandarshan-4 (GD-4) called VYAS–the higher educational channel of UGC was launched on January 26, 2004. The 24 channel, managed, coordinated and operated by Consortium for Educational Communication (CEC) and the University Grants Commission (UGC), telecasts 6 hours of fresh programming everyday with repeat transmission 3 times daily on regular basis. The programmes telecast are produced by the 17 UGC media centres EMMRCs (formerly AVRCs and EMRCs) located in various universities. The programmes are either based on UGC model syllabi for various undergraduate courses or are purely enrichment type. The enrichment type programmes are meant to broaden the mental horizons of students of various UG and PG streams. The fact that the UGC media centres are located in various geographically, socially, linguistically, and culturally distinct areas they bring in a lot of heterogeneity and variety to VYAS channel. From February 2002, VYAS became fully digital and server based. The programmes are also now carried through Ernet and Infonet and have a potential to benefit over "10 million students enrolled in 17,625 colleges and 348 universities" (Prakash : 2006)[40]. all across the country. With the quantitative expansion of institutions of higher education in India, devoid of quality teachers and worthwhile infrastructure, use of VYAS channel, by taking quality education to the students in remotest areas, can make a very significant difference.

Though slow and unorganized, educational television in India has shown a significant growth, but the broadcasting is invariably one way; with the exception of a few experiments and Gyandarshan-2 which offers some interaction. The one-way traffic of broadcasting educational television programmes on television had students at a disadvantage. They could never clear their doubts nor could they express their own ideas to the "tele-teacher". As back as 1991, UGC with the active support of Indian Space Research Organisation, Space Application Centre, Ahmedabad, conducted first National Talkback experiment, called UGC-ISRO National Talkback Experiment, "to test the viability of two-way interactive communication to enhance and enrich the quality of educational content for undergraduate students". For one week, from 25th to 30th November, 1991, 835 students from eight selected locations across the country, viz. Jodhpur, Imphal, Hyderabad, Kolkata, Ahmedabad, Roorkee, Madurai and Patiala, watched 12 prerecorded ETV programmes produced by various media centres, uplinked from Delhi earth station (Final Report, UGC: 1992).[41] Soon after the telecast the students interacted, through two ways audio and one way video, with the subject experts located at the studio created for the purpose at Delhi Earth Station. For interaction students made use of satellite based remote talkback at two centres, Jodhpur and Imphal, and conventional or temporarily dedicated STD telephone lines at the other six centres. Some students also asked questions using FAX facilities kept available for the purpose.

During this period research teams, using various elaborate and well designed research tools, measured and examined technical, operational, educational, enrichment, and economical aspects of the experiment. The analysis of the data, collected by the researchers from various locations, clearly suggested that "the interactive mode of television should become a regular feature of the countrywide classroom". The study further revealed that the successful completion of the experiment "demonstrates the operational feasibility of making interactivity a part of countrywide classroom", and suggested that "such interactivity on one hand will help students in providing update information and on the other, increase the audience for countrywide classroom". (Final Report, UGC : 1992)[42]

As a follow-up to the National Talkback Experiment 1991,

Consortium for Educational Communication (CEC) in collaboration with Indira Gandhi National Open University (IGNOU), Indian Space Research Organisation (ISRO), Doordarshan and UGC media centres conducted another national talkback experiment in 1994. This time, however, the experiment was conducted by including programmes on a single theme; a course on new information and communication technologies. 9 interactive sessions each of one hour's duration, with 20 minutes of ETV programmes followed by 40 minutes of interaction using STD lines, were conducted from December 15, 1994 to December 24,1994. The programmes were uplinked from Ahmedabad and broadcast at National Network of Doordarshan. For interaction organized viewing of students was arranged at 15 smaller cities and towns across the country, viz., Mysore, Sagar, Jammu, Shillong, Shirur, Berhampur, Modinagar, Tiruchirapally, Bhuj, Nasik, Darjeeling, Calicut, Malerkotla, Kavaratti and Jamshedpur. (Reddi et al. : 1995).[43]

After watching the programme students interacted with the panel of experts located in the studio at Ahmedabad who answered a lot of questions raised by the captive audience at the 15 remote locations. During the last four days of the experiment telephone lines were also thrown open for the general audience and a number of questions were raised by people watching programmes at their own places. After detailed analysis of the experiment, based on observations of the researchers and the data collected from the 15 locations using various research tools, Reddi and others found a "general enthusiasm and positive attitude toward this educational innovation". The report suggested "enhanced educational outcomes which would be even more if the technical snags are worked out". The experiment demonstrated a "successful attempt to reach out to the targeted viewers of CWCR in the small towns of India" and the participants were overwhelmed by the "spirit of participation and the feeling of involvement in learning process". It was also reported that, "the package concept" was "very well received" by the students as they feel it helped in "improving retention and understanding". The experiment also showed that such interactive sessions can be "introduced into the regular transmission at a relatively low cost" and shall be of immense value "benefiting a very wide audience". (Reddi : 1995)[44]

The report provided valuable suggestions for making interactivity more effective, suggested to "increase in number of telephone lines at the teaching end" to ensure fast connectivity and provide "more time for interaction". If the programmes are telecast in a package mode then every care must be taken to achieve "uniformity in programme content, quality, and information overload". The report suggested that the students must be enrolled for such courses and the enrolled students shall be provided, "supplementary reading material" before the telecourse begins. The "telecourses must be open to the general viewing audience". It lays stress on the "need for improvement of the technical quality of both the programmes and the interaction". The report while recommending use of teleconferencing for educational television, more frequently in a more organized manner concludes that "interactive television" increases "participatory communication that brings about motivation and commitment" among the teacher and the participant students.

The launch of EDUSAT, an exclusively dedicated educational satellite, by Indian Space Research Organisation on September 20, 2004 marks yet another milestone in the history of Educational Television in India. With the objective of supporting the formal and non-formal education system in India through low cost, IT based, systems, EDUSAT provides an extended C-B and National Beam, a Ku Band National Beam and 5 Ku Band Regional Beams. EDUSAT has been designed to integrate advanced space technology with the Information and Communication Technology (ICT) at the ground. This has paved the way for convergence of media which is considered very effective for education through distance mode. EDUSAT with inbuilt interactive features using ICT shall help reach distance learners in an effective, interesting and cost-effective manner.

EDUSAT, targeted at schools, colleges, and institutions involved in higher education, both formal and non-formal, is a boon for students as well as teachers, in the country as it will breach new frontiers and take quality education to the doorsteps of every one irrespective of their location. For effective utilization and enhanced scope EDUSAT, as envisaged in the project report (Shekhar : 2004)[45] shall pass through three phases :

1. In the first phase, the pilot project phase, EDUSAT was implemented in Karnataka, Maharashtra, and Madhya Pradesh even before the launch of EDUSAT using INSAT-3B. During this phase Visveswaraya Technological University in Karnataka, conducted regular classes for 100 engineering colleges; Y.B. Chavan Open University, at Nasik in Maharashtra, conducted contact classes for its study centres located at 75 places across the State; Rajiv Gandhi Technical University, Madhya Pradesh conducted classes over 25 locations. The encouraging results of conducting classes in virtual mode, using satellite links, are indicative of EDUSAT making a significant contribution in taking quality education across geographical barriers to the remotest areas for overall educational development.
2. The second phase of the project, also known as the semi-operational phase, shall start with the launch of EDUSAT in orbit. This will facilitate the use of new technology and the network would expand to cover two more States and a national institution. Around 100-200 classrooms will be connected in each beam.
3. In the third phase of the project, the entire country would be covered using six regional beams and one national beam. EDUSAT network is expected to become fully operational by 2008. ISRO will provide technical and managerial support in the replication of EDUSAT ground systems to manufacturers and service providers. End-users are expected to provide funds for this. In this phase, ground infrastructure to meet the country's educational needs will be built and during this period, EDUSAT will be able to support about 25 to 30 uplinks and about 5000 remote terminals per uplink. (*Hindu Online Edition*)

After the launch of EDUSAT in September 2004, the Ku Band National Beam of EDUSAT was assigned to Consortium for Educational Communication (CEC) and the University Grants Commission (UGC) for higher education. 58 Satellite Interactive

Terminals (SITs), also known as Virtual classrooms, were established at various locations in the country, which include 17 UGC-CEC media centres, 12 Academic Staff Colleges, 9 Universities/colleges of potential excellence and 19 universities/colleges in remote areas, with CEC as the nodal agency. A collaboration project of ISRO, UGC-CEC and the educational institutions having SITs, this unique interconnection of institutions provides an opportunity for the users to share their expertise through a two-way audio/video mechanism.

The UGC-CEC EDUSAT National Beam became operational in September 2005 for virtual classroom operations with CEC, New Delhi as the teaching end. Students across the country at various SITs attended the lectures delivered from CEC and interacted with the expert through a two-way video conference. Over a period of time teaching end is rotated among various media centres and teachers and experts from various institutions across the country share their knowledge and expertise with the students and scholars across the country. The national beam is also used by CEC and the media centres for organizing various workshops/seminars and meeting in the virtual mode. Three workshops on, "capacity building programmes in e-content and multimedia development" were conducted at CEC and extended to some media centres through EDUSAT. The centres in turn enrolled teachers from the local institutions, who attended the lectures and conducted practical sessions with the help of local demonstrators and experts at CEC through virtual guidance. The experiment was a great success as the teachers who were trained in virtual form were able to develop e-content and multimedia at par with the teachers who were actually trained at CEC, New Delhi.

Taking advantage of VYAS, SITs, and Internet CEC in 2005 also launched some online part time courses. Hundreds of students, across the country, enrolled for the online courses. The course material was packaged in the form of video courses telecast on VYAS channel, the interaction with the expert was organized through EDUSAT on weekly basis, additional reading material was kept available for the students on the CEC website and the assignments and evaluations were conducted using internet. The successful conduct of workshops and online courses through EDUSAT demonstrates the capability and the capacity of virtual teaching and training. It is established beyond any doubt in a country like India, which is scattered mostly in villages and remote areas, a proper use of information and communication technology with solid application and judicious use of mind and machine, will bring the desired results and make dream of education for all come true in a real sense.

EDUSAT, with inbuilt facility for two-way audio and video interaction, also brought in much desired and recommended talk back facility for the students. The quality of video/audio, especially during interactivity, however, is still far from satisfactory and requires improvement at par with, if not better than, the quality of interactivity seen on various national satellite news channels, viz., Aaj Tak, NDTV, Zee News, Star News, etc. The fact that private news channels and even Doordarshan are able to conduct live video conferences, on daily basis, with a fine quality of two-way audio and video across the country and even across the borders, proves that the technology is already in place for such endeavours for educational television. EDUSAT, together with the convergence of technologies and growth and spread of Information and Communication technologies in rural India, if properly used promises a great future for educational television in India.

Problems and Prospects of Educational Television in India

Referring to radio and television as the most powerful tools to provide education to the masses, Emery and others, as far back as 1955, wrote in their book *Introduction to Mass Communication* [46]:

> "Television and radio are electronic magic carpets that transport millions of persons each day to far away places. They are the twentieth century creation of the technological revolution that has been transforming much of the world for almost two centuries and their impact on our social, political and cultural life has been profound." (p. 249)

The Indian television, since then, has seen a phenomenal growth.

Four and a half decades later Sonia Livingstone, in her book *Making Sense of Television* (1990)[47] observed that:

> "Television has come to dominate homes in our day, the organization of our living rooms, the topic of our conversation, the conceptions of pleasure, the things which one looks forward, the ways we amuse and occupy our children and the way we discover the world we live in."
> (p. 102)

As Marshall McLuhan[48] makes us believe "medium is the message" Livingstone also argues that television dominates our thinking, how we think and what we think about. Adler considers television "not as a medium but a mediator between fact and fantasy, between our desires to escape and our need to deal with the real problems, between our old values and new ideas, between our individual lives and the life of the nation." (Aaliya 2000, p.103)[49]

Despite the above quoted lofty definitions, which project television as an angle with the divine power of bringing the whole world in our drawing rooms and making a great difference the way we think and believe, we are yet to make a proper use of the power of television for the spread of education. In India like other developing countries, even like developed countries, educational TV programmes are drawing a relatively very small audience. 22 million audience for countrywide classroom programmes telecast over India's gigantic Doordarshan, that claims coverage of around 90 per cent area of the country's land mass inhabited by over one billion population, is too meagre. Ironically the programmes, essentially meant for students who are less educated, students from lower social strata, students living in distant and rural areas – who do not have access to good teachers, libraries, laboratories and other resources, are mostly watched by highly educated people, bright students living in urban areas keen to know more and opinion leaders in some areas to keep themselves informed. It is also not always that people watch educational programmes for learning. Wilbur Schramm (1960)[50] in a research report writes that, the audience for Educational Television are, "some refugees from the parts of commercial TV which they do not like, some seekers after self-improvement, some intellectually curios persons, some aesthetically hungry persons, and so forth". (p. 96)

Prior to cable and satellite television, in 1980s/1990s, in India, when Doordarshan had a complete monopoly, educational television programmes telecast on it were being seen by a sizable population of general masses. The reasons for watching of UGC Countrywide Classroom by non-students though were different. The first and the foremost reason was the non-availability of other sources of entertainment on Indian television, those days, during the telecast of educational programmes, so the audience had a very little choice to watch. The second reason was that these programmes were telecast in the day time when the retired, the old and the housewives were always in the audience and had nothing else to do. Even today educational television is being watched by a large group of non-students in the rural areas where cable and satellite does not have much penetration. The growth of private satellite and cable channels in Indian urban areas has changed this equation; with more and more people flowing towards popular entertainment channels. In suburban and rural India also the equation is changing in favour of entertainment television as the cable and satellite are spreading to these areas.

The reasons why educational television could not achieve much success in India and for that matter allover the world are many. At the base of this lies the perception of the general masses that television is an entertainment media. Kent Geiger and Robert Sopol (1965)[51], after conducting a study on ETV in Boston found that people want recreation, relaxation, and entertainment, and educational television does not provide this. He also remarked that educational television is usually dull. Right from the childhood we are trained by parents and peers that television is for entertainment, as we grow our attitude towards serious broadcasting becomes negative, therefore, most often we see programmes which are more amusing and entertaining than educating. As they say education is a serious business and "television viewing is a non-serious, often interrupted and frequently non-exclusive activity for which the measure in hours and minutes serves only as the outer boundary of possible attention", (Comstock : 1991)[52] the two, therefore, cannot go together ?

The problem is further compounded by the fact that people judge the educational television in comparison with the commercial television. The fact, however, is that the two are totally different media. The biggest difference between the two is their access to resources primarily in terms of funding. The total yearly budget of educational television programming of entire America will in no case be more than one popular television series on a national network. The same is case with India, the total budget for the production of programmes for the CWCR for a production centre for one year is less than one single episode of a soap opera on the prime time on Doordarshan. Access to resources has a direct bearing on the quality of programmes. Discovery and National Geographic with deep pockets are able to commission programmes with huge budgets and the results are for everyone to see. Quality leads to acceptance by the audience and to the change in perceptions about the medium.

The absence of a concrete or solid policy for educational television in India and other countries has resulted in a haphazard growth of this otherwise important medium. Though the growth in India seems tremendous yet it does not serve much purpose for those for whom the ETV programmes are essentially made or telecast, the students living in remote and far-flung areas. Despite a year long SITE experiment, which to a great extent was a success, "India could not come out with a broadcast policy on education(al) television" primarily due to "political instability" and "heightened political power struggle". The government's indifference towards educational television led to gross misuse of television (read Doordarshan) for political propaganda. In the early eighties "Doordarshan was used more as a tool of government propaganda as it enjoyed a captive audience of over 12 million people" (Rani : 2006).[53] Television that started in India with the agenda of education gradually changed its policy for entertainment television by 1965. Despite the launch of many channels, some exclusively for entertainment, Doordarshan remains pre-occupied with dishing out entertainment and film based programmes, besides news and sports programmes. It pushed its mandate of educational programmes to the back burner. In early 1980s, with the launch of soap operas and serials like *"Hum-Log"*, *"Buniyad"*, *"Nukkad"*, etc., Doordarshan embraced commercial television and got swayed away in revenue generation forgetting its social agenda. The revenue generation potential of television resulted in pushing back educational television programmes produced by UGC media centres and other educational institutions to insignificant and inconvenient slots. In fact, the mandarins of the State television started viewing educational programmes as a liability because of their inability to attract advertisements and generate revenue. Despite claiming to be the flagship of a welfare state the Doordarshan could not find any worthwhile time slot for educational television programmes and successive governments failed to realize the importance of this important medium for education.

The non-availability of proper time slots for educational television on Doordarshan remains a matter of concern for those who view educational television as highly important for a developing society. The timings of these programmes are such that the target audience gets hardly any time to see them. This could have been overcome, though, with much ease had the educational institutions scheduled educational television viewing in their daily timetable. One argument for not doing so is that the programming is haphazard and choice of programmes on the air is limited. Therefore, every student cannot find it useful and interesting. Lack of television sets in schools and colleges, non-availability of electricity or viewing space in the educational institutions and the non-serious approach of the teachers also contribute to ineffectiveness of educational television programmes on Doordarshan. Yet another reason could be that the programmes are not integrated with teaching involving the institutions and the teachers with the broadcast.

The launch of Gyandarshan, a satellite channel by IGNOU, and other educational channels like EKLAVYA, VYAS, etc., under the umbrella of Gyandarshan made a good beginning but could not make a significant contribution as its reach is limited to some cable areas, if at all it is carried by the cable operator. Moreover, the cable operators assign weaker frequencies to Gyandarshan which results in poor reception quality of the programmes, adding to the disappointment of the students; as viewers' engagement with the programme is also related to the quality of transmission they receive.

The neglect of the educational television can be gauged by the fact that even the country's much hyped DTH service does not bother to carry the programmes offered on the Gyandarshan bouquet. In view of the importance of educational television programmes for the students, especially from the poor/weaker and distant areas of the country, these programmes should have been preferred over the commercial television. In fact, with the launch of so many free to air channels by now India must have launched at least one national terrestrial television channel exclusively for the purpose of education. That would have allowed a hassle free reception by the audience. The launch of EDUSAT promises some hope but again the service, as of today, is meant to be received through special antennas. The EDUSAT in fact is a closed circuit educational television and is not available freely to all. The services are still confined to major institutions that have been provided the reception facilities. The service is far from satisfactory as operations through EDUSAT are still evolving. The poor quality of audio and video telecasts through EDUSAT and poorer interactivity through net meeting software is at times disappointing and discouraging for the students.

The quality of educational television programmes produced by the media centres and educational institutions has always remained a case of concern. Out of 17,000 programmes produced by various UGC media centres for CEC in over 49 subject categories almost 50% are below average quality. The same is the case with the programmes produced by the CIET, SIETs, and the EMPC, etc.

The poor quality is attributed to two reasons, one the lack of enough resources and second the lack of talented manpower for production of educational television programmes. While the need of attracting talent is one of the primary requirements of educational television, it remains one of the major problems. The reason for not attracting talented manpower is rooted in lack of proper economic resources. One of the requirements for attracting the talent is to pay attractive salaries and remuneration. So if educational television can strengthen its financial base, it will be in a better position to offer better incentives to producers and academics resulting in excellent professional quality programmes to achieve its objectives. What is required is the pooling of all the resources to attract more and more of talented manpower and involving experienced media professionals, teachers, writers and even engineers and the technicians to create a movement for the uplift of educational television.

Shortage of funds for research, one of the most important aspects of educational television, always results in poor quality of programmes. Then there are requirements of facilities, production equipments and other essential requirements that are available to commercial television and remain a distant dream for educational television. All these factors put together result in the production of mediocre programmes by production centres involved in production of educational programmes. The programmes that, perhaps, no one likes to see and a very few watch.

Multiple languages in India is yet another major problem for educational television at the national level, owing to the fact that India is a multilingual country with 18 officially recognized languages. The programmes are mostly produced in English and a very small percentage in Hindi and local/regional languages, like Bengali, Kannad, Marathi, etc. The poor knowledge of English language especially in the rural areas results in poor reception of these programmes and, therefore, leads to general indifference of the audience towards these programmes. The launch of regional language channels by Doordarshan was seen as an opportunity to carry educational programmes in regional languages but again the opportunity for education has succumbed to commercial television. In fact lack of vision for regional channels by DD has resulted in making these channels redundant as they only depend on the reruns of entertainment programmes from other channels. For most of the day, these channels show the same programmes simultaneously being shown on the national network and the other local channels of Doordarshan. There is enough time available on these channels which could have been utilized for the purpose of educational television especially in regional languages.

The greatest problem for educational television is the indifference of educationists and academics towards educational television. A majority of them believes that, "television is irrelevant to the educational content as it corrupts its intellectual quality." (Gilbert Seldes : 1962).[54] In McLuhan's[55] classification of media as "hot and cold" television is categorized as a "cold medium". He argues that television is most often used with less intellectual involvement, therefore, making it less relevant for educational purposes, which requires a serious and attentive viewing. Television audience he feels are not always very attentive. But if educational television programmes are made and meant for a specific audience, and viewing is organized with a proper schedule, television can serve as an efficient tool to reach thousands of students scattered over a vast geographical area.

Despite the above drawbacks and problems faced by the Educational Television, it still retains its importance in imparting education to thousands who seek it. "A well designed ETV programme is more likely to be more effective than a poorly designed book" (John Carey : 1991).[56] A well designed educational television programme can motivate the students to watch more, inculcate their reading habits, encourage independent learning, develop new insights, but that is possible only when the traditional method of teaching through lectures is replaced or augmented with more exciting television programmes in the form of demonstrations and discoveries. The poorly designed content of educational programmes is an impediment in its growth as a powerful supplement to traditional teaching.

The challenge lies in developing skills for writing and producing educational programmes with the understanding of the requirements of audience in mind. Today when the modern teacher has all the facilities ranging from books to highly advanced computer and audio/visual services available for teaching, television remains a small tool in teaching resources. The effective way of maximizing the benefits of educational television is to blend it with other activities in the total learning process.

Ironically educational television remained only rhetoric for policy-makers in India, and nothing concrete has been done in terms of planning necessary to achieve the goals. In the West, particularly in USA various public pressure groups like the "Action for Children's Television", led by its dynamic and firebrand Peggy Charren, American Congress and FCC are taking some steps in this direction. Gore Commission, under the chairmanship of Al Gore, then American Vice President, indicated that the commercial broadcast stations would be required to carry a certain hours of programmes per week to meet the public interest obligations in the new digital system. FCC regulations require broadcast stations to telecast a minimum of 3 hours a week core programming for the children. Unfortunately, more than often, networks resort to pre-emption of these programmes for other sports and live coverages.

In India, though television is mostly government controlled or regulated and DD is considered the flagship on public service broadcasting in the country, educational programmes fail to reach the audience through the huge network of Doordarshan. The telecast of educational programmes, viz., UGC Countrywide Classroom, NCERT, etc., over DD national network are most often cancelled to make way for coverage of sports and political events. The government in India has utterly failed to prioritize education and this has adversely affected the production and telecast of quality education television programmes on Doordarshan and other private channels. In a welfare state like India, that is one of the emerging countries, this must have got the highest priority. India must take the full advantage of INSAT/ EDUSAT satellites and vast technical expertise available in the country to expand educational television and make a professional use of this wonderful medium for reaching students in distant areas. With educational expertise and facilities limited to major cities spread of TV provides an opportunity to share the educational resources at national level. But this can only happen if bold initiatives are taken making education a priority and removing the bottlenecks to integrate educational institutions and DD network for a holistic growth of society.

The closed circuit educational television in use in America and yet to reach India is one of the many possible solutions for making educational television a rewarding experience. Notwithstanding the fact that closed circuit television does not reach mass audience at the same time, it has the obvious advantage of offering a wide variety of programmes designed for a specific audience and the viewers can choose the programme of their choice.

The digital era in television technology together with the convergence of media promises some growth for educational television also. With the multiplication of channels leading to fragmentation of audience and the advertisers increasingly looking for quality audience, educational television, in the very near future, may attract more advertisers to strengthen its financial base, a requirement to improve the quality of programmes, which in turn will attract more audience. Even the modest viewership for educational programmes at present may be very attractive for the advertisers, in the coming years, in comparison to other popular programmes. 10 million for "Sesame Street" or 20 million for "CWCR programmes", though very small now may constitute a good portion of the audience in the fragmented universe to lure the advertisers to educational television. This will motivate the commercial channel operators to plunge into educational market.

The interactive aspects of new technology will further boost the chances of educational television becoming an attractive and rewarding experience for the audience on one hand and the broadcast stations to make maximum profits from these services on the other. The mutual benefit of the two is a key to the success of educational television. But before that happens government may have to take the initiative of making amendments in broadcast laws that prohibit the State governments and educational institutions in running television channels. In fact, the government must encourage and support the best educational institutions located in various States to launch educational television channels in their areas. Today when narrowcasting, due to fragmentation of audience, is the order of the day, local educational television channels can make a wonderful contribution in strengthening the development education in distant and far flung areas. Again telecast of educational TV programmes on private television channels for specific hours in a week must be enforced by legislation and private cable operators should be forced to carry at least a few educational channels on prime band, the way national and local networks in USA are forced under "must carry" practice. Broadcasting must be made interactive and backed by a strong mechanism where students from anywhere can participate in a discussion or get their doubts cleared by a liberal use of information and communication technology, viz., telephone, fax, e-mail, SMS, chatting and video conferencing, etc. The technology is already in place for such ventures what is required is a strong will with a solid political backing.

Educational television must not be confined to telecasting of programmes alone but must be mixed with production of valuable reading material and written content that is distributed among the students before and after the programmes. Printing and distribution of reading material has always been a problem but with revolution in ICT it has become easier. Tons of reading material in the form of e-content can be made available to students on dedicated websites. The websites can even be made more interactive by creating discussion platforms or blogs which today's generation is already familiar with. A multimedia approach, including joint use of television, radio, cable, telephones, cell phones, and the new media, together with strong satellite connectivity holds promise of a very bright future for educational television in India.

Statement of Purpose

From the above discussion it is clear that television is a potent medium for education, the technology is in place and the expertise is available in abundance. The experiments have shown that educational television can make a big difference if integrated with teaching. Some serious efforts have been initiated particularly by IGNOU and UGC to make use of television for higher education. Nonetheless educational television in India has not been able to establish itself in an effective and meaningful way, owing to various reasons. This study shall try to thoroughly examine the problems and prospects of educational television in India, analyse various educational television endeavours, particularly UGC Countrywide Classroom, and find out ways and means to make effective use of educational television and the new technologies for teaching and learning. An attempt shall also be made to study the problem with a special reference to the valley of Kashmir.

References

1. *UNESCO. World Communication : Press, Radio, TV and Film.* (Paris : 1964) in *Behra, S.C. Educational Television Programmes : Impact on Teachers', Competency* (New Delhi : Deep & Deep Publication, 1991), p. 7.

2. Kinder, James S., *Audio Visual Materials : Television* (New York: American Book Company, 1959), p. 19.
3. Kinder (1959), *ibid*, p. 27.
4. Dominick, Joseph R. *The Dynamics of Mass Communication*. 5th ed. (New York : McGraw-Hill Company, 1996), p. 317.
5. Ford Foundation. *Attitudes Towards Instructional Television*. (New York : International Research Associates, Inc, 1965).
6. Carnegie Commission USA. *Report on Educational Television in USA*. (New York : Carnegie Corporation, 1967)
7. Wikipedia, website, Public Broadcasting Service viewed on 17 March, 2008. <http://en.wikipedia.org/wiki/Public_Broadcasting_Service>
8. Ball, S. and G.A. Bogatz. *The First Year of 'Sesame Street': An Evaluation*. (Princeton NJ : Educational Testing Service, 1970).
9. Engelman Ralph. *Public Radio and Television in America : A Political History* (New York: Sage Publications, 1996), pp. 213-219.
10. About PBS, Website Public Broadcasting Service viewed on 17 March, 2008. <http://www.pbs.org/aboutpbs/>
11. Rasool, Shahid. "Educational Television in India : Present Scenario and Future Prospects". *Insight Journal of Applied Research in Education*, Vol.1, No. 8 (Srinagar : Faculty of Education, University of Kashmir, Spring 2002), pp. 93-101.
12. Moir Guthrie. *Teaching and Television : ETV Explained*. (London : Pergamon Press, 1967).
13. Masterman, Len. *Teaching About Television*. (London : The McMillan Press Ltd., 1980).
14. Wittich, W.A. and C.F. Schullar. *Audio Visual Material : Their Nature and Use*. (New York : Harper and Row Publishers, 1968).
15. Gordon, George N. *Classroom Television : New Frontiers in ITV*. (New York : Communication Art Books, 1970).
16. Behera, (1991), *ibid.*, pp. 8-11.
17. Raina, Rajindra Singh Eds., *Srinagar Doordarshan : 24 Years*. (Srinagar: Doordarshan 1997), Preface.
18. Mohanty J. *Educational Broadcasting : Radio and Television in Education*, (New Delhi: Sterling Publishers 1984), p. 7.
19. Report of the Study Group on INSAT Television Utilization for Education and Development. (New Delhi : Ministry of Education and Culture, Government of India (1981), p. 157.
20. Rani, Usha N. *Educational Television in India : Challenges and Issues*. (New Delhi : Discovery Publishing House, 2006), pp. 2-11.
21. Rani, Usha N. (2006), *ibid.*, p. 10.
22. Website indianetzone viewed on January 20, 2008: <http://www.indianetzone.com/3/doordarshan_dd_india.htm>
23. Phadnis Atul, "The two in one nation !" The *Hindu* Daily Newspaper website viewed on 12 March 2008 <http://www.thehindubusinessline.com/catalyst/2004/12/30/stories/2004123000050300.htm>

24. Website Indianetzone. *ibid.*
25. Chander, Romesh and Kiran Karnik. *Planning for Satellite Broadcasting : The Indian Instructional Television Experiment.* (*UNESCO Report,* 1976), p. 51.
26. Aggarwal, Binod C. *SITE Social Evaluation: Results, Experiences, and Implications.* (Ahmedabad : Space Application Centre ISRO, 1981).
27. Chander and Karnik (1976). *Ibid.,* p. 25.
28. Doshi, J. K., "Indian Television and Rural Children" in Agarwal, Binod, C. and Arbind Sinha (Eds.). *SITE to INSAT.* (New Delhi : Concept Publishing Company Pvt. Ltd.,1986), p. 43.
29. Aggarwal B.C. and M.R.Malek. *Television in Kheda.* (New Delhi : Concept Publishing Company Pvt. Ltd., 1986), p. 71.
30. Agrawal *et al.,* 1986 *ibid.,* p.73.
31. Rani, Usha N. (2006). *ibid.,* p. 22.
32. Rani Usha N. (2006). *ibid.,* pp. 29-30.
33. "DD more popular than private channels". (New Delhi : Outlookindia.com. May 19, 2007). <http://www.outlookindia.com/pti_news.asp?id=385755>
34. ADMAR Report. *Viewership Study on UGC Country Wide Classroom Programmes.* (New Delhi : Consortium for Educational Communication. 1993), pp. 8-24.
35. ADMAR Report. *National Viewership Study* (New Delhi : Consortium for Educational Communication, 1997), p.15.
36. Mishra, Rajendra. "Countrywide Classroom Viewership", *CEC Newsletter.* Vol. 1 No. 1". (New Delhi : Consortium for Educational Communication, 1997) : p. 3.
37. Rani, Usha (2006). *ibid.,* p. 29.
38. IGNOU. "Vice Chancellor's Report, Fourteenth Convocation". (New Delhi: Indira Gandhi National Open University, 2003). p. 37.
39. Rani, Usha N. (2006), *ibid.* p. 38.
40. Prakash P. Jt. Secretary UGC. Power Point Presentation (New Delhi: University Grants Commission 2006)
41. Final Report. *UGC-ISRO National Talkback Experiment, November 25-30, 1991.* (New Delhi: University Grants Commission, 1992): pp. 6-18.
42. Final Report. (1992), *ibid.,* pp. 14-17.
43. Reddi, U. V. *et al.* Final Report, CEC-IGNOU-ISRO National Talkback Experiment, New Information and Communication Technologies (New Delhi : UGC Media Centres and the Consortium for Educational Communication, 1995) : p. 10.
44. Reddi, *et al.* (1995) *ibid.,* p. (See Executive Summary).
45. Shekar, G.L. "EDUSAT–Indian Satellite in Education : Edusat a boon for students, teachers". *Online Edition of Hindu Newspaper.* Wednesday, August, 4th, 2004. URL <http://www.hinduonline.com/essay/2004/08/04/Article/2004080400090130.htm>
46. Emery, E., P.E.Ault and W.K. Ager. *Introduction to Mass Communication.* (Bombay: Vakils, Feffer and Simons Pvt. Ltd, 1955), p. 249.

47. Livingstone, Sonia M. *Making Sense of Television* (*Oxford*: Pergamon Press, 1990). in Aaliya A. *Television and Social Change.* (Srinagar: Computer City, 2000), p.102.
48. McLuhan, M.C., *Understanding Media : The Extension of Man.* (London : Routledge and Kegan Paul, 1964), p. 7.
49. Aaliya A. *Television and Social Change.* (Srinagar: Computer City, 2000), p. 103.
50. Schramm, Wilbur. *The Impact of Educational Television.* (Urbana Ill : University of Illinois Press, 1960) in Rasool, Shahid. "Educational Television in India: Present scenario and future prospects". *Insight Journal of Applied Research in Education,* Vol.1, No.8, Spring 2002. (Srinagar : Faculty of Education, University of Kashmir, 2002): p. 96.
51. Kent Geiger & Robert Sopol "Educational Television in Boston". *Educational Television* in Gordon, George N. (1965). *ibid,* pp. 39-67.
52. Comstock, G. *Television and the American Child.* (San Diago : Academic Press, 1991), p. 107.
53. Rani, Usha N. (2006), *ibid.*, p. 6.
54. Gilbert Seldes. "ETV's Community Job" *Educational Television : The Next Ten Years* (Standford : The Institution for Communication Research 1962). In Comstock, G. (1991), *ibid,*. p. 119.
55. McLuhan, Marshall. (1964), *ibid.*, pp. 24-35.
56. John Cary. "Plato at Keyboard: Telecommunication Technology & Education Policy". *Links for Learning.* Vol. 514 ed. Vivian M. Horner & Linda G. Roberts,1991), in Rasool, Shahid (2002): *ibid.*, p. 98.

Chapter - 2

Studies on Television

Television as a Tool for Education–A Literature Survey

The famous American communication researcher and commentator George Gerbner is quoted to have said, "if you can write a nation's stories, you needn't worry about who makes its laws. Today television tells most of the stories to most of the people most of the time"(Dizard : 1997)[1] This statement aptly demonstrates that television is the most powerful and most persuasive medium in the world. Yet the former chairman of the Federal Communication Commission (FCC) of USA, Newton Minow, characterised television as a "vast waste land"(Dizard : 1997)[2] a phrase that is mostly used to refer to this powerful mass medium and rightly so. Television arrived, in India, as a medium for education in 1959. Since then while the medium saw tremendous quantitative and qualitative growth in terms of transmission, production, reach, accessibility, acceptance and overall impact on the society, it forgot its mandate and put education on the back burner. Today when television is ubiquitous and occupies central space in almost every household in the urban areas and a majority of homes in rural areas, it is mostly used for entertainment and information. According to a survey, there are 98.96 million TV homes in India. They include 49.09 million cable and satellite homes and 40.87 million non-cable and satellite homes (Outlookindia.com).[3] Another survey shows that "300 million viewers", watch Doordarshan programmes at home. With "TV sets established under various schemes in community centres in villages" and people watching programmes at offices and other public places it is estimated that "a total of 450 million viewers" watch Doordarshan programmes on any day. (Indianetzone : 1998).[4] With such a powerful presence in the country, television is used to dish out entertainment programmes, live sports coverage and a host of news and current affairs programmes day in and day out. With the penetration and mushroom growth of global television channels, bringing the whole universe in our drawing and bed rooms the "global village" concept has long been realized. The sensual power of communication that television facilitated and the fact that growth and speed of television far exceeds the reach of any other media, it has resulted in creation of a new "global village". Today people across the globe are exposed to events happening in other parts of the world within no time. Television with the power of visuals and the strength of sound also assumed the role of educating and instructing the society as a whole and students in particular. Carrying a mixture of content rich fantastic, and at times dull, educational programmes, relating to science, history, geography, social sciences, literature, adventure, health, environment, sports, religion, technology and many more, to students in distant areas television has in a subtle way made a great difference in our lives.

Despite the lofty definitions and facts, which project television no less than an angel with the divine power of bringing the whole world in our drawing rooms and making a significant difference in the way we think and believe we are yet to make a proper use of power of television for the purpose of education. While this is mostly attributed to commercialization of television and television assuming the shape of an industry; churning huge revenue by selling advertisements, it is also linked to the mindset, that has unfortunately developed, that television is primarily an entertainment medium and cannot serve as an effective medium for education, as education is a serious business and television viewing by nature is "a non-serious, often interrupted and frequently non-exclusive activity for which the measure in hours and minutes serves only as the outer boundary of possible attention" (Comstock : 1991).[5] Again we are made to believe that from television "people want recreation, relaxation, and entertainment, and educational television does not provide this" (Kent Geiger *et al.*, : 1965).[6]

The irony is that an overwhelming majority of the academics even believe and advocate that "television is irrelevant to the educational content as it corrupts its intellectual quality." (Gilbert Seldes :1962).[7] Berkman (1976)[8] commenting on Instructional Television (ITV), a decade after Ford Foundation invested $ 25 million for the development of ITV in USA, wrote that, "I defy anybody to show me where this multi-megabuck-backed experiment–by far, still, the largest ever in American education – rates even a footnote in the education texts". But contrary to Berkman's view ITV in America has shown a sure growth, learning from previous mistakes and constantly improvising and evolving to gain a very strong position in American educational system. That said television is no magic wand that it can solve all the problems facing education, it can at best be used as tool to assist in teaching on micro or macro level. Skinner (1958)[9] commenting on the use of television, films, phonographs and tape recorders, etc., in a classroom, laid emphasis on the use of these gadgets to "supplement and supplant lectures" resulting in a meaningful and highly productive exchange of ideas between the teacher and the student. He further emphasized and cautioned about the real danger that it will be wholly obscured if use of the equipment is simply made to present materials; the students may become more and more passive receiver of the instruction, resulting in less involvement and reduced scholastic achievements. That is where the real danger of using technology, particularly television, can harm the very cause of education if not used with proper precautions. The television shall be seen as partner in teaching alongside the teacher, a means to end and not an end in itself. While teachers generally feel that the educational television can make a positive contribution they are divided on the type of programmes that must be telecast. Seth (1983)[10] reported "64.58 per cent teachers prefer syllabus based programmes" and another "35.42 per cent have a preference for enrichment type programmes". Though syllabus based programmes are mostly done in the form of lectures, demonstrations or discussions, Seth reported that the teachers have observed the lecture format was not liked by most of the children and that different teachers preferred different programme formats for the educational television. Singh and Singh (1983)[11] reported that a majority of teachers subscribe to the thesis that the educational television programmes should supplement the classroom teaching or they should be syllabus-based. A sizable number of teachers, however, feel the programmes shall be of enrichment type and that is how television can make the process of teaching and learning an exciting and enriching process. But need assessment study by Singh and Singh (1984)[12] reported 75 per cent teachers prefer syllabus-based programmes and 20 per cent favour programmes of general nature. The demand for syllabus-based programmes, the teachers believe, will help the students learn more effectively and enjoy the programmes as they are already familiar with the subject and also inculcate a habit of reading textbooks to get more information about the topic.

Though television and society has been a hunting ground for researchers for the past many decades resulting in voluminous research material on the topic, yet research on educational aspect of TV is scanty and material directly related to the subject hard to come by. Again the published research work on educational television is mostly confined to school education, young children and school teachers. The relevance, impact and utilization of television for higher education in India does not find much research support, except a few publications and in house research reports produced by the UGC media centres. Under the circumstances one is compelled to make inferences from research done on the mainstream television or instructional television for school teachers and students. For the purpose of this study, therefore, the studies reviewed can be classified or arranged in the following four groups :

1. Studies on impact of television on society in general and children in particular.
2. Studies on educational or instructional television and their impact on students and teachers.
3. Studies on impact of various production techniques, technologies and modes of programme delivery on the audience.
4. Studies pertaining to the use of television in higher education in India.

Television research can also be classified into "rating research" and "non-rating research". While the former is a quantitative technique, encouraged by the advertisers, to find the size of audience for particular channel or programme, the later is a scientific qualitative and quantitative research to understand the whole gamut of communication through television. Rating research, like "TAM", i.e., "Television Audience Measurement", was pioneered by A.C Nelson of USA. Nelson through various methods, including installation of "people meters" in television households and sending weekly booklets to select viewers, collects data regarding audience size and viewing habits of people. The data is sold to the advertisers that help them to choose a programme and/or a channel for the advertisement of their products. The non-rating research is mostly conducted by media scholars, sponsored either by public or private agencies in terms of funding, to asses the needs of audience, find the use and utility of technology, understand the effects of exposure to television and measure the impact of technology and programmes on audience.

1. Studies relating to Impact of Television on Society in General and Students in Particular

Research on television 'effects' and 'impact' has caught the imagination of researchers allover the world resulting in voluminous research reports and publications helping media scholars understand the role of television in bringing about behavioural and attitudinal changes in the viewers. Alvin Toffler (1980)[13] sees "home as an electronic cottage" and says, "people no longer have to commute but can send their work to office electronically". The wider effect of television is making it superior to other media and as Grossberg sees television as, "indifferent to us, it does not demand our presence, yet it is always waiting for us". (Dizard :1997)[14]

Television viewing is generally believed to have changed the time schedule that people normally followed prior to its arrival. It determines when we eat, sleep, socialize, read, or spend our leisure time. Belson (1967)[15], Himmelweit, Oppenheim, and Vince (1958)[16], Coffin (1955)[17], Schramm, Lyle, and Parker (1961)[18] and Furu (1971)[19] studied the effect of introduction of television on the leisure time patterns. These studies provide evidence to television usurping leisure time of people in general and children in particular. Dobb and Macdonald (1979)[20], Gerbner and Gross (1980)[21], studied television viewing and arousal of fear factors among children and adults and found a positive correlation directly proportional to the amount of television viewing. The heavy viewers of television see world outside as more dangerous. Dorr (1981)[22] also found that television viewing plays an important role in arousal of emotions and feelings among children. Scott (1956)[23] found that television viewing directly affects children's studies at home and their performance and academic achievements at school. Surprisingly Clark (1951)[24] and Childers and Ross (1973)[25] could not find any significant effect of television viewing of children at home on their overall academic achievements. The conflicting reports of the latter seem unpalatable as the time that children spend with entertainment television could have better been spent in reading and writing resulting in better academic achievements. Bailyn (1959)[26] found that children who spent more time watching television or engaging themselves more with mass media tend to inculcate certain 'stereotypes in their thinking'. This results in damage to their 'cognitive characteristics' and creative ability. Stern (1974)[27] conducted an elaborate experiment involving 'mentally gifted children'. The students were divided in seven groups and each group was directed to see a particular type of programme on television for three weeks. The control group was not given any specific instructions with regard to viewing of programmes. The results of the experiment showed that the students of the experimental groups showed a definite and significant signs of decline in their creative ability as compared to the control group, who "showed an increase in creative ability". The review of studies on television by Maccoby (1963)[28] suggest that "children's attitudes and beliefs can be shaped by what they see on television" and portrayal of certain characters on television lead to raising similar "emotions and impulses" among them.

The study of the impact of television on the behaviour of the rural children in India by Kanade (1982)[29] indicated "positive attitude" of children towards educational television stimulating their "inquisitiveness", "creative behaviour" and to some extent influencing "verbal and non-verbal aspects" of their behaviour. Mohanty (1986)[30] also found "favourable impact of educational television on the scholastic achievements of school children". The study of relationship of educational television and educational development by Seth (1983)[31] indicated that the scholastic achievement of the students exposed to educational television programmes with intervention of teachers or parents was higher than the non-educational television group.

Television viewing has a direct bearing on the behaviour of young children. Shahid (2004)[32] reported a deluge of research findings on violent portrayals on television and their effect on children and teenagers. The studies including, Bandura, A. (1979); Belson, W. (1978); Berkowitz, L. (1974); Comstock, G. and Paik H. (1991); Gunter, B. (1994); Lconard, J. (1995); Malamuth, N.M. and Donnerstein, E. (1982); Milavsky, J. R. (1988); Van Evera (1998); Van der Voort, T.H.A (1986); and Williams, T. (1986); have established that television is a highly violent medium, as it shows lot of violence on the screen, and also that the viewing of violent portrayals by children and teenagers on television have a direct bearing on them; affecting their overall behaviour depending on the degree of viewing, age and other factors. Some of these studies also show that heavy viewing of violent scenes on television has a bearing on the learning behaviour of children resulting in low scholastic achievements; however the effects on children can be minimized by parental interventions.

The above review, therefore, shows a definite influence of television on people in general and children in particular. A safe conclusion or inference can be drawn that television affects the lives of students and the effects are in tune or proportionate to the amount of television they watch. If the influence is directly related to the type of programmes students watch then it can be inferred that viewing educational programmes must have a bearing on the cognitive learning ability and the scholastic achievement of the students.

2. Studies on Educational or Instructional Television and their Impact on Students and Teachers

Educational or instructional television utilization, the world over, is seen as a non-serious activity and marred due to lackadaisical approach of the teachers, programme makers and the end-users. Akutsu *et al.* (1971)[33] studied the frequency of the use of television in elementary level schools in Japan and found that the facility was more used by the female teachers, the teachers in general did not learn anything from the school television programmes and those teachers who used school television did not necessarily show any improvement in their instructional design. The appeal and relevance of school television was not universal for all subjects and in fact most of the teachers were of the opinion that the school television was not uniformly effective for all the subjects and only certain subjects can be effectively taught using television.

The study of utilization of educational television in public schools in Mississippi, USA, by Bostik (1984)[34], revealed a very positive attitude towards activities surrounding Instructional Television. In another study of effects of television on 400 prospective teachers in USA, it was found by Torres (1984)[35], that the attitude of teacher students towards use of ETV for training was 'favourable' and the 'level of knowledge acquired' through the use of television was 'significantly higher' than its non-use. Similarly, Wittich and Schuller (1968)[36] found that majority of television teachers in Chicago were very favourable towards this new medium and most of them enjoyed the innovative way of organizing their subject matter. They also found television courses superior. The study, however, reported that a small number of teachers was 'skeptical' about the use of educational television. Phutela (1984)[37] reported that teachers in India are mostly receptive to the idea of using educational television as they feel that, "teachers too learn about better methods of teaching and subject matter" and students "learn more" than teachers. Contrary to the above Choat, Griffin and Hobart (1986)[38] after studying educational television in England found that the teachers did not show much enthusiasm and only a very few teachers were seen using the medium effectively. They also advised a formal initial training of teachers in the use of educational television. The evaluation of Delhi Television Project by Neurath (1966)[39] indicated better overall performance by students taught through television, with the performance on questions based on visuals the best and performance on factual questions the least. The recall and understanding after one month was also significantly better in television taught students than the others, but the difference in delayed tests was less. The use of television for education is also being related to the educational level of teachers. Ghiassi (1978)[40] studied the attitudes of teachers towards educational television programmes in Iran and reported that the teachers with higher academic degrees tend to use more of instructional television than the teachers with associated degrees or diplomas. The interest of teachers was also inversely proportional with the length of their service. Those with 0 to 5 years of service were far more interested in use of educational television than the teachers with over 10 years of teaching experience. Similarly students' interest in the programme and learning outcome also varies among various age groups. Schramm (1962)[41] studied various research works and found that students' attitudes at younger age are appreciably more favourable for educational television; their attitudes towards educational television show a steady decline as they move to high school and college.

Studies on SITE experiment in India revealed that negative attitude of teachers in utilization of educational programmes, more or less, is a single factor that contributed in a big way towards the "failure" of the experiment for the purpose of school education. Shukla and Kumar (1977)[42] "noticed that the teachers did not teach around the broadcast of the day". Bhaskaran and Patel (1977)[43] found that pre - and post-telecast discussions did not take place in the majority of the schools. In Karnataka also, Chandra and Karnik (1976)[44], "only 13 per cent of the teachers conducted" such discussions. However, Behra (1991)[45] reported such discussions were conducted in Andhra Pradesh, Karnataka and Orissa. Rahman (1977)[46] found teachers 'insensitive' to the new technology and 'incapable' of making a proper use of it. He links their negative attitude with their traditional beliefs, lack of enough knowledge of the content, and their inability to 'stand to reason'. From the post-telecast activities it emerged that, "most of the teachers were in a very autocratic way of dominance over the children. It needed considerable change in teachers' attitudes towards teaching learning situation". Therefore, reason for most powerful and most persuasive medium like "television being kept down in education is teachers rather than any limitation of the medium itself" (Husain, M. : 2004).[47]

The results of a survey by Mohanty (1986)[48] in Orissa, revealed that television sets installed in the schools of the State are mostly out of order and the schools have either no or often disrupted power supply. Mohanty suggested "involvement of teachers and students in production" of educational programmes to increase the participation of more and more teachers and students in an effective way. He also recommended "better incentives to the custodians" of television sets and stressed the need for using "appropriate language" and dialect in the programmes. Singh (1983)[49] cited similar reasons and problems facing utilization of educational television programmes in Sambalpur and recommended that since the television villages are selected by Doordarshan without consulting education department there is lack of coordination. For better results and proper utilization of educational programmes a proper coordination between the two is highly desirable and strongly recommended.

Sudame and Goel (1985)[50] surveyed over two hundred schools in Maharashtra, which were equipped with television sets. Though the study found a very positive reaction of students and teachers towards school television programmes yet proper utilization of these programmes was impaired due to logistic reasons and the lack of seriousness on the part of school administration, teachers and even the managers. While the 'teachers were not properly trained in the utilization' of educational television programmes, 'no pre- and post-telecast' activities were organized, the use of English language was a strong barrier especially for teachers and students of rural areas, there was 'not enough space' in the schools to accommodate students, the programme 'schedules were not available' prior to telecast, the school 'timetable had no provisions' for the telecast and as usual the 'sets were frequently out of order' with no maintenance backup.

The detailed study of SITE by Agrawal (1978)[51] is a solid document on ETV programme utilization during SITE operations. The report suggests different approaches that are required to be taken to make ETV relevant and useful for all age groups. The report indicates that the students showed a great liking and fascination for programmes on cities, tourist places and industrial areas. Agrawal lays stress on various production techniques, telecast styles and curriculum development that would ultimately increase the teacher-student interaction which is very essential for broadening the mental horizons of students.

Research reveals that teachers favour use of television for teaching some courses and feel that all the subjects cannot be taught effectively by using television. The effectiveness of teaching through television also varies from subject to subject. To find effectiveness of educational television in teaching of elementary science for teachers and students Frazier and Evans (1976)[52] conducted experiments and reported that the teachers who saw television programmes exhibited "a significantly greater confidence in teaching of science" and the students also showed interest in it. But surprisingly children's achievement scores were not found "significantly higher" after the use of television.

Chau and Shramm's (1967)[53] comparison of television teaching with normal classroom teaching did not show much significant difference between the two, nonetheless comparison is skewed in favour of television teaching as more respondents felt that television can be more effective as a tool for learning when used in a suitable context of learning activities and under favourable conditions, children can certainly learn effectively from television. The study also indicates that television can be used effectively to teach various subjects at school, and college level. In contrast Herminghaus (1957)[54] studied and found face to face teaching significantly superior to the television teaching. Notwithstanding these findings, it is generally believed and seen that television does enhance the learning outcome if the viewing is done for the purpose. Ogawa (1963)[55] reported a substantial increase in the knowledge of the students after allowing them to watch an educational television programme on the Tokyo city. Schramm's (1962)[56] review of studies, comparing classroom teaching with instructional television, did not find any difference between the two, except a small percentage (14 per cent) favouring classroom teaching over television teaching. Comparisons were more favourable in studies on elementary schools than in high schools.

The contention that television is relevant for teaching of some subjects and not all has also drawn the attention of researchers. Many subject specific studies were conducted, majority of them support use of television for teaching of certain subjects, however, some studies did not favour teaching through television. Teaching of physics through television was studied by Barrington (1964)[57] in comparison to traditional teaching. Five groups of students, four experimental and one control group, were taught same subject matter, involving five different combinations of teaching techniques. First group was taught with "television integrated with laboratory lessons", second group had "conventional laboratory lessons", the third group saw "television lessons in classroom", the fourth group had "conventional textbook lessons in classroom" and the fifth was a control group with normal school teaching. While the study did not find any significant difference in learning of the first two groups, it did find a significant difference between the third and the fourth, skewed in favour of the third, i.e., television lessons in a classroom. Similarly, Gordon's (1960)[58] study favours use of television for teaching of languages. He found that the students taught through television showed an average gain as compared with those students who were taught in conventional way by their own teachers. Shukla and Kumar (1977)[59] evaluated the impact of Satellite Interactive Television Experiment (SITE) on cognitive development and behaviour of primary school children and attitudes of the teachers. The study indicated a clear and significant improvement in the language of SITE exposed students, though on the whole studies have shown that SITE either did not affect children's achievements at all or it affected their scholastic achievements to a very small extent.

In teaching of social studies to class 9th and 10th through the medium of television, Kornadt and Abankova (1975)[60] found higher achievement scores as compared with normal classroom teaching. Singh and Singh (1983)[61] reported that children of the television schools did better on the achievement test in social studies and science compared to the children of the non-TV schools. Similar potential, however, could not be found in language development and the attitudinal change in the students.

Similarly in study of Zoology, Greenhill (1959)[62], after 5 years' long experimentation, concluded that television was more effective in teaching of zoology as compared to conventional methods. Exposure to science education programmes through television normally stimulated an interest among the students, (Agrawal and Malek : 1986)[63], who became 'high performers' from 'low performers' compared to conventional students who moved from 'low performance' to 'medium performance' and from 'medium performance' to 'high performance'. The study of Kheda experiment by Space Application Centre (Aghi : 1977)[64] indicated that majority of the students exposed to a series of science programmes on television correctly replied the questions on hygiene and their immediate environment as compared to the students of the control villages. Woodward (1964)[65] on the other hand favours teaching of biological sciences through face to face teaching, as the achievement scores of the students taught in conventional form are significantly better than those taught through television. Johnson and Harty (1960)[66] also found that performance of high school students taught geometry in conventional style was significantly higher than those taught through television lessons.

From the above it is clear that research studies with almost similar parameters, variables and other factors tend to differ in results, though marginally, but are more or less consistent in establishing the superiority of teaching through television over the traditional face to face teaching under certain conditions. Cronbach (1975)[67] attributes the difference in the results to the interactive nature of television. Learning he says depends on the involvement, attention, and interaction between the television screen and the viewer. At no time can two students have similar interaction with the screen. Even the same student at two different times cannot have a same degree of attention or involvement in the programme. This relationship between the student and the television is momentary and is directly related with the learning outcomes, hence, the variation in results is justified. The television teaching, if not always better, is comparable to classroom teaching, provided the students watch programmes as captive audience and keep interest. A comparison of over 250 studies on educational television by Stickwell (1963)[68] concluded that neither the television nor the face to face teaching can be considered superior from the comparison of achievement scores of students who study through various means.

3. Studies on Impact of various Production Techniques, Technologies and Modes of Programme Delivery

One of the important factors that is directly related to the learning out comes, is the quality of educational or instructional programme shown to the students. Various production techniques and styles are used to make learning through television an enriching experience. There has always been a tussle between the content, treatment and sleekness of the programme. The more sleek and attractive a programme the poorer the content load, the more the content the duller the programme. Talk head or discussion based programmes are rich in content but not very attractive for the target audience, i.e., the young viewers. Dramatised versions or documentaries in story telling format with a lot of visual and music support tend to attract more students but the learning outcomes are significantly less. Television offers a host of techniques and use of various kinds of equipment and styles, each creating a certain aesthetic appeal and having a profound effect on the audience. Zettl (1973)[69] studied "contextualistic aesthetics" for television and recommended that a television programme should be live and artistic, so as to elevate viewers' involvement and appreciation. Various elements related to aesthetics of television have been examined to understand the complexity of the medium. Arnheim (1974)[70] and Millerson (1972)[71] studied role of lighting and colour in television and also identified four distinct elements of television programming concerning aesthetics as: space, time, motion, light and sound, which have a direct bearing on the involvement of audience. Similarly composition of shots, camera angles, image sizes and placement of objects on screen have been studied by Baggaley *et al.* (1976)[72], Coldevin (1978)[73], Kipper (1986)[74] and Wurtzel *et al.* (1972).[75] The movement on screen and various time factors were studied by Schlater (1970).[76] The studies have shown that the elements of a television programme have a direct bearing on cognitive experience and learning gains of the viewers. This was reported by researchers including Anderson (1972)[77], Dwyer (1971)[78] and Salomon (1974).[79]

It is claimed by many that since educational television programmes have a very dull on screen background and presentation, that impairs the learning process, they are low at cognitive learning process. Ellery (1959)[80] studied the effect of the background of a televised message on cognitive behaviour and did not report any significant differences in the cognitive gains when the viewers watched the presenter against a normal classroom setting or a well-decorated background. Similarly, Schlater (1970)[81] and Nielson (1979)[82] found neither the "positive or negative" nor "any significant differences in the learning process", when they tested different backdrops or juxtaposition of the presenter against a variety of unrelated simple or abstract settings. This, however, is disputed by the study conducted by Baggaley and Duck (1976)[83], who after conducting elaborate tests on effects of background on students' perception of the presenter against a plain grey background and a background decorated with a photograph of an archeological site. It was found that the presenter against the decorated background was perceived by the viewers "as more honest, profound, reliable and fair than the same presenter against a plain background". The replication of the same experiment with three different backgrounds by Coldevin (1978)[84] also showed similar results. Coldevin prepared three different versions of the same material; presenter against plain background, presenter against a background shot of stadium projected on a rear screen placed above the shoulder, and shot of stadium shown on full screen behind the presenter. The analysis revealed that the viewers rated the presenter in the second and the third case significantly higher than the first. The presenter in third case, i.e., full screen background was rated highest on all the factors including, "credibility, clarity, interest, relaxedness, professionalism, straightforwardness and strength". Again Sinha *et al.* (1994)[85], observed, "that students expressed their dislike for plain monotonous background used during the teleconferencing sessions and they preferred either a classroom environment or use of some appealing pictures or backdrops to make screen more attractive".

The placement of objects on screen also drew the attention of many researchers. Metallinos & Tiemens (1977)[86] and Metallinos (1984)[87] found that viewers pay more attention to one side of the screen than the other, and placement of various items on screen are perceived differently. Both the studies concluded that visual retention data supports the "theory of asymmetry in favour of left hand placement of objects" and that viewers pay more attention to the left of screen than the right.

McLuhan's (2001)[88] classification of television as "cold media" against films as "hot media" and Schramm's (1977)[89], book, titled *Big Media, Little Media,* made many believe that small size of television makes it a poor medium of education as viewers are less attentive and, therefore, gain very little in terms of education. The availability of television screens in many sizes, ranging from 4 inches to 74 inches, encouraged researchers to find out the effect of television screen size on viewers. Lombard, Reich, Grabe, Bracken and Ditton (2000)[90] studied the effect of screen size on the viewers and concluded that while "the screen size played a critical role in generating the responses that constitute presence or participatory experience", however, "the viewers of the large screen did not report any greater enjoyment of the stimulus than the viewers watching the same stimulus on the small screen". This view, from the perspective of real life experience, looks faulty as bigger the screen size, much pleasant the viewing and, therefore, higher the enjoyment level. Whether or not that enjoyment is translated into higher learning or better understanding remains to be seen.

Skornia (1965)[91] analysed the impact of television on values, education, language, mental/physical health, catharsis, passivity, etc. and found the influence of television profoundly persuasive and subtle but the persuasive power of the television, at the same time, is not too powerful to leave much negative effect on the educated, who he believes are mature enough to form their own opinion. He, therefore, warned the educationists and sociologists about the negative effects of television on viewers who are not yet properly matured and equipped with enough education. Television also leaves powerful and staying effect on people. It is this quality of television that makes it an effective tool for education but requires a proper balance between where television and teacher are seen as partners.

Actual presence of teacher in a classroom results in higher involvement of the students thereby leading to better understanding, as 'social presence' makes the connection more lively and the teacher is seen taking note of and showing concern for the student. In education through television this is seen as a disadvantage. So the organizers of ETV programmes must try various ways and means to make ETV as realistic as possible to bring it at par with the social presence of a teacher. In making virtual look real, two-way audio and video interactions between the 'tele-teacher' and the students is seen as one of the possibilities. Boverie and others (1997)[92], suggested that due to interaction through television screen it can be understood that satellite based television courses are as effective as face to face instruction. This may be an exaggeration, especially in our settings as the quality of interaction, in terms of audio-video and connectivity, offered by IGNOU or UGC is far from satisfactory, and as of now nothing can replace the 'social presence' of a teacher in the class. Dublin and Hedley (1969)[93] "found instructional television with talkback significantly superior to the instructional television without talkback, but not significantly different from conventional instructions." The fact, however, remains that it does make difference depending on "the degree to which the on screen instructor is seen as a real person, with a genuine interest in the distance learner's progress" (Boverie *et al.*, 1997).[94]

Production techniques, including camera placement, camera movement, use of lenses of varying focal lengths, editing techniques, use of graphics, animations and digital effects have also drawn attention of researchers. As far back as 1963, Grant and Merril[95] studied the effects of subjective *versus* objective camera angle. A programme on nursing skills, shot from subjective and objective angles was shown to two groups of audience. The group that saw the programme made of the shots taken from the subjective angle performed significantly better on recognition learning than the group that watched the programme from the objective angle. Camera angles in terms of height above or below the eye level creates a dramatic effect of the subject. While above the eye level angle (high angle shot) makes subjects look weak and inferior, the below the eye level angle (low angle shot) makes it look more powerful and superior. The use of low or high angle shots create a strong aesthetic reaction in the viewers who readily assume the camera's viewpoint and identify with its superior, above the eye level position, or its inferior, below eye level position. While Mandell and Shaw (1973)[96] supported this argument, McCain, Chilberg & Wakshlag (1977)[97] also concluded "that a low angle shot, if used sparingly as a referent, may increase a speaker's credibility and attractiveness." However Tiemen (1970)[98], in an earlier study, failed to demonstrate any relationship between camera angle and communicative ability or knowledgeability of the newscaster. Like camera angles, camera movements also lead to better understandability of a subject on screen. In Kipper's (1986)[99] study of camera movements *vis-à-vis* the fixed shots, the groups of viewers were shown video tapes of a 'cluttered bedroom of a child' shot with a moving or a fixed camera. The groups that saw the moving camera video reported, "significantly higher scores than the fixed camera groups." The study concluded that the moving shots "provide more information about the physical form or properties of the objects as compared to the fixed shots." Kipper, therefore, recommends, "that camera movements can be used as a powerful technique for structuring the experience of viewers in situations where the task requires them to learn about the physical nature of the scene or to perceive its three dimensional depths." (pp. 299-300). Zettl (1978)[100] had also speculated that "camera technique that leads viewers into the scene" can influence their "comprehension and understanding of depth".

Telephoto lens and wide angle lens make objects look closer or farther from each other, due to different focal lengths and create an illusion. This property of lenses is being used to create or achieve a certain dramatic effect on the screen. Acker (1983)[101] studied the effect of different lenses on 'perceptual judgments of the subjects'. Shots of two moving trains were taken using a wide or a telephoto lens and shown to two groups of students. The group that saw the train on screen shot with wide angle lens was able to better judge the velocity of trains as against the group that was shown the trains shot with a telephoto lens. The experiment, therefore, demonstrated that "the focal length of a camera lens affects perceived velocity and distance" and, hence, the use of lenses for educational programmes must be handled with utmost care. Singh, Prasad, Bajpai and Kuar (1984)[102] found that "too much reliance on long shots at times adversely affects the comprehension and close-up shots may serve a better purpose."

Graphics and animations are considered a great help in educational television programmes, as they help in comprehending complex statistical details and understanding of twisted techniques and phenomena. This finds enough support in research. Coldevin (1975)[103] found that, graphics that are superimposed to reinforce news content produce better retention and recall than no graphic version of the same newscast. Findahl and Hoijer (1976)[104] also found that the superimposed captions of keywords significantly improved recall of news items. Schwardzwalder (1960)[105] had also got similar results in an experiment in which a newscaster was either accompanied by captions or was shown without any captions. Recall in case of the former was found for higher than the latter. Captions, as a rule, however, do not always make a significant difference. Bernard and Coldevin (1985)[106] found that use of captions or graphics in recapitulation do not make any significant difference to learning, while recapitulation in general did make a difference to learning than no recapitulation at all. Edwardson, Kent & McConnel (1985)[107] suggested that the use of repeated graphics provide a conceptual basis that helps in retention and recall of what was seen or heard. Contrarily, Singh *et al.* (1984)[108] found that, "use of too many graphics made a programme monotonous and uninteresting, particularly when much attention was not given to the quality of the graphics." The study further revealed that children particularly 'liked the use' of 'puppets', 'masks', 'animation sequences' and those programmes in which 'children participated and played the characters'.

"Films are either made or marred on the editing table", goes the maxim. No matter how well the film or ETV programme is shot, if it is not edited properly it will not make any significant difference to the audience. Educational television programme makers have, therefore, been using various editing techniques to achieve the desired effect on the audience, most of the time they depend on the individualistic tastes of the editor and his personal experience.

Numerous studies have been conducted to find the effect of various editing techniques. Use of simple or complex methods of enriching the programmes with visual inputs *vis-à-vis* the learning gains of the students have also been studied. Salomon & Cohen

(1977)[109] conducted an experiment with five differently edited versions of the same story using five distinct editing techniques with varying emphases on size, movement and placement of shots. One version was made using zoom ins and zoom outs, second version with close ups and long shots, third with shots from different viewpoints, fourth by leaving gaps in continuity of plots and the fifth with no unique emphasis. The results of the experiment indicated that the knowledge acquired from each version was different. The students who watched the fourth version, 'logical gaps' showed a better understanding of the structure and continuity of the story; the students who watched third version, 'fragmented space', required special 'skills for relating details to the conceptual whole' and demanded to close the visual gaps. The version with close-ups helped students better than the zoom version, in understanding 'relations between the parts and the whole'. The experiment clearly indicates a high correlation between editing techniques and the learning outcome and suggests special care in editing keeping in view the requirements and objective of the programme. Mitchell (1978)[110] experimented through three different versions of video programmes with same audio track. The first was a 'simple' video, and the other two 'complex' —using either film footage and slides or graphics for enhancement. Attention of the viewers was found higher for the 'complex' versions of the programme. Contrary to this, Moris (1984)[111] experimenting with a simple "straight classroom presentation" in comparison with two "innovative versions" of the same programme did not find any significant difference in the overall performance of the two groups, though on "conceptual questions" the group that saw the "innovative version" did better than the other group. Similarly, Silbergleid (1992)[112] studied the phenomenon with three versions of the same video programme that he termed as 'Basic', 'Advanced' and 'Extravagant'. The results, surprisingly, did not show any significant differences in 'comprehension' or 'liking' by the three groups. Keeping in view the time and money required to produce 'advanced' or 'extravagant' versions of the programme in comparison to the simple programmes and the limited or no significant gains for the viewers, media scholars suggest that these techniques shall be used by the producers only if they find them logistically convenient and economically viable. This is especially true for educational programmes that are invariably faced with a very low budget.

The study of the famous US television programme for pre-school children, "Sesame Street" by Pezdek and Steven (1984)[113] concluded that while visuals do not interfere with the audio clips they are certainly more predominant and always more memorable. Kozma (1991)[114], therefore, suggested a combined audio-visual approach as a learning pedagogy.

Despite research supporting the use of various editing techniques for enhancing learning compatible with the objectives of the programme, ETV in India is devoid of much thought on editing. An overwhelming percentage of educational programmes are simple lectures with little or no graphic or video support, discussion or interview, or at best simple documentary format with a beaten track treatment. Very few ETV programmes are made using proper shooting/editing techniques to enhance the learning process. The studies also confirm that the television news research has consistently shown the informational superiority of items that are enriched by the pictorial material in comparison to talking head presentations. (Edwardson, Grooms, and Proadlove (1981)[115], Gunter (1979)[116] Television programmes embellished with graphics and video clips, either supporting or redundant, have shown a significant increase in recall of the events but not necessarily in the understanding of the stories (Son, Reese & Davie, 1987).[117] Drew & Grime (1987)[118] also came out with similar findings. Study of educational television programmes by Mohanty (1976)[119] reported a non-serious attitude on the part of programme makers and broadcasters. The sudden "deviation of ETV" telecast schedule made the pre- and post-test difficult. The programmes were marred by "lack of synchronization", "overlapping of Hindi and Oriya tracks", "difficult language", "inadequate pauses and quick speed" that acted as barriers in communication. Further, students failed to understand the content of various science programmes as the steps were not properly explained and the demonstration of the equipment used was not very clearly understood.

After survey of literature on educational media, Berry (1983)[120] concludes that, "effects of television visuals on the uptake of information are important for TV practice and for the design of educational A-V material'. Therefore, production of ETV programmes must be done with absolute care taking into account the interests of audience, their prior knowledge of the subject and language and also the objectives to make teaching through television a worthwhile activity.

4. Studies pertaining to the Use of Television for Higher Education in India

Use of television for higher education in India is limited to UGC Countrywide Classroom on Doordarshan, IGNOU's Gyandarsahan, VYAS —the higher educational channel of UGC and EKLAVYA — the technology channel managed by Indian Institutes of Technology (IITs). Mohanty and Rath (1990)[121] studied UGC Countrywide Classroom (CWCR) and found that "the knowledge objective has been realized to a great extent in all the programmes whereas understanding and application objectives have been realized in 60 per cent and 52 per cent programmes respectively." Again Jaiswal, Kiran and Goel (1991)[122] referring to the CWCR programmes suggested that different pedagogical fields such as methods, media, techniques, devices, aids and formats have to be well selected." Referring to the need and importance of television for higher education, Ranganathan (2002)[123], contrary to the popular notion that people watch television only for entertainment, found that some people watch television for education. A significant number of these people seek information and education from television to update their knowledge regularly which "will enhance their general awareness" and effectively help them in their "academic pursuits". The study of Reddi, *et al.* (1991)[124] of the Countrywide Classroom suggested the need to be conscious of the entry level skills of the target group, advised student participation in the programmes and advocated that the UGC countrywide classroom programmes must be integrated with the college education.

With the enrolment of students for higher education in India increasing manifold in the last few decades, estimated at 15 million by the end of Eleventh Plan, the proportionate enhancement of infrastructure and quality human resource, owing to limited financial support, remains a matter of concern. Under the circumstances television has assumed much important significance, owing to its wider reach and tremendous potential, in improving the quality of education at all levels across the geographical boundaries. Bates (1980)[125] remarked that television can be an effective educational medium when used in conjunction with the other forms of teaching. He classifies the general factors that tend to influence the learning outcome from television as :

(a) Organisation of teaching which includes the organizational, administrative, and managerial contexts in which educational programmes originate, pedagogical approaches, and the availability and selection of media;
(b) Programme content, modes of presentation and production quality; and
(c) Learners' profile, context of learning and the learning process. (Bates : 1980, pp. 395-396)

Despite the tremendous growth and reach of television, its potential for education has not been yet realized. Arulchelvan and Vishwanathan (2006)[126] studied the "pattern of usage of various electronic media by higher education" and remarked :

> "While the growth of the electronic media of radio and TV in terms of reach, popularity and variety has been phenomenal, there has not been a corresponding growth in their education related usage. Lack of publicity about the contents and timings of the programs, inability of one's electronic equipments to receive the signals and lack of interactive nature of their programs have contributed to the underutilization of these educational media."
>
> (Arulchelvan *et al* : 2006, p. 100)

The Arulchelvan *et al.* (2006)[127] study of the countrywide classroom in Tamilnadu, revealed that 96.31% of their sample possesses television sets, majority of them (74.76%) spend more than half an hour daily watching television. 35.08% of them watch television for education. Results also revealed that "68.12% watched subject based programmes on TV, 38.12% watched scientific programmes and expert lectures, 46.77% watch interactive programmes, while 58% watched career guidance, higher education information on TV". It is disturbing and a matter of serious concern to note that despite a good response to the educational television programmes only "14.61% watch UGC countrywide classroom" and whooping "85.39% do not watch UGC CWCR" on television. Even those who watch UGC programmes, majority of them do not see them more than once a week. The reasons for not watching UGC programmes are many including; "they are not interesting", provide "inadequate interaction", "lack of periodic information", students have "little awareness about the telecast", and most important the inability of the TV sets to "receive the signals". Countrywide classroom programmes that are essentially meant for the students living in remote and rural areas of the country, the study found, are being watched "more by the urban students than their rural counterparts." The researchers found a significant association between medium of instruction and watching of UGC programmes and recommended the production of programmes in local language. They concluded that the "initial negative attitude towards educational television is likely to lessen over time and become more positive or neutral."

Kirkwood (1990)[128] argued that, "the most exciting feature of television lies in delivering educational material to a national audience and its increased potential to enhance students' learning." The countrywide classroom was launched, therefore, to deliver educational content to national audience scattered across the vast geographical areas. After two decades of broadcasting the UGC CWCR is yet to make people excited as it is yet to meet the expectations. To study the expectations of students and teachers from the UGC countrywide classroom programmes and to examine the pattern of viewership for the countrywide classroom a lot of in-house research studies have been conducted by the UGC media centres located across the country. The findings of the research are published in voluminous research reports or in the form of articles in some academic journals, besides small pamphlet, brochures or annual reports published by various media centres. Most of the reports have enumerated the problems facing educational television in India in general and countrywide classroom in particular. The researchers have also tried to find out the utilization of educational programmes by college / university students and teachers, study their impact on and relevance to students, study various modes of programme delivery including interactive mode of broadcasts and understand the needs and requirements of the student community. Through both formative and summative research the researchers tried to find out the entry levels of students, the content load in programmes, suitability of various programme genres for a particular subject and also tried to illicit opinions from the target audience regarding their preference for syllabus-based or enrichment type programmes. The following passages briefly enumerate various research reports on Countrywide Classroom :

> "Profile of the UGC's Countrywide Classroom : A feed-back survey of universities in the State of Maharashtra" by Pendharkar (1988)[129] is a consolidated study of four periodic feedback reports to find out the awareness of students about the Countrywide Classroom and also try to "understand the difficulties and obstacles" students face in watching these programmes. The study revealed a majority of the students (60.96%) watch programmes and most of them are from science stream. Though 86% out of those who watch programmes found them useful, but only 17.58% students watch the telecast regularly. About half of the students get information of the programmes from newspapers. The major reason for not watching is "unsuitable" time slot on DD, some students did not find programmes interesting and useful and some others did not understand the programmes fully due to language barrier.

Kumar (1990)[130] conducted a summative feedback on a programme "Fibonacci Numbers Part 1" with the objective of studying the understanding of programme content by students and get valuable suggestions for improving the programme quality. While '68%' reported that the programme 'generated interest' in them, '44% felt the information was too much'. The report suggested the objectives of the programme should be made very clear in the beginning, equations shall be explained properly, giving enough time to students to understand and the music if used should be chosen and mixed properly to avoid any distraction.

Mishra (1990)[131] conducted a feedback study in the colleges of Himachal Pradesh with the objective "to gather viewer's assessment" of CWCR, "evaluate the programme preferences", "assess the utility and relevance of CWCR" and also "investigate the viewing arrangements". The study reported that '92.7%' respondents have TV sets at home, 84% respondents watch UGC telecast with '9.1%' watching programmes regularly. An overwhelming percentage, "96.9%" of those who watch these programmes find them very useful and "helpful for their overall mental and intellectual development." The language was again found an important barrier in understanding of the programmes. The researcher found that the TV sets provided to colleges are not utilized as there is no proper space available for them; they are either installed in Principal's office, residence, science labs or the store and are never used for the purpose of viewing CWCR programmes. The viewing of programmes by students is mostly at home. Yet the researcher concludes that, while the countrywide classroom has in a broad sense fulfilled its aim to "update, upgrade the knowledge", there are several steps that can be taken to make its impact felt more effectively by the target audience.

Kumari and Ali (January 1991)[132], undertook the programme evaluation of two programmes—one enrichment programme of general interest and the other specifically meant for the science students. The idea was to see if it made any difference to both the levels of comprehension and the general enthusiasm. The enrichment programme was played first to generate enthusiasm that may enhance the learning outcome of the second programme. The researchers found the students reluctant to watch the programmes and most of those who saw first programme left without watching the second programme making one or the other excuse. The study revealed "a general apathy" in the attitudes of students and they did not find any apparent excitement leave alone enthusiasm about getting an opportunity to see a film on something new. In yet another study Kumari and Ali (July 1991)[133] monitored countrywide classroom programmes for a week to "analyse how the capsules were structured and to assess the quality and content of programmes" for the benefit of producers and researchers. The study revealed that while the countrywide classroom credo envisages "to fully exploit the potential of medium" with regard to "immediacy", "omnipresence", "animation and special effects", "visual power", and "intimacy", these remain the "weakest" areas of countrywide classroom. Study further revealed that the constraints of language, time and speed rarely create a feeling or involvement amongst the viewers. The potential of technology is not properly utilized owing to limitation of resources. Govindaraju (1993)[134] after conducting programme evaluation with respect to technical qualities of educational programmes in some colleges of Anna University, Madras found that the quality of programme content is ranked high when the programme content is well organised, meets high pedagogical standards and is presented in a learning context.

National Talkback Experiment 1991 was the first major national level research project in the history of Countrywide Classroom. The two-way audio and one-way video experiment was conducted across the country at eight remote locations involving 35 colleges and 1835 students. For the experiment three experimental groups and one control group was used. The first Experimental group watched programmes and had the benefit of talkback, the group two discussed the programmes among themselves after it was telecast and the group third watched the programmes and talkback but could not ask the questions and the control group simply saw the programmes only. The broader objectives of the study were to test the feasibility of introducing talkback on regular basis and also to find the optimum duration of the talkback, determine to what extent it enhances comprehension, clarify ideas, bring focus to the subject, increase knowledge base, increase questioning ability, increase retention, remove or reduce the problems caused by language, reinforce learning and increase participation (Reddi *et al.* : 1992).[135] Each day two programmes were telecast in normal Countrywide Classroom slot on DD followed by interaction with the expert through two audio and one-way video by the experimental group one. The study found a "conclusively superiority of the talkback approach in improving the quality of classroom participation", "created a new interest, among the students, in the countrywide classroom" and stressed the need for improvement in the quality of programmes and the quality of the talkback (p.119). They suggested the talkback should be made a regular feature with increase in time for interactive sessions. The 'language' was established a problem in reducing the learning outcomes. Findings, however, were inconclusive about the effectiveness of the talkback. Thus the researchers attributed to the influence of some "extraneous factors affecting" the results. The novelty of the experiment may be one among them. As the "emphasis shifted from attention to the programme to the asking of questions and the competition to get most questions through." (p.118)

The talkback experiment was repeated in 1994 with some changes in the design. The repeat of talkback experiment had one experimental group (with talkback through STD lines) and one control group (without talkback), and used a package of tele-course on new communication technologies. The experiment yielded much encouraging results. The telephone lines were also thrown open to general public during the last four days of the experiment and each day only one 20 minutes programme was played and rest of the transmission time i.e. 40 minutes were utilized for interaction. The focus this time was on "passive viewers" concept of telecasting "package of programmes" on same or similar theme and the "cost-effectiveness" of talkback in Indian settings. Reddi, U. V. and Others (1995)[136] reported that the package concept was well taken by the viewers. The report also provided valuable suggestions for making interactivity more effective. Report suggested to "increase in number of telephone lines at the teaching end" to ensure fast connectivity and provide "more time for interaction." If the programmes are telecast in a package mode then every care must be taken to achieve "uniformity in programme content, quality, and information overload". The report suggests that the enrolled students shall be provided, "supplementary reading material", before the telecourse, the "telecourses must be open to the general viewing audience" and lays the stress on the "need for improvement of the technical quality of both the programmes and the interaction." The report while recommending use of teleconferencing for educational television, more frequently, in a more organized manner concludes that "interactive television" increases "participatory communication that brings about motivation and commitment" among the teachers and the participant students.

A national survey on UGC Countrywide Classroom was conducted by an independent agency ADMAR (1993)[137] , engaged by CEC, involving a sample size of "20,000 listing interviews and 15,300 detailed interviews", scattered in 27 cities and towns. The study, conducted across the country projected the viewership of the countrywide classroom, in the target cities and towns with an estimated potential viewership of 121.78 million, at 21.29 million, who have watched UGC programmes at least once. However, on an average day, the viewership is estimated at 3.99 million. The majority of the viewers watch UGC programmes at home and the "viewership is skewed towards higher income households and socio-economic groups." The study also found that students have a preference for watching programmes from 6:00 a.m. to 8:00 a.m. in the morning or any time after 5:00 p.m. The repeat of the survey by ADMAR (1997)[138] , 4 years later with a sample size of 26,600 in 50 cities and towns found a viewership of 22 million "spread in 10,000+ population towns." The survey also found higher viewership in "non-metros" and again most of them males "from higher income and socio-economic groups." Viewership was skewed towards "viewers with English medium school background." The majority of the viewers this time, however, preferred evening time slots for CWCR, which in fact are highly commercial time slots on DD.

To understand the reasons of students for not watching UGC Countrywide Classroom programmes, to determine the interests and expectations of students, to examine the viewership pattern and effectiveness of CWCR, Govindaraju (1996)[139] conducted a 'social survey' involving 954 undergraduate and postgraduate students of 12 colleges in Tamilnadu. The study reported that despite a very high daily exposure of 68.45 per cent to television, only 7.13 per cent students watch CWCR programmes daily and 7.65 per cent frequently.

The low exposure to CWCR is mostly attributed to inconvenient time slot on DD, lack of enough information about the programmes, poor institutional back-up for arranging and encouraging the viewing of these programmes and language. Language again remains a factor as most of the students, especially from the semi-urban and rural areas are not very comfortable with the English language programmes. The study also found that students from arts and social science streams prefer documentary mode programme while the science students like demonstrative formats. Students on the whole feel the programmes are useful, they desire programmes that help them prepare for competitive examinations and other career-oriented vocations.

With regard to reasons for non-viewing of UGC countrywide classroom programmes, Rao Jagadeeshwar (1998)[140] also reported that lack of proper information and "awareness" about the telecast, "non-availability of TV sets", "language of CWCR " and "lack of interest" contributes heavily for students not watching the CWCR programmes. Rao Jagadeeshwar (2004)[141], however, reported that majority of the students are aware of various educational television programmes including CWCR but still less than 10% of them watch CWCR programmes regularly. Students prefer programmes that offer something more than that is not taught in the classroom and that will enrich their knowledge and help them in self-development. The study concludes that CWCR shall offer programmes that are a judicious mix of direct teaching, enrichment and general awareness.

The launch of VYAS —the 24- hour satellite higher educational channel of UGC offers flexible time slots to students as the programmes are repeated after every 6 hours in a day. Jan Salima (2007)[142] , reported though 47.75% of the respondents have seen some UGC CWCR programmes on Doordarshan but they are yet to see "VYAS channel" as it is neither available in the colleges nor is it being shown by the cable operators. Even after two years in operation majority of the respondents have heard the name of the channel for the first time. The study further revealed that while majority of the students, 52%, want to see programmes of general nature including a mixture of enrichment and syllabus-oriented, 41.75% want pure enrichment type programmes, 23.25% want pure syllabus-oriented programmes. The teachers are divided in their opinion, with equal number 45.5%, for enrichment and syllabus-based programmes. The use of multimedia i.e. visuals, graphics and animations, the majority said, make the programmes more interesting. The study also revealed that none of the colleges have facility for receiving VYAS-Channel nor is the college administration, in any college, aware about such a channel some of them have, however, heard about the Gyandarshan.

The above research studies and surveys reveal that television has an impact in shaping the attitudes, behaviour, and learning of an individual and television has established itself as the most persuasive medium and potent weapon in bringing about a change. The use of television in education has been experimented and studied the world over, with some research in the use of television in higher education, and it has been established that television can play a significant role in education and enhance the learning outcomes. In a country like India, with a huge population scattered over a vast area mostly in rural and remote areas, where the resources in terms of infrastructure and expertise are meagre, the role of educational television can neither be undermined nor overemphasized. Yet, the educational television like Countrywide Classroom, despite 25 years of its existence has not yet been able to create a dent in the hearts and minds of people. Majority of the people even today are not well aware about these programmes. Some scholars attribute this to lack of enough publicity and yet many others to centralized mode of the project, which is more or less an isolated effort.

As Bates (1987)[143] says, "for areas as large and diverse as India, there is a need for national, regional, and local programming; this means decentralized production and delivery to match the needs of local areas, and a flexible network arrangement that provides a national, regional, and local coverage." The illustrative potential of television has been shown beyond doubt and the power of audio-visual presentations in education are no longer in question. What remains to be found is how to make the best use of this wonderful technology in higher education? Educational television in India, as the surveys and the research studies reveal, is facing a general apathy on the part of students, teachers, programme producers, broadcasters and the planners alike. In a welfare state, that India claims to be, the national television has almost no time for educational television programmes, the government cannot afford or does not want to pump some money to make at least one educational terrestrial free to air channel that can be easily received by the people, the cable operators do not carry the educational channels as they feel there are no takers for such programmes, parents and teachers do not ask for such programmes from the cable operators, the teachers neither themselves see nor encourage students to watch educational programmes on television, the programme producers and broadcasters mostly do not take the work serious enough to create a dent on the general psyche that these programmes are useful and serve an important function in educating a society where enrolment in higher education is still less than 10 per cent.

The research also reveals that people are well aware about the educational potential of television both in urban and suburban areas, and a very healthy trend is quite evident that the people increasingly want to update their knowledge. So it is required to find out ways and means to reach these people with quality educational programmes in a flexible and meaningful way. The general perception and consensus among the researchers is that television can contribute to the teaching learning situation as a complementary or supplementary service but the "perceptions vary on the use of television in higher education. Specifically they differ on the use of television as a means of quality enhancing medium in education." (Govindaraju : 1996)[144]

But the research as conducted so far is neither thorough nor does it reflect how perceptions vary from person to person. It also does not provide any clues how television under the given circumstances can be used as an effective medium for higher education. As Gandhi (1995)[145] remarks :

> "It seems to be widely agreed that a great deal of the research that has been carried out in the general field of educational and instructional television has, to put it mildly, been of less use than it might have been. It is suggested here that this is so quite simply because often the right questions were not asked. Even when we recognize in this research area the inadequacies in design, the impression of techniques and instruments, the uncontrolled variables, we are still forced to the

> conclusions that, even in the unlikely event of all these snags being ironed out, time talent and money would still be wasted unless more attention were *(sic)* given to theoretical foundations, the wide social context, and to the nature of questions asked."
>
> (pp. 138-139)

The studies conducted so far have tried to find out the utilization of the "Countrywide Classroom" programmes and the reasons for underutilization. Not a single study has been conducted to find out the perceptions of broadcasters, programme producers and senior academics about the educational television. Nor has any study tried to find out how the "UGC Countrywide Classroom" programmes can be utilized in a better and effective way taking into account the perceptions of those who are directly connected with it. This study, therefore shall aim at studying the perceptions of two important sections concerned with the use of television in higher education, i.e., the broadcasters and academics. The perceptions with regard to educational television in higher education in general and UGC Countrywide Classroom in particular shall be collected and analyzed thoroughly to determine how to make the best use of television for higher education. The study shall be conducted in a holistic manner together with the opportunities that television and new technologies today offer to make effective use of television for higher education.

The literature survey also shows a very little research has been conducted on educational television in the valley of Kashmir. The efforts shall, therefore, be also made to study the role of educational television in higher education in the valley of Kashmir.

References

1. Dizard, Wilson Jr. *Old Media New Media.* 2nd Ed. (New York : Longman Publishers, 1997), p. 89.
2. Dizard, Wilson. (1997), *ibid.*, p. 90.
3. "DD More Popular than Private Channels", *Outlookindia.com*, viewed on January 18, 2008. <http://www.outlookindia.com/pti_news.asp?id=385755>
4. Indianetzone Website, viewed on January, 20, 2008. <http://www.indianetzone.com/3/doordarshan_dd_india.htm>

5. Comstock, G. *Television and the American Child.* (San Diego: Academic Press, 1991), p. 107.
6. Kent Geiger & Robert Sopol. *Educational Television in Boston.* (1965) In Gordon, George N. *Classroom Television: New Frontiers in ITV.* (New York: Communication Art Books, 1970), pp. 39-67.
7. Gilbert Seldes. *ETV's Community Job in Educational Television: the Next ten years.* (Stanford: The Institution for Communication Research, 1962) in Comstock, G. *Television and the American Child.* (San Diego: Academic Press 1991), p.119.
8. Berkman (1976) in Husain, M. *Distance Education through Television,* (New Delhi: Anmol Publications Pvt. Ltd. 2004), p. 26.
9. Skinner, B.F. "The Teaching Machine". *Science,* Vol. 128, Issue 3330, October 24, 1958, pp. 969-977.
10. Seth, Indu. *A Study of the Effectiveness of Educational Television on the Educational Development of Primary Children.* Baroda: Ph.D. Thesis, University of Baroada. (1983) pp. 169-170.
11. Singh, J. and A.K Singh. *A Study of the Impact of ETV Programmes on Children of classes iv-v, in Sumbalpur District Orrisa.* INSAT Evaluation series-3, Mimeographed, (New Delhi, CIET, NCERT, 1983).
12. Singh, J. and A.K Singh. *Reports of the ETV Utilization in Orissa* (Period ending December 1983). Evaluation series-4, Mimeographed, (New Delhi: CIET, NCERT, 1984).
13. Toffler, Alvin. *The Third Wave: the classic study of tomorrow.* (New York: William Morrow, 1980), p. 210.
14. Grossberg in Dizard (1997), *ibid.*, p. 114.
15. Belson, W.A. *The Impact of television* (Melbourne: Cheshire, 1967).
16. Himmelweit, H., A. N Oppenheim, and P. Vince. *The television and the child – an empirical study of the effects of television on the young.* (London: Oxford University Press, 1958).
17. Coffin, T.E. "Television's Impact on Society". *American Psychlogist.* Vol 10, (1955): pp. 630-641.
18. Schramm, W.; J. Lyle, and E.B Parker. *Television in the Lives of our Children.* (Stanford: Stanford University Press, 1961).
19. Furu, T. *The Functions of Television for Children and Adolescents.* (Tokyo: Sophia University Press, 1971).
20. Dobb, A. and G.E Macdonald. "Television Viewing and fear of victimization – Is the relationship casual". *Journal of Personality and Social Psychology,* Vol. 37. (1979).
21. Gerbner, G. and L Gross, "The violent face of television and its lessons". In E. L. Palmer and A. Darr (Eds.). *Children and three faces of television - teaching, Violence and Selling.* (New York: Academic Press, 1980).
22. Dorr, A. "Television and effective development and functioning: may be this decade". *Journal of Broadcasting,* Vol. 25 (1981): pp. 335-345.
23. Scott, L.F. "Television and School Achievement". *Phi Delta Kappan,* Vol. 38 (1956): pp. 25-28.

24. Clark, W.J. *Off Children and Television*, (Cincinnati OH: Xavier University, 1951).
25. Childers, P. and J. Ross. "The Relationship between Television and student's Achievement". *Journal of Educational Research*, Vol. 66 (1973): pp. 317-319.
26. Bayline, L. "Mass Media and Children: A study of exposure habits and cognitive effects". *Psychological Monograph*, Vol. 73. Whole No. 471 (1950).
27. Stern, S.L. "Television and Creativity: The Effect of Viewing Certain Categories of Commercial Television Broadcasting on the Divergent Thinking Abilities of intellectually gifted children". *Dissertation Abstract*, (1974), 34, 3716A.
28. Maccoby, E. "The Effects of Television on Children". In W. Schrall (Ed.). *The Science of Human Communication*, (New York, 1963), pp.110-127.
29. Kanade, H.M. *A Study of the Impact of Instructional Television on the Behaviour of the Rural Elementary School Children*. (Baroda: Ph.D Thesis, University of Baroda, 1982) in Behra, S.C. *Educational Television Programmes* (New Delhi: Deep & Deep Publication, 1991), p. 55.
30. Mohanty, P.C., *A Critical Study of the Educational Television Programmes for the Primary School Children in the State of Orissa*., (Bhuneshawar: Ph.D Thesis. Utkal University, 1986 in Behra (1991) (*Ibid.*), p. 56.
31. Seth Indu, *ibid.*, p. 169-170.
32. R. Shahid. "Television Violence and its effects on children and teenagers – the global perspective" *INSIGHT Journal of Applied Research in Education*, Vol 9, No.1. (Srinagar: Faculty of Education, University of Kashmir, 2004): pp. 125-140.
33. Akutsu, Y. *et al.*, "An analysis of factors related to use of school television at the elementary level". *The Japanese Journal of Radio-TV Education*. (1971): pp. 69-80.
34. Bostik, R.N.R. *The Extent of Use of ITV in Mississippi Public Schools and Factors which Encourage, limit or Prevent Usage*. Ph.D thesis, University of Mississippi (1984).
35. Torres, Migdalia. *Effect of Video Tape Modules in sensitizing prospective Teachers to the Problems inherent in the Acquisition of Knowledge and Goal Perception of Bilingual Education and Attitudes towards Pre-service Training*. Doctoral Dissertation. Pennsylvania State University of USA. (1984).
36. Wittich, W.A. and C.F. Schuller. *Audio-Visual Material : Their Nature and Use*. New York: Harper and Row Publishers, 1968.
37. Phutela, R.L. *A Study into Utilization and Comprehensibility of School Television Programmes in Delhi*. Mimeographed. New Delhi: CIET, NCERT, 1984.
38. Choat, E., H. Griffin, and D. Hobart. "Educational TV and the curriculum for children up to the age of seven years". *British Journal of Educational Technology*, Vol. 17(3), London Council of Educational Technology. October, 1986: pp. 53-66.
39. Neurath, P. "School Television in Delhi". (New Delhi: All-India Radio, 1966) in Behera, S.C. (1991), *ibid.*, pp.52-53.
40. Ghiassi, Jahrome. *Survey of the opinions of social studies teachers in Shiraz (IRAN) regarding the potential use of Instructional Television in middle school.* Doctoral Dissertation, the Florida State University, 1978.

41. Schramm, W. *What we know about learning from Instructional Television, Educational Television: The Next 10 Years.* Stanford, CA: Institute of Communication Research 1982., pp. 52-76.
42. Shukla, S. and K. Kumar. *Satellite Instructional Television Experiment: Impact of SITE on Primary School Children.* Bangalore: Indian Space Research Organisation, August, 1977. p.23.
43. Bhaskaran, P. and I. Patel. *SITE for Children: Morning Feedback.* Mimeographed, (Ahmedabad: Space Applications Centre, 1977).
44. Chandra, R. and K. Karnik. *Planning for Satellite Broadcasting: The Indian Instructional Television Experiment.* Paris: UNESCO, 1976, p. 49.
45. Behera, S.C. *Educational Television Programmes: Impact on Teachers Competency.* New Delhi: Deep and Deep Publications, 1991, p. 54.
46. Rahman, S. *Satellite Instructional Television Experiment –A Study in Educational Television (Udaya-Bhanu).* New Delhi: Ministry of Education and Social Welfare, GOI, 1977 in Husain M. *Distance Education through Television.* New Delhi: Anmol Publications Pvt. Ltd. 2004, p. 21.
47. Husain, M. *Distance Education through Television.* New Delhi: Anmol Publications Pvt. Ltd. 2004, p. 26.
48. Mohanty (1986) in Behra (1991), *ibid.*, p.57.
49. Singh, J. *A Report on ETV Utilization with special reference to TV Maintenance in Sumbalpur.* INSAT Evaluation Series-2. Mimeographed, New Delhi: CIET, NCERT, 1983.
50. Sudame, G.R. and D. R. Goel "Educational Television in India: Organization and Utilization", *EPA Bulletin*, Vol. 8 No.1 & 2, New Delhi: NIEPA. April-July, 1985).
51. Agrawal, C. Binod. *Television Comes to Village: An Evaluation of SITE.* Bangalore: ISRO, 1978.
52. Frazier and Evans (1960). In Behra (1991), *ibid.*, p. 45.
53. Chu, G.C. and W. Schramm. *Learning from Television: What the Research Says.* (Stanford, CA: Institute for Communication Research. 1967) in Arulchelvan and Vishwanathan (2006). "Pattern of usage of various electronic media by higher education students", *International Journal of Education and Development using Information and Communication Technology.* Vol. 2 Issue 4 (2006): p.101.
54. Herminghaus, E.G. "Large Group Instruction Television by Television and Experiment", *School Review.* (1957), pp. 119-133.
55. Ogawa, T. *Learning from Educational Television.* Nagano City, Japan: Institute for Educational Research, 1963.
56. Schramme, W. *What we know about learning from Instructional Television: Educational Television the Next 10 Years.* Stanford, CA: Institute of Communication Research, 1962, pp. 52-76.
57. Barrington, H. *The Teaching of Elementary Science by Television and other methods,* M.Ed. Dissertation, University of Manchaster, in H. Barrington (1964), "A Survey of Instructional Television Researches", *Educational Research,* (1964), Vol. 8.
58. Gordon, G. N. *Educational Television.* New York: The Centre for Applied Research in Education, 1960.

59. Shukla and Kumar. August, 1977. *Ibid.*, p. 34.
60. Kornadt and Abankova. (1975). In Gerhard Tulodziecki, "Educational Television in Federal Republic of Germany", *Programmed Learning and Educational Technology*, Vol.14., May 1977.
61. Singh J. and A.K. Singh. *A Study of the Impact of ETV Programmes on the Children of classes IV-V in Sambalpur District* (*Orissa*). (INSAT Evaluation Series-3). Mimeographed (New Delhi: CIET, NCERT, July, 1983).
62. Greenhill, L.P. *TV in University Science Instruction*. (Pennsylvania : State University of Pennsylvania, 1959).
63. Agrawal, B.C. and M.R. Malek. *Television in Kheda*. (New Delhi: Concept Publishing Company Pvt. Ltd., 1986), p. 62.
64. Aghi, M.B. *Impact of Science Education Programme on SITE Children of Rajasthan*. (Ahmedabad: Space Application Centre, 1977).
65. Woodward (1964). In Behra (1991), *ibid.*, p. 48.
66. Johnson, G.N. and F. Harty. "The Norfolk city experiment in Instructional Television: The Big Picture" September, 1957, June 1960 (Norfolk, VA: *Vision Project*, 1960).
67. Cronbach, L.J. "Beyond the two Disciplines of Scientific Psychology". *American Psychologist*, 1975, pp. 116-127.
68. Stickwell, D.W. (1963). "A critical review of the methodology and the results of research comparing televised and face-to-face instructions". *Dissertation Abstract*, 24, 3239A.
69. Zettl, H. *Sight, Sound, Motion: Applied Media Aesthetics*. (Bellmount Cliff : Wadsworth Publishing, 1973).
70. Arnheim, R. *Art and Visual Perception*. (Berkley: University of California Press, 1974).
71. Millerson, G. *The Technique of Television Production*. (New York : Hastings House Publication, 1972).
72. Baggaley, J.P. and S. W. Duck. *Dynamics of Television*. (Farnborough : Saxon House, 1976).
73. Coldevin, G. "Experimentation in TV presentation strategies II: Effectiveness of full Screen *vs* Corner Screen, symbol establishment background visuals". *Educational Broadcasting International*, Vol. 23. (1978) : pp. 289-303.
74. Kipper, P. "Television camera movement as a source of perceptual information". *Journal of Broadcasting and Electronic Media*, Vol. 30. (1986) : pp. 295-307.
75. Wurtzel, A.H. and J. R. Dominic. "An evaluation of television Drama : Interaction of acting styles and shot selection". *Journal of Broadcasting*. Vol.16. (1972) : pp. 103-110.
76. Schlater, R. "Effect of speed of presentation on recall of television messages". *Journal of Broadcasting*, Vol.14. (1970): pp. 207-214.
77. Anderson, C.M. "In Search of a Visual Rhetoric of Instructional Television". *AV Communication Review*, Vol. 20. (1972): pp. 43-63.
78. Dwyer, M.F. "Colour as an Instructional Variable". *AV Communications Review*. Vol.18. (1971): pp. 399-416.

79. Salomon, G. "What is learned and how it is taught: The interaction between media, message, task and learner". in D. R. Olson, (Ed.). *Media and Symbols : The Forms of Expression, Communication and Education.* (Chicago: University Press. 1974), pp. 383-406.
80. Ellery, J.B. *A Pilot Study of the Nature of Aesthetic Experience associated with Television and its Place in Education.* (Detroit : Wayne State University, 1959).
81. Schlater (1970), *ibid.*, pp. 210-211.
82. Neilson, J. "Does the background affect televised message reception"? *Educational and Instructional Television*, Vol.11(2), (1979): pp. 61-64.
83. Baggaley and Duck (1976), *ibid.*, 79.
84. Coldevin (1978) *ibid.*, pp. 289-303.
85. Sinha, A., D. Kishore and J.N. Hashmi. *Report of Training and Development Communication Channel Experiment.* (New Delhi: EMPC, IGNOU, 1994).
86. Metallinos, N. and R. K. Tiemens. "Asymmetry of the screen: the effect of left *versus* right placement on television images", *Journal of Broadcasting*, Vol. 21,1, (1977): pp. 21-33.
87. Metallinos, N. "Children's Perception, Retention and Preference of Asymmetrical Composition in Pictures". *Canadian Journal of Communications*, Vol 13, (1984): pp. 10-15.
88. McLuhan Marshal, (1964), *ibid.*, pp.24-35.
89. Schramm, Wilbur. *Big Media, Little Media.* (California: Sage Publications, 1977).
90. Lombard, M.; R; Reich; M. Grabe; M. C. Bracken; and T. Ditton. "Presence and television : The role of screen size". *Journal of Broadcasting*, Vol. 26 (1). (2000): pp. 75-98.
91. Sakornia, H.J. *Television and Society.* (New York: McGraw Hill Publications, 1965).
92. Boverie, P.; W.G. Murrell; C.A Lowe; R.H Zettl; and C. H. Gunawardena. *Live versus taped: New Perspective in Satellite based Programming for Primary Grades.* (Albuquerque: University of Mexico, 1997) ED 407939.
93. Dublin, J. and T. Hedley. (1969) "Interactivity in Instructional Television", in *The SITE Experience No. (9). The Reports and Papers on Mass Communication* (Paris: UNESCO, 1983), p. 8.
94. Boverie *et al.* (1997), *ibid.*, p. 9.
95. Grant, T.S. and I. R. Merill, "Camera Placement for Recognition of Complex Behaviours". *Television in Health Science Education.* (Washington : US Office of Education, 1963).
96. Mandell, L.M. and D. L. Shaw. "Judging people in news unconsciously: effect of camera angle and bodily activity", *Journal of Broadcasting*, Vol.17, (1973): pp. 353-362.
97. McCain, *T., A.J* Chilberg and J. J. Wakshlag. *The Effect of Body Type and Camera Shots on Interpersonal Attraction and Course Credibility.* (1977) (ED 099917), p. 34.
98. Tiemen, R.K. "Some relationships of camera angle to communicator credibility", *Journal of Broadcasting*, Vol 14. (1970): pp. 483-490.

99. Kipper (1986), *ibid.*, pp. 299-300.
100. Zettl, H. "The rare case of television aesthetics", *Journal of the University Film Association*, Montreal, Vol 3., (1978): pp. 3-8, 30.
101. Acker, S. "Viewers' perception of velocity and distance in televised events", *Human Communication Research*; Vol. 9(4); (1983): pp. 335-348.
102. Singh, J.; S. Prasad; A. Bajpai; and R J. Kuar. *Pre-telecast Testing of the ETV Programmes: Some Observations*. INSAT Evaluation Series, Mimeographed. (New Delhi : CIET, NCERT, 1984).
103. Coldevin, G., "Spaced, massed and summary treatments as review strategies, for ITV production". *AV Communication Review*, Vol.23, (1975): pp. 289-303.
104. Findahl, O. and B. Hoijer. *Fragments of Reality: An Experiment with News and TV News*. (Stockholm: Swedish Broadcasting Corporation, 1976).
105. Schwardzwalder, J.C. "An investigation of the relative effectiveness of certain specific TV techniques on learning". (1960) (ED 014913).
106. Bernard, R.M. and G. O. Coldevin. "Effects of recap strategies on television news recall and retention". *Journal of Broadcasting and Electronic Media*, Vol. 29 (4), (1985): pp. 407-419.
107. Edwardson, M.; K. Kent; & M. McConnel. "Television new information gain: Video text *versus* a talking head". *Journal of Broadcasting.*, Vol. 29(4). (1985): pp. 367-378.
108. Singh, *et al.* (1984), *ibid.*, 37.
109. Salomon, G. & A. A. Cohen. "Television formats, mastery of mental skills and the acquisition of knowledge". *Journal of Educational Psychology*, Vol. 69. (1977): pp. 612-619.
110. Mitchell, P.D. "Do Students pay more attention to complex than simple ETV images"? (London: Paper presented to Canadian Educational Researcher's Association, 1978).
111. Moris, J.D. "Florida Study: improving achievements through the use of more dynamics in TV production", *Technological Horizons in Education*, Vol. 12(3). (1984): pp. 104-107.
112. Silbergleid, M.I. "Instructional television: visual production techniques and learning comprehension". (1992) (ED 349942).
113. Pezdek, K. and E. Stevens. "Children's memory for auditory and visual information on television". *Developmental Psychology*, Vol. 20(1-3) (1984): pp. 212-218.
114. Kozma, R.B. "Learning with Media", *Review of Educational Research*, Vol. 61 (2) (1991), pp. 179-211.
115. Edwardson, M.; D. Grooms; and S. Proadlove. "Talking news information gain from interesting video *vs* talking heads". *Journal of Broadcasting*, Vol. 25 (17), (1981), pp. 367-378.
116. Gunter, B. "Recall of brief television news items: effects of presentation mode, picture content and serial position". *Journal of Educational Television*, Vol. 5 (2). (1979): pp. 57-61.
117. Son, J.; S. Reese; & W. Davie. "Effects of visual-verbal redundancy and recaps on television news learning". *Journal of Broadcasting and Electronic Media*, Vol. 31(2). (1987): pp. 207-216.

118. Drew, D. G., and T. Grimes."Audio-Visual redundancy and TV news recall". *Communication Research*, Vol. 14(4) (1978): pp. 17-26.
119. Mohanty, J. "A study of ETV programmes under SITE". (Bhubaneswar: Educational Technology Cell; Directorate of Higher Education, 1976. In Behra (1991) *ibid.*, p-59.
120. Berry, C. "A dual effect of pictorial enrichment in learning from television News: Gunter's date revisited". *Journal of Educational Television*, Vol. 9(3). (1983): pp. 171-174.
121. Mohanty, J. and A. Rath. "Countrywide Classroom TV Programmes : An Appraisal Study". (1990) in Arulchelvan and Vishwanathan (2006), *ibid.*,101.
122. Jaiswal, Kiran and Goel "Improving Countrywide Classroom Programmes" (1991) in Arulchelvan and Vishwanathan, (2006), *ibid.*, pp. 101-102.
123. Ranganathan Y. (2002). "Information Based Education in Rural Schools", Chennai: ICCD 2002 in Arulchelvan and Vishwanathan (2006). *ibid.*, 102.
124. Reddi, U.V., Sai Prassad, A. and V. Rukmini. *Final Report National Talkback Experiment* (New Delhi: University Grants Commission. 1992).
125. Bates, A.W., "Towards a better Theoretical Framework for studying learning from Educational Television", *Instructional Science,* Vol. 9, (1980): pp. 393-415.
126. Arulchelvan, S. and D. Vishwanathan. "Pattern of usage of various electronic media by higher education students." *International Journal of Education and Development using Information and Communication Technology* (IJEDICT), Vol. 2, Issue 4 (2006), p. 100.
127. Arulchelvan *et al.* (2006). *ibid.*, pp.107-109.
128. Kirkwood, A. "Into the Video Age: Open University Television in the 1990s", *Journal of Educational Television* Vl 16(2), 1990, pp 77-85. in Govindaraju P. *Educational Television (ETV) in Higher Education: An Evaluation of UGC Countrywide Classroom.* (Madras: Audio Visual Research Centre, Anna University, 1996), p. 2.
129. Pendharkar, Sushama. *Profile of the UGC's Countrywide Classroom : A Feedback Survey of Universities in the State of Maharashtra,* (Pune: EMRC, University of Pune, 1988).
130. Kumar, Usha. *Postproduction Feedback Report, on Fibonacci Numbers Part 1* (Roorkee: Audio Visual Research Centre, University of Roorkee, 1990).
131. Mishra, Rajendra. *Countrywide Classroom: Feeback Study from Himachal Pradesh,* (New Delhi: UGC, INSAT TV Project, Teachers Training College, Jamia Milia Islamia, 1990).
132. Kumari, Abhilasha and Athar Ali. *Programme Evaluation Series Report-1* (New Delhi: Mass Communication Research Centre, Jamia Millia Islamia, Jan. 1991).
133. Kumari, Abhilasha and Athar Ali. *Monitoring Report-1* (New Delhi: Mass Communication Research Centre, Jamia Millia Islamia, July 1991).
134. Govindaraju, P. *Research Report: 6, Programme Evaluation Series II,* (Madras: Audio Visual Research Centre, (CEMDC), Anna University 1993).

135. Reddi, Usha, V. *et al*, 1992), *ibid.*
136. Reddi, Usha, V. and others. *Final Report, CEC-IGNOU-ISRO National Talkback Experiment, New Information and Communication Technologies,* (New Delhi: UGC Media Centres and the Consortium for Educational Communication, 1995).
137. ADMAR Report of the "Viewership Study on UGC Countrywide Classroom Programmes". (New Delhi: Consortium for Educational Communication, 1993).
138. ADMAR Report of National "Viewership Study 97 on UGC Countrywide Classroom Programmes". (New Delhi: Consortium for Educational Communication, 1997).
139. Govindaraju, P. *Educational Television (ETV) in Higher Education: An Evaluation of UGC Countrywide Classroom.* (Madras: Audio Visual Research Centre, Anna University, 1996).
140. Rao, Jagadeeshwar. *Needs Assessment and Reasons for Non-Viewing of Countrywide Classroom Programmes: A Research Report.* (Hyderabad: Audio Visual Research Centre. Osmania University, 1998).
141. Rao Jagadeeshwar. *Needs and Expectations of Primary Target Viewers of Countrywide Classroom Programmes : A Research Report.* (Hyderabad : Audio Visual Research Centre, Osmania University, 2004).
142. Jan, Salima. *Regional Report on VYAS Channel.* (Srinagar : Educational Multimedia Research Centre, University of Kashmir, 2007).
143. Bates, A. W. *Television, Learning and Distance Education,* (Milton Keynes, UK: The Open University, Institute of Educational Technology, 1987). In Khan, M.I. and S.R. Sharma. *Instructional Technology: Media and Theory.* (New Delhi: Kanishka Publishers and Distributors, 1993), p. 280.
144. Govindaraju, (1996), *ibid.*, p. 2.
145. Gandhi, V.P. *Media and Communications Today : Policy, Training and Development.* Volume 2. (New Delhi: Kanishka Publishers Distributors, 1995): pp. 138-139.

Chapter-3

Television for Higher Education

From Countrywide Classroom to Virtual Classroom—The Analysis of UGC's Experience of using Television for Higher Education

With the rapid growth of Doordarshan in early eighties, owing to satellite broadcasting, Doordarshan experienced a huge dearth of programmes to feed the transmission. Around the same time there was a strong feeling that television, with its dynamic and versatile character, can be an economical and effective medium for taking quality education to the students across the country. Taking advantage of the Indian experience from SITE experiment and Doordarshan's growing demand for television software, University Grants Commission (UGC), the apex body of higher education in India, decided to exploit the potential of television for the cause of higher education and launched "UGC Countrywide Classroom", on Doordarshan National Network, on 15th August, 1984. Under the Countrywide Classroom, on Doordarshan, special educational television programmes were produced and telecast for the benefit of undergraduate and postgraduate students across the country.

The need for using television for higher education was necessitated due to enormous growth in student population in higher education. The enrolment for higher education by the end of Tenth Plan was estimated to cross 10 million. Though there was a significant increase in number of higher educational institutions in the country but there was not enough matching growth in terms of proper infrastructure and manpower. While some colleges in cities and urban areas had a proper infrastructure in terms of manpower and facilities to conduct the courses, most of the colleges, especially in rural areas were experiencing shortage of trained teachers, dearth of equipped laboratories and libraries. There was a great disparity among the colleges located in various parts of the country, which continues with greater magnitude today, that resulted in imbalance in the quality of teaching between rural and urban colleges. Under the circumstances, it was thought that television may be able to remove some of the disparities and make quality education available to the students irrespective of their location. The idea, therefore, was to make use of television technology for taking quality education to students especially in rural, remote and underprivileged areas of the country.

The countrywide classroom also meant to provide students a 'ringside view of the latest developments in various fields' taking place around the globe. The programmes are meant to "upgrade", "update" and "enrich the knowledge" of students, "broaden their mental horizons" and "stimulate their urge" to know more. The credo for the countrywide classroom reads :

> "The programmes will aim to upgrade, update and enrich the quality of education while extending its reach. They will attempt to overcome the obsolescence of the syllabus and present the latest advances in all fields. The programmes will seek to arouse the interest of the viewers, whet their appetite and broaden their intellectual horizons. The aim is to stimulate but not to satiate. The programme will not be based on or restricted to a syllabus. Instead they will seek to provide new insights, interrelatedness of various disciplines and highlight developmental problems so that the sum is greater than the whole of the parts". (CEC, 1993)[1] p.5

A special cell, UGC INSAT Television Project (which later became CEC in 1993) was established, to coordinate the production and transmission of educational television programmes, housed at Teachers Training College building, Jamia Milia Islamia University, New Delhi and six programme production centres, "four Educational Media Research Centres and two Audio Visual Research Centres" (CEC :

1993)[2], were also established at different educational institutions of the country. By 1995, the number of these media centres rose to 17 and all of them were established in universities and educational institutions in 14 States. Equipped with broadcast quality equipment and professional manpower these media centres were called Media Education Research Centres (MERCs) or Audio Visual Research Centres (AVRCs), conveniently referred to as "Media Centres". The AVRCs were smaller centres with minimum equipment and a small number of staff whereas the EMRCs were relatively bigger centres with more production facilities and staff.

The centres were initially equipped with a relatively low cost production technology including, U-matic low band recording systems. The U-matic equipment had been a reliable tool for industrial programme production in the developed countries but was already on its way to obsolescence. Since the state broadcaster Doordarshan, at that time, was using the U-matic technology for telecast, the U-matic equipment served the purpose of countrywide classroom. In fact, most of the production centres used the equipment for more than a decade. Gradually, the CEC and media centres were equipped with advanced CCD cameras and Betacam recording and production technology in the early 1990s. This tendency to go for the best and the latest production technologies continued into the era of non-linear editing, computer animation facilities, multimedia platforms and now much advanced tapeless digital XD-cam technology.

In 2004, the centres were upgraded and renamed as Educational Multimedia Research Centres (EMMRCs). These media centres are located at University of Kashmir, Srinagar; Punjabi University, Patiala; Jamia Millia Islamia, New Delhi; Jai Narain Vayas University, Jodhpur; Devi Ahilya Vishwa Vidyalaya, Indore; Gujarat University, Ahmedabad; Harisingh Gour Vishwa Vidyalaya, Sagar; University of Poona, Pune; Osmania University, Hyderabad; English and Foreign Languages, University, Hyderabad; University of Mysore, Mysore; Anna University, Chennai; Madurai Kamraj University, Madurai; University of Calicut, Calicut; St. Xaviers College, Kolkata; University of Manipur, Manipur and Indian Institute of Technology (then University of Roorkee), Roorkee. The centres are distributed throughout the country covering major geographically and culturally distinct areas. The wide distribution of the centres brings in a unique diversity to countrywide classroom from across the country (See Map 3.1).

The primary reason of locating these production centres in the universities is to help them make the best use of the expertise of academics and scientists working in these institutes. The university

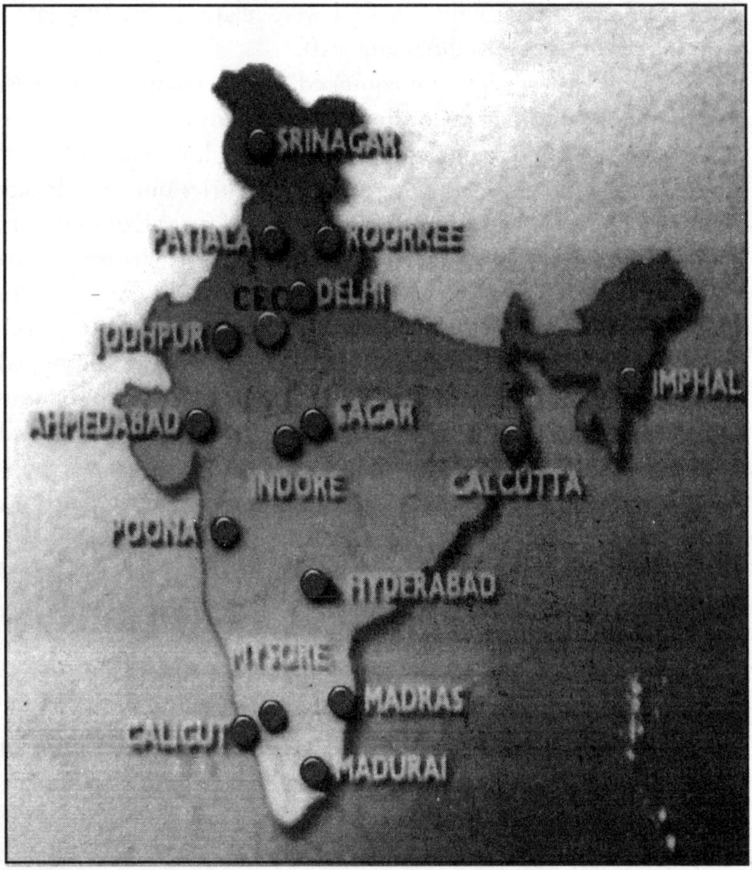

Map 3.1 : UGC, Media Centres (Educational Multimedia Research Centre) in India.

teachers and academics are involved in the production of programmes as subject experts and script writers. The type or kinds of programmes that must be produced and telecast during countrywide classroom always generated debates among the producers, academics, general audience and the planners. Some favoured enrichment type programmes while others thought syllabus oriented programmes will serve the cause of higher education in a better way.

Though there was a strong need to formulate a solid programming strategy, the UGC followed an open programming strategy that allowed production of both the types of programmes. Having an open programming strategy was considered a boon by the producers. Although the decision to create programming not tied to a specific syllabus or curriculum was quite disconcerting for some academics and students, especially those who needed clear instructions as to what to do with the content viewed, the production staff loved the creative freedom it provided. Planners argued that not all television viewers were students. Viewers would like to see educational programmes on TV even without the promise of certificates, diplomas and degrees; merely for the sake of increasing their knowledge. But another sizable section of the people demanded strictly syllabus-oriented programmes that will help students pass the exams. Therefore, to bridge this gap the UGC, in addition to enrichment type programmes, decided to produce video programmes meant specifically for colleges. These were not to be telecast, but used as transportable videos in VHS tape format for viewing by students who did not have access to good lecturers. The best professors, from allover the country, were involved to design and deliver lectures that were recorded creating a series of model video lectures in around nine subjects.

Gandhi (1995)[3] reported that "the countrywide classroom programmes seek to exploit fully the potential of the medium in following ways :

1. *Immediacy* : For bringing to viewers the latest and exciting new findings.
2. *Omnipresence* : For taking the viewers to where action is, such as a research laboratory, a hospital, a village or conference.

3. *Animation and special effects* : To help in clarifying the concepts, highlight built structures or invisible process.
4. *Intimacy* : To serve the viewers and make them a part of the voyage of discovery of wonders and of enquiry." (p.120)

The research based programmes with rich academic content produced by the UGC media centres were telecast on national network of Doordarshan, under UGC Countrywide Classroom. Initially, from August 1984 to February 1985, the programmes were telecast on national network of DD1, six days a week between 12:45 hours to 13:45 hours. From February 1985, the telecast was repeated at 16:00 to 17:00. The repeat telecast was made to enable the students watch programmes as per their convenience after they return from the colleges. The timings since then have been changed back and forth by DD-1, obviously to accommodate other commercially viable programmes, sports coverage and political coverage programmes. In 2008, the UGC programmes were telecast on DD-1 between 05:30 hours to 06:00 hours seven days a week, and by 2010 the slot was also withdrawn. What an irony. In an educationally backward country the state owned TV network has no space for educational programmes.

Some of the UGC ETV programmes, however, were also shown on DD Bharti. While the UGC programmes under "Healthline Category" were shown on DD-Bharti for around one hour five days a week, Monday through Friday, programmes on culture (DD-Bharti Culture) were shown every Sunday at 7:00 p.m. to 7:30 p.m.

To enable students and teachers watch UGC countrywide classroom programmes in the colleges, UGC during the Seventh Plan period provided colour television sets to over 7,000 colleges in the country. (Rao : 2004)[4] Sadly most of these sets were not used for the purpose for which they were sanctioned. While most of the sets remained non-functional due to one or the other reason, some of them were misused by the principals of the colleges by installing the sets in their offices or at their residences.

The countrywide programmes were telecast primarily on national network of Doordarshan and mostly these were in English and some in Hindi, however, with the launch of many local and regional channels by Doordarshan, some of the UGC centres, including EMMRC Mysore, EMMRC Calcutta, EMMRC Pune and EMMRC Hyderabad started telecast of UGC programmes on regional channels in the regional languages. EMMRC Srinagar telecast programmes on Doordarshan Srinagar besides local cable channels.

Establishment of the Consortium for Educational Communication (CEC)

For better co-ordination among the media centres and to take the educational television to newer and more meaningful heights with cooperative planning, involving universities and academics, the UGC in 1993 constituted an interuniversity "Consortium for Educational Communication" (CEC). Located at New Delhi, CEC is the apex body to oversee and coordinate the activities of all the media centres. Over a period of time, the role and mandate of CEC underwent a drastic change, owing to tremendous growth of information and communication technologies in India. The CEC in addition to use of television for education is also envisaging using various new communication technologies for enhancing the standards of higher education in the country. The current objectives of the CEC are :

1. Close Coordination, facilitation, overall guidance and direction to the activities of the media centres setup by UGC in various universities.
2. Dissemination of educational programmes through both the broadcast and non-broadcast mode.
3. Production of educational programmes (especially video and audio) and related support material and the setting up of appropriate facilities.
4. Research related to optimizing the effectiveness of the programmes.
5. Providing a forum for the active involvement of academic and other scholars in the creation of appropriate educational programmes.
6. Studying, promoting and experimenting with new techniques / technology that will increase the reach and / or effectiveness of educational communication. (CEC : 2006, p. 2)[5]

The role of CEC has been to provide direction for countrywide classroom, coordinate the development of centres, ensure the quality of programmes produced by the media centres, collect programmes from the media centres, conduct proper preview and technical check of the programmes, make programme capsules as per the requirements of transmission slots, prepare proper programme schedules and send the programmes to Doordarshan for telecast at national network. Simultaneously CEC organizes qualitative and quantitative research on various aspects of countrywide classroom, including production techniques, transmission, needs assessments of the target group, utilization of countrywide classroom programmes at national level. The CEC also encourages research at the media centre level to enhance the quality of the programmes and increase the utility of countrywide classroom. To achieve uniformity in quality of programmes and provide additional skills to media production and research staff CEC has been organizing various workshops and training programmes.

The CEC has maintained a video tape library of the programmes produced by the media centres, by now the number of these programmes has crossed 17,000, with around 1000 fresh programmes added every year. These programmes, in English and Hindi, include enrichment and syllabus based programmes covering 50 subject areas. The library also has a collection of e-content modules and Reusable Learning Objects developed by CEC and media centres. The library is on path to full digitalization for creation of a video data base for streaming in various forms. The complete digitalization of video programmes is aimed at creation of a virtual video library for retrieval by students through internet / Ernet / Infonet in the form of what is called "Video on Demand". The video on demand with a limited choice is currently available through internet at <http://www.cec-vod.edu.in>

The CWCR programmes, till recently, were more of enrichment type programmes, and not necessarily, based on syllabi. For the last few years the centres are concentrating more on lecture and discussion format programmes based on UGC model syllabus for the undergraduate students. The programmes are, however, embellished with graphics, animations and other visuals to make them more attractive and comprehensible. Initially the programmes were mostly produced in English language but later programmes were also made in Hindi and some other regional languages.

Viewership and Utility of Countrywide Classroom

Various viewership surveys conducted by the media centres showed these programmes were being watched by a sizable population of students and teachers besides a very high percentage of housewives, retired persons and senior citizens.

National Viewership Survey conducted by ADMAR Services (P) Ltd., New Delhi in (1993)[6] and (1997)[7] also showed very encouraging results. As per the report the overall viewership of UGC countrywide classroom in 1993 was 21.29 million viewers with an average daily viewership of 3.99 million. About 1.57 million were regular viewers watching UGC programmes over 4 days a week. The report produced by ADMAR in 1997 showed viewership of countrywide classroom as stagnant at 12% with increase in the viewership base from 21.29 million to 22 million. "At the height of its popularity the CWCR (countrywide classroom) on Doordarshan enjoyed a viewership of 20 million people with a daily viewership of 4 million people" (Rani : 2006).[8] It may be noted, however, that in a country of one billion people, this is a very small percentage. The fact is that the programmes are being watched by a very small percentage of students across the country. Arulchelvan & Viswanathan (2006)[9] reported that a small percentage of 14.61 per cent respondents in Tamilnadu watch UGC CWCR programmes while a huge population of students 85.39 per cent do not watch the programmes. "Even those who watch the programmes, majority of them do not watch even twice a week". The researchers suggest that, "top priority should be given to strengthen the educational usage of the powerful electronic media" and "creation of awareness among students about educational media should be taken up on a massive scale with a sense of urgency." (Arulchelvan *et al.*- p. 116)

The in-house research conducted by CEC, Media Centres and some independent researchers show that the UGC Countrywide Classroom programmes remain underutilized for a variety of reasons. Some of the in-house research studies including Peddharkar (1988)[10],

Kumar (1990)[11], Mishra (1990)[12], Kumari and Ali (Jan. 1991)[13], Govindaraju (1996)[14], and Rao (1998)[15], etc., have detailed the reasons for underutilization of UGC programmes and the overall apathy facing the use of television for higher education. Majority of the researchers have reported that lack of proper information about the programmes, indifference of teachers, non-availability of television sets, lack of proper space for the viewing, lack of electricity in the colleges, difficult language used and improper mode of delivery of programmes are some of the reasons that undermine the utility of educational television programmes. The students have also reported that "they have never heard of VYAS —the higher educational channel of UGC even after two years of it being in operation". (January 2007, p. 6)[16]

Interactivity and Talkback Experiments

Television is essentially a one-way medium, while the requirements for education demanded an interactive communication between the teachers and the taught. The lack of interaction was seen as a major disadvantage for UGC countrywide classroom programmes on Doordarshan. UGC, therefore, supported experimentation in interactivity during countrywide classroom telecasts. As far back as 1991, UGC with the active support of Indian Space Research Organisation (ISRO) conducted first National Talkback experiment, called UGC-ISRO National Talkback Experiment, "to test the viability of two-way interactive communication to enhance and enrich the quality of educational content for undergraduate students".

"For one week, from 25th to 30th November, 1991, 835 students from eight selected locations across the country, viz., Jodhpur, Imphal, Hyderabad, Kolkata, Ahmedabad, Roorkee, Madurai and Patiala, watched 12 prerecorded ETV programmes produced by various media centres, uplinked from Delhi earth station" (Reddi *et al.* : 1992).[17] Soon after the telecast the students interacted, through two-ways audio and one-way video, with the subject experts located at the studio created for the purpose at Delhi Earth Station. For interaction students made use of satellite based remote talkback at two centres, Jodhpur and Imphal, and conventional or temporarily dedicated STD telephone lines at the other six centres. Some students also asked questions using FAX facilities kept available for the purpose. During this period research teams, using various elaborate and well designed research tools, measured and examined technical, operational, educational, enrichment, and economical aspects of the experiment. The analysis of the data, collected by the researchers from various locations, clearly suggested that the interactive mode of television should become a regular feature of the countrywide classroom. The study further revealed that the successful completion of the experiment demonstrates the operational feasibility of making interactivity a part of countrywide classroom, and suggested that such interactivity on one hand will help students in providing them up-to-date information on various subjects and on the other create awareness and increase the audience for the countrywide classroom.

Encouraged by the results of National Talkback Experiment 1991, Consortium for Educational Communication (CEC) in collaboration with Indira Gandhi National Open University (IGNOU), Indian Space Research Organisation (ISRO), Doordarshan and UGC media centres conducted another national talkback experiment in 1994. This time, however, the experiment was conducted by including programmes on a single theme; a course on new information and communication technologies. Nine interactive sessions of one hour duration each, with transmission of 20 minutes of specially designed educational television programme followed by 40 minutes of interaction using STD lines, were conducted from December 15, 1994 to December 24, 1994. The programmes were uplinked from Ahmedabad and broadcast at National Network of Doordarshan. For interaction organized viewing of students was arranged at 15 smaller cities and towns across the country, viz., Mysore, Sagar, Jammu, Shillong, Shirur, Berhampur, Modinagar, Tiruchirapally, Bhuj, Nasik, Darjeeling, Calicut, Malerkotla, Kavaratti and Jamshedpur. (Reddi *et al.* : 1995).[18] After watching the programmes students interacted with the panel of experts located in the studio at Ahmedabad, who answered host of questions raised by the captive audience at the 15 locations. During the last four days of the experiment telephone lines were also thrown open for the general audience and a number of questions were raised by people watching programmes at their own places. After detailed analysis of the experiment, based on observations of the researchers and the data collected from the 15 locations using various research tools, Prof. Usha V. Reddi and others (1995) reported the results on many aspects of the experiment which include :

- The general enthusiasm and positive attitude toward this educational innovation.
- Enhanced educational outcomes which would be even more if the technical snags are worked out.
- The very successful attempt to reach out to the targeted viewers of CWCR in the small towns of India.
- The spirit of participation and the feeling of involvement in learning process expressed by so many of the participants from these small towns who wanted many more such experiences.
- The package concept which has been very well received and which has gone a long way in improving retention and understanding on the topic chosen, especially when the concept matches participants needs and current enrichment topics with quality programming.
- That such telecourses can be easily introduced into the regular transmission at a relatively low cost while benefiting a very wide audience

(Reddi *et al.*, p. 3)

While providing valuable suggestions for making interactivity more effective the report suggested "increase in number of telephone lines at the teaching end", to ensure fast connectivity and provide "more time for interaction". If the programmes are telecast in a package mode then every care must be taken to achieve "uniformity in programme content, quality, and information overload". The report suggests that the enrolled students shall be provided, "supplementary reading material", before the telecourse; the "telecourses must be open to the general viewing audience" and it also lays stress on the "need for improvement of the technical quality of both the programmes and the interaction". The report while recommending use of teleconferencing for educational television more frequently, in a better organized manner, concludes that "interactive television" increases "participatory communication that brings about motivation and commitment" among the teacher and the participant students. (pp. 89-90)

VYAS—The Higher Educational Channel of UGC

Owing to commercialization Doordarshan forgot its mandate of service to educational sector and sadly pushed the UGC Countrywide Classroom programmes to insignificant and odd telecasting hours further reducing the viewership and utility of these programmes. To tide over the problem of transmission of programmes, the CEC with the support of Ministry of Human Resource Development (MHRD) and The University Grants Commission (UGC) launched Gyandarshan-4 (GD-4) called VYAS —the higher educational channel of UGC, on January, 26, 2004. VYAS is a satellite channel and can be received either directly by installation of a dish antenna or through the cable network. The 24 channels, managed, coordinated and operated by Consortium for Educational Communication and the University Grants Commission, telecast 6 hours of fresh programming everyday with repeat transmission 3 times on a regular basis. The programmes are telecast on the channel on various subject bands during the week as per the fixed point chart. (See Table 3.1)

The ETV programmes, a mix of syllabi based and enrichment type, in the form of documentaries, lectures, discussions and some other formats are telecast on the VYAS channel under various programme categories including Heritage India, Contemporary Issues, Women Empowerment, Hall of Inspiration, *Guru Devo Bhava*, India for the World, Window to the World and other subject based categories. The programme schedules drawn are published in CEC News Letter and distributed among various institutions and viewers.

Table No. 3.1 : Fixed Point Chart of the VYAS Channel of CEC.

Days/Timings	*5.30-7.30,11.30-1.30, 17.30-19.30,0.30-1.30*	*7.30-9.30,13.30-15.30, 19.30-21.30,1.30-3.30*	*9.30-11.30,15.30-17.30, 21.30-22.30,3.30-5.30*	*Band would be blended with programme on*
Monday	Maths	Fine Arts	Geography	India for the World
Tuesday	Economics and Commerce	History	Zoology	Heritage India
Wednesday	Political Science	Home Science	Botany	Contemporary Issues
Thursday	Physics	Sociology	Language and Literature	Women Empowerment
Friday	Physiology	Chemistry	Education	*Guru Devo Bhava*
Saturday	Functional English	Environmental Science	Anthropology/Medical Science	Hall of Inspiration
Sunday	Music, Art & Culture	Technology	Career Watch	Window to the World

A copy of the programmes telecast over VYAS during March 2008 is appended. (See Appendix No.1)

The syllabi oriented programmes are based on UGC model syllabi for various courses. The enrichment type programmes are meant to broaden the mental horizons of students. The fact that the UGC media centres are located in various geographically, socially, linguistically, and culturally distinct areas they bring in a lot of heterogeneity and variety to VYAS channel. From February 2006, VYAS became fully digitalized and server based. The programmes are also now carried through multicast on Ernet / Infonet and are capable to benefit over '10 million students' and '0.5 million teachers', enrolled in '17,625 colleges' and '348 universities' (Prakash, 2006)[19] all across the country depending on Ernet and Infonet connectivity. With the quantitative expansion of institutions of higher education in India, devoid of quality teachers and worthwhile infrastructure, use of VYAS for taking quality education to the students in remotest areas can make a significant difference.

But research suggests that the channel remains underutilized as the signal cannot be received without the help of cable or dish antenna and people are not fully aware about the channel despite being in operation for over two years. (Jan : 2006)[20]. The channel, therefore, requires enough publicity to create awareness about it among the target audience so that they are motivated to either ask cable operators in their areas to provide the channel or install a dish, costing from rupees 3 to 4 thousand to directly receive the programmes. The involvement of college teachers is also required to make viewing part of classroom activity. The viewing of the programmes in the classroom with the intervention of the teacher will greatly enhance the scholastic achievements of students. The launch of VYAS, though seen as a significant development for taking quality teachers and education to the students, has not been yet able to mark its presence in the educational institutions; precisely because the signal is not available and the people are not yet aware about the richness of ETV programmes telecast on the channel. The CEC is trying hard to convince "Prasar Bharti Corporation" to include VYAS channel in DTH, but the efforts sadly could not yet yielded much results; as

Prasar Bharti failed to understand the significance of educational television for higher education in India. Thankfully Prasar Bharti finally agreed to carry VYAS on DTH in 2009. The inclusion of VYAS on DTH of Doordarshan, DD Direct Plus, is seen as a possibility to reach a wider audience and help students see the programmes at their own convenience. But DTH with limited market share may again not prove very effective.

Virtual Classroom through EDUSAT

The lack of interactivity during telecast of educational television programmes on Doordarshan and VYAS is seen as a major impediment in the utility of the programmes. Because interaction is seen as a major factor for the overall scholastic achievements of students from educational television programmes. (Reddi *et al.* :1992)[21], (Reddi *et al.* :1995)[22]. The launch of EDUSAT, a dedicated satellite for education in India, in September 2004 has provided much needed opportunity for interaction between the expert teachers and students across the country. After the launch of EDUSAT the Ku Band National Beam of EDUSAT was assigned to Consortium for Educational Communication (CEC) and the University Grants Commission (UGC) for higher education. With the help of ISRO 58 Satellite Interactive Terminals (SIT), also known as Virtual Classrooms, were established at various locations in the country, which include 17 UGC-CEC media centres, 12 Academic Staff Colleges, 9 Universities/ Colleges of potential excellence and 19 Universities/Colleges in remote areas, with CEC as the nodal agency. A collaboration project of ISRO, UGC-CEC and the educational institutions having SITs, this unique interconnection of institutions across the country provides an opportunity for the users to share their expertise through a two-way audio/video mechanism. (See Map 3.2).

The UGC-CEC EDUSAT national beam became operational in September 2005 for virtual classroom operations with CEC New Delhi as the teaching end. Students across the country at various SITs attend the live lectures, of one to one and a half hour duration, delivered from CEC and each lecture is followed by a live interaction with the expert through a two-way video-conference through net meeting. The

Higher Education EDUSAT Network

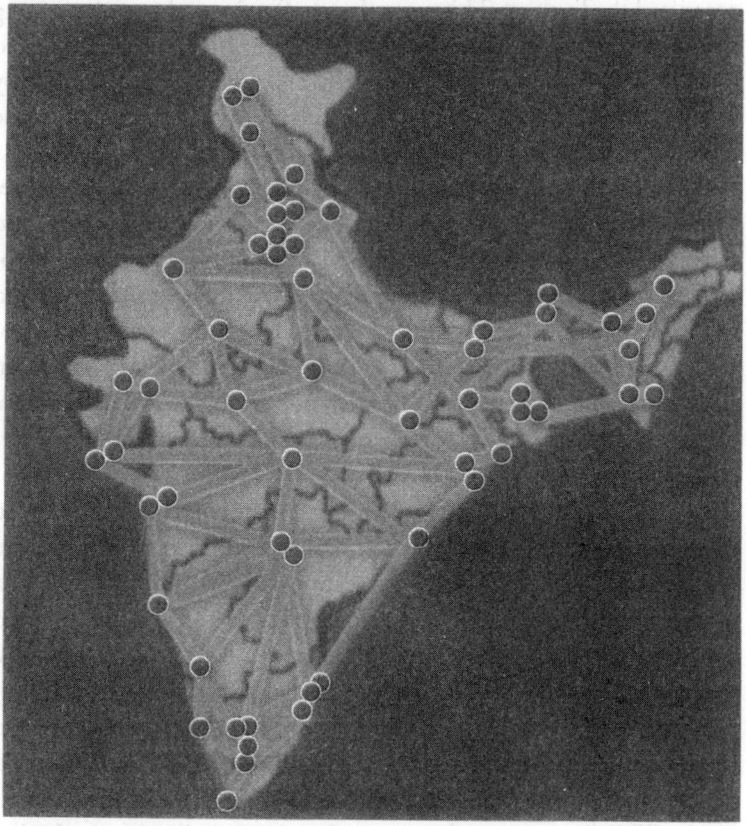

Source: CEC-New Delhi

Map. No. 3.2 : Satellite Interactive Terminals (SITs) or Virtual Classrooms for Higher Education in India.

questions are also taken from students using e-mails, SMSs, Phone or Fax calls. Over a period of time teaching end is rotated among various media centres and teachers and experts from various institutions across the country share their knowledge and expertise with the students and scholars across the country. To make virtual classrooms more need based Educational Multimedia Research Centre (EMMRC) Srinagar with the help of CEC launched the "Lectures on Demand" from May 2007. The students and teachers at Kashmir University, suggested topics and experts and the EMMRC with the help of CEC organised the lectures. This proved very effective and popular among the students and teachers and huge demands for lectures started pouring in from most of the university departments. Encouraged by the success of "Lectures on Demand", UGC Chairman dedicated the scheme to the nation on Teacher's Day on 5th September, 2007.

The national beam is also used by CEC and the media centres for organizing various workshops/seminars, online courses and meeting in the virtual mode. EDUSAT, with in-built facility for two-way audio and video interactions, brought in much desired and recommended talk back facility for the students. The quality of video/audio, especially during interactivity, however, is still far from satisfactory and requires improvement at par with, if not better than, the quality of interactivity seen on various national satellite news channels, viz., AajTak, NDTV, Zee News, Star News, etc.

If the enthusiasm of teachers and students towards virtual classrooms at some of the SITs (Virtual Classrooms) is an indicator, one can safely imagine a very bright future for educational television in higher education. All it requires is a serious approach and cooperative planning involving all the academics, students, teachers, media professionals and institutions of higher education.

From one hour UGC countrywide classroom programmes on Doordarshan in 1984 to launch of 24-hour VYAS in 2004 and establishment of Virtual Classrooms through EDUSAT in September 2005, CEC has come a long way; but its contribution to higher education in terms of access and reach is still far from satisfactory. Under the circumstances CEC has started some new initiatives with a revised vision to package knowledge and reach target audience in a much better and effective way.

The New Initiatives

EDUSAT, together with the convergence of media and growth of Information and Communication Technologies in rural India, promises a great future for educational television in India.

In the changed scenario and with a view to make significant contribution in creating a vibrant knowledge society, CEC has launched several new activities with a revised vision. The CEC vision for 2020 reads as :

> "Vision 2020 envisages India to be a knowledge superpower. To achieve this vision higher education has to play a key role. Universities and colleges provide higher education to nearly nine million students. To enable India to become knowledge superpower, education and knowledge resources have to reach out a large number of people through various means in a seamless way. During 80s with the expansion of television the electronic media reached different parts of the country with the receiving stations dotting the skyline. The new information and communication technology has further expanded its reach through internet. Our vision, therefore, is to electronically reach out to a large number of students, teachers and general public with quality educational material, so as to address the issue of access to higher education with equity and quality. This in turn CEC believes will contribute to overall vision of making India a Knowledge Superpower by 2020".
>
> (CEC 2006)[23]

To achieve the above vision CEC has taken serious initiatives to engage academics, media professionals and multimedia experts allover the country in packaging of knowledge in various forms. These initiatives include :

Development of e-Content and Multimedia

With the advent of new information and communication technologies and great demand for reliable and authentic educational content in electronic form CEC recognized the need to develop e-content and multimedia involving teachers and subject experts from various parts of the country. A "Technology Incubation Cell" was, therefore, established at CEC for the purpose of capacity building and training for development of e-content material on higher education. The "incubation cell" helps in training of teachers and integration and development of e-content, with a solid video base, on UGC model syllabi for the undergraduate students; besides developing and experimenting new software to make e-content data base universally available to students and teachers.

With the training of teachers in e-content development, CEC also announced a scheme inviting college teachers to develop e-content in their own subjects with financial support and incentives. The scheme, however, could not take off in a significant way due to indifference of teachers or their lack of knowledge about such a scheme. CEC is therefore currently devising a mechanism of involving teachers allover the country to develop e-content and multimedia in their own field. For this purpose each media centre shall be allotted one subject area, depending on the strength of the faculty in a particular subject in their areaa, and the centres shall involve the best college and university teachers to develop e-content and multimedia modules. The e-content generated shall be properly checked, by a peer group of experts at national level using a standardized educational effectiveness scale, and fully authenticated before it is placed on server for the use of students and teachers. Currently the e-contents available at CEC can be accessed through internet at <http://www.cec-econtent.edu.in> (See e-content template, Appendix-II)

Training Teachers in e-Content Development

For the training of teachers in development of e-content, CEC organized a number of long and short duration workshops at CEC and some universities. During the workshops teachers were sensitized about the use of new technology in teaching and learning and provided a solid training, with hands on equipment, in the development of educational multimedia and e-content. By the end of each workshop teachers developed e-content modules and Learning Objects. Some of the three week workshops held at CEC were also extended through EDUSAT to media centres and SITs at Pune (Maharashtra), Mysore (Karnataka), Coimbatore (Tamil Nadu), Srinagar and Baramulla (J&K). The lectures and demonstration at CEC were carried to teachers enrolled at remote locations through EDUSAT. The teachers saw the lectures and participated in interaction with the experts at CEC with two-way audio and video. The practical sessions at remote centres were conducted with the help of local demonstrators under constant guidance of experts through EDUSAT.

The experiment was a huge success, in terms of training through EDUSAT, as the teachers who were trained in virtual form were able to develop e-content and multimedia at par with the teachers who were actually trained at CEC New Delhi. But these training programmes, on the whole, did not achieve the desired results as teachers who took the training and produced e-content modules during the workshops could not continue the actual development of e-content when they returned to their places. They also did not show any significant response towards CEC e-content scheme. Their indifference towards e-content requires a deeper analysis but it seems that since e-content development at present is neither directly related to teaching pedagogy nor it is linked with the promotional avenues of the teachers, like publications, the teachers are not motivated enough to devote time for e-content development. The technophobia that afflicts majority of our teachers can be the other reason.

Development of Learning Object Repository (LOR)

CEC with a very strong library collection of over 15,000 educational television programmes on various subjects is in the process of developing a Learning Object Repository (LOR) with video and graphic inputs. Each reusable learning object shall have a 60 to 90 second video and a paragraph or two written content for the download. LORs being developed by CEC and media centres are in essence a "video glossary" on the basic concepts. This brings students an added advantage of seeing a video alongside the written content thereby making learning more enjoyable and enriching. The Learning Objects Repository shall be available to the students through internet. Currently the LORs developed by CEC and the media centres are available at <http://www.cec-lor.edu.in>. (See LOR Template, Appendix III)

On-Line Courses

Taking advantage of VYAS, SITs, and Internet CEC in 2005 also launched some online part-time courses, viz., Certificate course on scriptwriting for television and other electronic media; Certificate Course on Marketing Communication and Salesmanship; Certificate Course on Digital Library and Information Science and Certificate Course on Editing for Films and Television. Hundreds of students, across the country, enrolled for the courses. The course material was packaged in the form of video courses telecast on VYAS channel, the interaction with the expert was organized through EDUSAT on weekly basis, additional reading material was kept available for the students on the CEC website and the assignments and evaluation was conducted using internet. The successful conduct of workshops and online courses through EDUSAT demonstrates the capability and the capacity of virtual teaching and training. It is established beyond any doubt in a country like India, which is scattered mostly in villages and remote areas, a proper use of communication technology, with solid application and judicious use of mind and machine, will bring the desired results and make dream of education for all, anytime anywhere, come true in a real sense.

Production of Syllabus Oriented ETV Programmes

With the aim of making VYAS —the higher educational television channel, more meaningful to students in distant areas and to help them overcome the disadvantages caused due to lack of proper infrastructure and expertise, CEC initiated the process of producing syllabi oriented programmes, based on UGC model syllabus, for the entire course under different subject categories. Each media centre, depending on the strength of the faculty of the institution in which the media centre is located, is assigned a subject to produce educational television programmes on the entire syllabi involving one or a group of teachers. The programmes are made using a variety of formats, more often lectures, demonstrations, discussions or interviews. The programmes are then enriched with multimedia inputs including graphics, animations, maps, video clippings, etc. The idea is to exploit the audio-visual potential of television for making teaching and learning more attractive and meaningful.

But in pursuing production of more syllabi oriented programmes production of enrichment programmes at the centres have dropped to the disadvantage of the students. The emphases now seem to have shifted to "satiate" rather than to "stimulate" and "broaden the mental horizons" of the students. With the production of syllabus based programmes each centre produces over 50 to 100 programmes a year. The bulk production of programmes in lecture format, without caring too much for the production values and elements, have reduced the importance and effectiveness of UGC programmes, thereby defeating the very purpose for which educational television was thought to be used. The producers at the centres, who were earlier trying to devise innovative ways of making programmes, have turned recordists and majority of them simply do not apply their production skills to make programmes attractive and effective. In the number game the centres are more after the quantity throwing the quality to dustbin. Nonetheless, the media centres have produced a considerable number of syllabus oriented, lecture/discussion format educational programmes with international standard content and quality.

Preview of Programmes

Marketing and utility of the educational television programmes, like other products, is directly linked to the quality assurance and benchmarking. For benchmarking of the programmes media centres and CEC organize preview of programmes. The programmes produced at the centres are mostly seen by a preview committee at the centre level. After incorporating the suggestions the programmes are revised and send to CEC. At CEC level programmes are again previewed by another group of people including two subject experts from the same field. The programmes found up to the mark as per the CEC standards are forwarded for telecast, the others with suggestions are returned to the media centres for corrections or revision. The CEC over a period of time has devised its own standards or mechanism to review the programmes, however, there is a need to devise and standardize the preview tools to achieve a globally accepted benchmark for the programmes.

International Cooperation and Linkages

For sharing of knowledge at global level and benefiting from experience of international agencies involved in the use of new technologies for education, CEC has started developing linkages with the global agencies. Through Commonwealth Educational Media Centre for Asia (CEMCA) numerous international delegations visited CEC premises at New Delhi and interacted with the staff. Commonwealth of Learning (COL) supported a five-day workshop on "adaptive learning systems" in which an expert from prestigious Massachusetts Institute of Technology (MIT), USA was engaged as a resource person. CEMCA also supported the visit of some CEC and media centre staff to educational institutions and broadcast agencies in Malaysia and Singapore.

Problems facing CEC and the Media Centres

The greatest misfortune of this nation is that technocrats, planners, bureaucrats, researchers, producers, students and teachers are all going their own ways in a seemingly chaotic and individualistic manner. This characteristic of our society has kept the benefits of the use of television and technology for higher education at the minimal.

CEC and the media centres are capable of making a very significant contribution to higher education, as billions of rupees have been pumped into the project by UGC during the last two decades. But the project on the whole has been facing serious problems from the day one which have considerably impeded its progress.

One of the major problems is that of governance and coordination. While CEC is responsible to coordinate the production and development of media centres, there management is still left to the institutions where they are located. The employees of the media centres at various institutions have different working conditions, nature of appointment, salary structure, avenues of promotion, etc. Most of the media centre staff has no service rules, no recruitment conditions and no promotion policies. This has led to discouragement of the staff members who fail to perform to their potential. The result is poor quality of programmes. So staffing the media centres with capable and talented manpower has remained one of the biggest problems for the countrywide classroom. In the absence of a proper recruitment, service and promotion policy the centres did not attract much of talented manpower, who mostly embraced the commercial and mainstream popular television. This also resulted in media centres remaining understaffed and nearly half the number of approved posts remained vacant at any given time. There are still no posts of audio recordists, video editors, computer animator. This meant that whoever was producing had to be good at all the skills required for production. Since there are no professional sound recordists and music composers, the centres at most places could not record and make use of specially designed music tracks for their programmes and rather depended on the existing music, most of the time resorting to violation of copy-right, that resulted in poor use of audio tracks.

With the increase in hours of transmission, particularly because of the launch of VYAS, the demand for number of programmes increased manifold. But in the absence of enough production staff at the media centres a situation arose where Research Scientists, Production Assistants, Technical Assistants and even Camerapersons were asked to produce the programmes to meet the targets. This undermined the position of the producers who lost interest in production. The demand for quantity also meant lack of attention to quality.

Since the centres were established in universities, the university system had the prerogative of appointments. "Usually directors of media centres were chosen from amongst the professors of the universities. Unfortunately, most had no previous exposure to production dynamics and some had no interest in it. But these posts had power and clout and some perks which were attractive" (Madhu K.P. : 2007).[24] This often led to underproductiveness of the staff and conflicts between the production staff and centre directors.

The media centre staff is staggering under a heavy pressure because there is no coherent salary structure or promotional avenues for them. Quite often these people were not accepted by the academic community. With trouble brewing in the ranks, a staffing and promotion policy was issued in 1996 but same was not implemented due to the indifference of institutions, UGC, CEC, media centres and the complexity of already existing designations, years of service and above all the bureaucracy. The absence of service rules and proper promotion policy for the staff still remains a problem for CEC and media centres.

Effective participation of CEC and Media centres in academic development is directly linked with their coordination and uniform administration at the national level. The scattered location of production centres and the fact that the centres are more under the control of the Universities, CEC is at times finding it too difficult to co-ordinate activities and productions. The CEC in essence was set up to provide leadership, vision and coherence but the organizational pattern that has developed over a period of time hampers its effectiveness and control. Though a "Memorandum of Understanding (MOU)" was signed between the UGC, CEC, Universities, and the media centres, in the past and very recently a new MOU has been signed, to give CEC more powers and control over the media centres but their implementation in letter and spirit is still caught in the complexity of bureaucracy and idiosyncrasies of the system. This has in fact further aggravated the problem of staff who are now seen outsiders even by their own universities. In 2009, the new MOU was withdrawn.

The educational television programmes of countrywide classroom are seen by Doordarshan "as a liability, rather than an asset", owing to their over-indulgence with commercialization (Rani : 2006).[25] The programmes were telecast at most inappropriate time, 05:30 a.m. to 06:00 a.m., with almost no audience and finally withdrawn in 2010. The VYAS Channel is hardly visible outside as it is not carried on the cable and people are not ready to install a separate dish to receive the programmes. The channel is also facing problems of publicity as most of the people do not know about the channel. Though CEC publishes the telecast schedule in its monthly newsletter but its distribution has not proved very effective. The efforts to convince Prasar Bharti to carry VYAS on DTH did not yield any results till 2009, when it was finally carried an DD Direct plus. As the teachers and students have not yet realized the importance of television or technology for education, the UGC CEC endeavour in this regard remains grossly underutilized. The indifference of planners and policy-makers has adversely contributed in making the best use of knowledge resources. The ministry it seems is interested only in "channel launching spree". "In India policy-makers are good at creating facilities but bad at creating access to the facility. Facility without access defeats the purpose for which it is created". (Rani : 2006)[26]

Though CEC claims to have over 17,000 ETV programmes in the library, Rani (2006)[27] reported that out of 13,000 programmes in CEC library, "over 50 per cent" are not telecast worthy and require "cosmetic surgery". The "free and open for all strategy of programming" followed by the CEC / UGC was in a way good, as it brought variety and different approaches to a subject. But the collection of programmes at CEC library reveals that there is abundance of some kind of programmes and at the same time dearth of many more. Madhu (2007)[28] reported, "32 programmes on remote sensing, but only 6 on agriculture". He adds that there are "a large number of cases where it had many programmes on the same topic". Admittedly some sort of redundancy is always useful in education, but on the whole the efforts could have been better utilized for covering some other areas where very few or no programmes are available. This requires better coordination among the media centres which till recently was not seen. Though CEC has recently allocated subject areas for production of syllabus based programmes and development of e-content to certain centres but the centres are producing programmes without caring too much for the guidelines and without knowing what the others are producing. This most often results in duplication of efforts, wastage of time and money.

The e-content scheme has not been able to attract many teachers, even the teachers who took training did not return to generate e-content in their subject areas. Out of 58 virtual classrooms established across the country less than 15 are active and only few are actively taking part in the virtual classroom operations. The general indifference of planners and policy makers at UGC and ministry towards the use of television for education can be judged from the fact that even after 24 years, CEC does not have a proper building of its own and is housed in the outhouse of another interuniversity centre. The ministry has pumped in a lot of resources in creating CEC and media centres but has failed to provide additional support and direction to make the best use of the facility. The flow of funds from UGC for production of programmes and other activities of the media centres has remained stagnant and mostly the grants are not released on time resulting in faulty planning for programme production.

Despite the above problems and many more that are beyond the purview of this study CEC and media centres hold a promise to make a significant contribution in the higher education through the use of television and other new technologies.

Prospects for Higher Education

While the Discovery Channel, which started around the same time as the Countrywide Classroom, without having its production facilities located at the Universities, but by concentrating on few chosen subjects, could establish itself as a global channel with expanded viewership, the Countrywide Classroom could not expand even within the Indian borders. If Discovery could carve out a niche for itself with a relatively small audience and could make a difference across the globe, one fails to understand why Doordarshan and the University Grants Commission could not explore the possibility of putting the best of Countrywide Classroom into a sponsored category. The possibility of such a venture had the support of the viewership survey conducted by Admar Services (P) Ltd. for CEC in 1997, which had shown a significant audience share, 22 million, for UGC Countrywide Classroom programmes. This could have boasted the prospects of educational television and made it an economically viable proposition for both the Doordarshan and the UGC.

Today when television penetration is very high, the technology is spreading across the rural areas, satellites and transponders are manufactured like cars, the Indian skyline is dotted with transmission towers of all kinds, there is a greater scope of using television technology for education. There are many wonderful ways to make use of television for education for all; 'anytime anywhere'. But the users have to be prepared to make effective use of these services. Such ventures, whether in education or other sectors, take time and effort; but sustained and constant efforts by planners, producers, managers and academics are a sure way to succeed in making effective use of television and new technologies for higher education.

With the new initiatives CEC and the media centres are making a humble beginning by packaging knowledge in various forms, viz., educational television programmes, Educational multimedia / e-content, Learning Object repository and live interactive sessions through EDUSAT. The initiatives are to be carried forward in a much serious and sustained manner. The CEC at the same time shall have to devise easy, flexible and effective ways of dissemination of knowledge among the students and teachers across the country for a meaningful teaching and learning. The delivery of knowledge resources shall be backed with a strong interactivity mechanism; also involving the teachers in the classroom. This will help students in better understanding and comprehension and will iron out all their doubts; making countrywide classroom and virtual classroom real in essence. In the long run this may help India to overcome the problem of equity and access to higher education without undermining the quality and help the country emerge as a global superpower by 2020.

For better understanding of the role and utility of UGC Countrywide Classroom and the new information and Communication technologies it is imperative to further examine and understand the phenomenon of teaching through television and new technologies. This is also more important because of the tremendous growth of new technologies together with the convergence of media and India's growing student population in higher education in the absence of a quality infrastructure for teaching.

References

1. "A window on the world: UGC Countrywide Classroom". *CEC, Brochure.* (New Delhi: Consortium for Educational Communication,1993): p.5.
2. *CEC, Brochure* (1993): *ibid.*, p.3.
3. Gandhi, V.P. *Media and Communication Today: Policy, Training and Development.* Vol. 2. (New Delhi: Kanishka Publishers, Distributors, 1995), p.120.
4. Rao, Jagadeeshwar V. *Needs and Expectations of Primary Target Viewers of Countrywide Classroom Programmes – A Report.* (Hyderabad: Audio Visual Research Centre, Osmania University, 2004): p.6.
5. CEC, *Annual Report 2005-06.* (New Delhi: Consortium for Educational Communication, 2006): p. 2.
6. Admar Services (P) Ltd. Report, "Viewership study on UGC Countrywide Classroom Programmes" (New Delhi: Consortium for Educational Communication, 1993).
7. Admar Services (P) Ltd. Report, "National Viewership Study" (New Delhi: Consortium for Educational Communication, 1997).

8. Rani, Usha N. *Educational Television in India –Challenges and Issues* (New Delhi: Discovery Publishing House, 2006), p. 29.
9. Arulchelvan, S and D. Vishwanathan. "Pattern of usage of various electronic media by higher education students". *International Journal of Education and Development using Information and Communication Technology* (*IJEDICT*), *Vol. 2, Issue 4*, (2006): pp. 100-118.
10. Pendharkar, Sushama. "Profile of the UGC's Countrywide Classroom: A feed-back survey of universities in the State of Maharashtra". *Quest.* (Pune: EMRC, University of Pune,1988).
11. Kumar, Usha. "Postproduction Feedback Report, on Fibonacci Numbers Part 1". *A Research Report.* (Roorkee: Audio Visual Research Centre, University of Roorkee, 1990).
12. Mishra, Rajendra. "Countrywide Classroom, Feeback study from Himachal Pradesh". *A Research Report.* (New Delhi: UGC-INSAT TV Project, 1990).
13. Kumari, Abhilasha and Athar Ali. "Programme Evaluation Series Report - 1". *A Research Report.* (New Delhi: Mass Communication Research Centre, Jamia Millia Islamia, Jan, 1991).
14. Govindaraju, P. "Educational Television (ETV) in Higher Education: An evaluation of UGC countrywide classroom". *A Research Report.* (Madras: Audio Visual Research Centre, Anna University, 1996).
15. Rao Jagadeeshwar. "Needs assessment and reasons for non-viewing of Countrywide Classroom programmes". *A Research Report.* (Hyderabad: Audio Visual Research Centre. Osmania University, 1998).
16. Jan Salima. "*Regional Report on VYAS Channel*". *A Research Report.* (Srinagar: Educational Multimedia Research Centre, University of Kashmir, 2007): p. 6.
17. Reddi, U.V., A. Sai Prassad, and V. Rukmini. *Final Report National Talkback Experiment* (New Delhi: University Grants Commission. 1992): pp.14-16.
18. Reddi, Usha, V. *et al. Final Report, CEC-IGNOU-ISRO National Talkback Experiment, New Information and Communication Technologies.* (New Delhi:UGC Media Centres and the Consortium for Educational Communication, 1995): p.10.
19. Prakash, P., Jt. Secretary, UGC, Power Point Presentation (New Delhi: University Grants Commission, 2006).
20. Jan, Salima (2007): *ibid.*, p.6.
21. Reddi et al. (1992): *ibid.*
22. Reddi et al. (1995): *ibid.*
23. CEC, *Annual Report* 2005-06, (2006): *ibid.*, p. Cover Page on the back side.
24. Madhu, K.P. "Use of Satellites for Education". *A Report.* (Kuala Lumpur: Asia-Pacific Institute for Broadcasting Development, 2007): p.12.
25. Rani (2006) : *ibid.*, p. 29.
26. Rani (2006) : *ibid.*, p 38.
27. Rani (2006) : *ibid.*, p. 26.
28. Madhu, K.P. (2007): *ibid.*, p.17.

Chapter 4

Educational Television : Potential

Perceptions, Potential and Prospects for Higher Education

Brian Groombridge (1972)[1], in the foreword to his book titled, *Television and the People,* writes :

> "television is a major educational force in our society, perhaps the chief one, even though most people do not think of it in that way; the criteria by which I criticize its present performance are fundamentally educational criteria, though much of my critique is shared by professional broadcasters who do not think of themselves as educators; and finally my main prescription is for development of a new kind of educational television, which I believe would have a benign influence on the medium as a whole and would certainly reduce the gap between those who make programmes and those who receive them". (p. 7)

From the very inception of television, perceptions and perspectives of scholars, teachers, students, broadcasters and programme producers, with regard to its potential as a medium of education, tend to be similar and different at the same time. While research is very much consistent in portraying television as the most powerful medium or agent of change, more so due to the belief that it shapes attitudes and behaviours, research is yet inconclusive to establish how television can effectively be used for education. Under experimental conditions, as reported in detail in the literature review of this study, the results for learning through television are most of the time significantly higher than learning without television, of course with varied degrees and also the results are not always very consistent, but educational outcomes of viewing television outside the experiment or without a captive audience is yet to be conclusively ascertained.

Though it is believed that exposure to television under normal viewing conditions also enhance learning outcomes yet it is not very significant and not always so. The literature examining the relationship between amount of television viewing and educational achievement is not consistent. While Williams *et al.* (1982)[2] believe the relationship is negative —more a student views television, lower are his educational achievements, Blosser (1988)[3] believes the relationship is positive. Scarborough (1989)[4] at the same time does not find any relationship between television viewing and educational achievement.

To examine the relationship between the amount of television viewing and educational achievement, Razel (2001)[5], analysed the data reported in six international and national studies of educational achievements that were published after 1985. Correlations between amount of television viewing and educational achievements were also computed. The researcher found that generally, "for small amounts of viewing, achievement increased with viewing, but as viewing increased beyond a certain point, achievement decreased" (p. 371) but the results were not always consistent and varied between various age groups. The inconsistency in the research findings about correlation of television viewing and achievements is attributed by Razel to the following facts :

(1) Various studies report statistics for children of different age groups;
(2) Correlations that were considered statistically insignificant were treated differently by different research scientists; and
(3) Function relating the two variables may not be linear.

(Razel : 2001, p. 371)

Literature in the recent years indicates that television viewing and educational achievements are related to the quality of the educational television material being viewed (St. Peters, *et. al.* : 1991)[6].

Viewing of high quality material for smaller duration of time may result in better achievements than viewing relatively low quality material for more time.

So while scholars believe that television is a strong medium that can be effectively used as a tool for education, they also differ about its actual potential and the circumstances under which it can be safely termed as a medium of education. There is also a dichotomy of sorts between the way we normally think about television and the way we make use of it for. People generally complain that television is showing too much of news and entertainment and very little educational content. Yet when we ask people what they watch, mostly they refer to the most popular entertainment or news programmes. People think of television as a fun medium, for entertainment and relaxation, as a viable and cheaper alternative to theatre or cinema of yesteryears. People after day's hard work wish to put their feet up and watch television to relax not to be educated. As Comstock and others believe that "television viewing is a passive activity"; he argues that while watching television people engage in all sorts of things that attention to the screen is "a non-serious, often interrupted and frequently non-exclusive activity for which the measure in hours and minutes serves only as the outer boundary of possible attention" (Comstock : 1991)[7]. This argument also finds support in "reactive theory of viewing", that is a notion in which, "the passive viewer entranced by the moving images, which in essence was a blank screen on which the broadcast was played" (Winn : 1985)[8]. This belief works contrary to the educational potential of television because for genuine understanding or learning, attention is paramount. The "reactive theory", however, was displaced by another theory, "cognitively active theory", which placed the viewers in much active role. (Anderson : 1983)[9] According to this theory, viewers are not mere receptacles, passively absorbing any and all content coming from the screen; instead they actively apply their experience and understanding to their viewing. The changing nature of television viewing can be attributed to the medium itself which has changed significantly over a period of time. The viewers have also mastered the art of viewing, as their visual literacy has increased over a period. The viewers now know when to tune in or out of the screen without losing much. But the fact still remains, the passive or active viewing does make a difference to the students with varying impacts on learning outcomes. In the context of casual effortless viewing, the characteristics of a passive viewer, learning tends to be shallow and short lived, but when viewing is more active, purposeful and serious, then deeper and more sophisticated learning can occur (Kozma : 1991)[10].

Peter Black (1968)[11] , who believes that television is fundamentally a non-serious medium, wrote in one of his reviews in daily 'Listener' that, "the trouble is that television is basically a frivolous medium". The frivolous nature of the television is in fact not rooted in the medium itself but attributed to it, rightly so, by the people who skilfully used the medium for commercial gains. As history bears testimony television was not introduced to be a medium of fun or frivolity but as a serious medium for education. Black's contention of television as a non-serious medium again goes against the seriousness that an educational programme requires or demands on the part of audience; as education by nature is a "serious business". Television, like other media in the past, viz., comic books, radio, telephone, movies, etc. is blamed for "corrupting values, wasting time, and causing a decline in taste, morality, self-discipline, learning and socialization". These attributes are now gradually shifting to new media like internet and it is increasingly felt and recommended, the world over, that the broadcasters and educators together can use the medium to enhance the educational effectiveness of television in the classroom and beyond.

The critics of educational television genuinely argue that the viewers have less or no control on the flow of information as compared with more static media, like books, pictures, etc. Their inability to recall or go back to passages that they may not have grasped the first time limits their educational outcome from television. But then television's potential to enable viewers to view actually or virtually objects; see realistic scenes and sequences in motion; see from various perspectives that are difficult and impossible to observe in real life and take viewers to places beyond their reach, is something unique about this medium. The unique audio-visual character of television makes it the most versatile medium and gives it an edge over the other media. As most researchers agree that, "when presented together, each source provides additional complimentary information" (Kozma: 1991)[12], thus increasing the chances of comprehension. The unique feature of television combining audio and visual information differentiates it from other media in representing knowledge. As the saying goes "seeing is believing" the research makes us believe that "seeing is remembering too"; as Wiman and Miechenry (1969)[13] found that, "people generally remember 10% of what they read, 20% of what they hear, 30% of what they see, and 50% of what they see and hear". This proposition puts television ahead of other media for comprehension and recall.

Television is also attributed to be an "easier medium than the books" and the attention lags when the content is either too easy, predictable or too challenging. Salomon (1983)[14] found that when a sample group of students were divided into two, one group watched an educational television programme and the other read a similar story in print form. The TV watchers visibly put in less effort as compared to the other group. Interestingly the result of both the groups showed a similar pattern. This dimension of television makes it an exciting medium of education especially for those who have a markedly less attention span.

The arrival of new media and its high penetration in the developed countries have led to another perception that it will make video based learning irrelevant and redundant. But evidences from the West indicate that video for from being supplanted is becoming an increasingly essential part of classroom learning. While the format, delivery channels, and storage options may change, video will continue to be an effective, engaging and essential tool of education. In fact, the improvement in video compression techniques, increasing digitalization and access to server based videos will enhance its use by teachers who can store chunks of video on their laptops or computers and integrate it with their own teaching material thereby making the overall teaching pedagogy more effective. In USA and most of the developed and developing world teachers are continuously finding innovative ways to incorporate the television or video medium into their teaching, resulting in more motivated students and improved learning outcomes.

The 'myth' that Television displaces reading and negatively effects reading habits, especially among the young readers, is not fully supported by the research. While there seems to be a general consensus that a positive correlation exists between the heavy viewers and a decline in reading habits but Flood and Lapp (1995)[15], citing the survey by Williams, *et al.* (1982), show no overall effect of viewing on achievements except for heavy viewers who watch over 40 hours of television per week. Wright and Huston (1995)[16] found that, "the content of television may be more significant to academic achievements than the amount of viewing time". The studies also fail to account for the other factors that may have resulted in lower achievements.

Some overzealous protagonists of educational television led people believe that television together with the new technology will replace the teacher, the way Thomas Edison is attributed to have remarked that "motion pictures would soon replace the books". But even over hundred years from Edison's prediction books continue to thrive and resist even bigger challenges offered by new media. The same way teacher will continue to remain central to teaching and learning, the technology shall only facilitate him teach with a better pedagogy and reach more students at the same time. It is, however, undeniable that learning technologies, television in particular, can be significant contributors to student's achievements. But in practice educational television rather than enhancing and extending the good things already happening in the traditional classroom, is simply copying and carrying the classroom teaching practices through television technology trying to replace the classroom teacher with a televised version. Educational television that competes rather than complementing the traditional teaching is bound to fail as Levin (1988)[17] wrote: "...claims....have been made for every new instructional technology which heralded them as having revolutionary implications for education. In every case their educational impact fell short of that promise", because he believes "they simply did not evolve in the way that were predicted." (p. 62)

Television today has become pastime for much of population in the country reducing its importance for education. The medium in itself is neither good nor bad for overall academic achievements. Its advantages or disadvantages as a medium are defined by its users. A survey of television research during the last 25 years (Thompson & Austin : 2003)[18], found that, if students are exposed to programmes with rich informational content, like news programmes or documentaries, they have a better opportunity to increase their knowledge and skills, but contrarily, "if most of the viewing is of low informational content like music shows, soap operas, feature films, an opportunity for detrimental academic impact is increased." (p.197)

Television in USA is used to support instructions in almost all the subjects at various levels. The subjects include science, the languages, arts, social studies, health, nutrition, and even mathematics, etc. The research indicates that the value of video is highly correlated to its integration with the curriculum. In other words how closely the video content fits into overall instructional design. The instructional use of television will be most effective when, "interwoven into an integrated teaching / learning system in the context of other learning activities." (Chu and Schramm : 1975)[19] This is where television can become a partner in teaching and learning alongside a teacher.

In the light of the above discussion and the overwhelming research support for use of television for education, discussed in detailed in the literature review of this study, it is established beyond doubt that television is one of the most potent tools available today for taking quality education to the students. The outcome, however, depends on the way we use it. While Comstock's theory of "passive viewing" or considering television "a pastime" is not totally unfounded but that does not reduce its importance as a means of education. The passive or casual viewing may yield a shallow understanding of things but active and purposeful viewing shall pay very high dividends and gratification in terms of educational achievements. While television viewing if unregulated may have some indirect disadvantages, for heavy viewers, but it surely can be used to the advantage of students and teachers, the difference lies in the way we use television.

If television is so important for education, especially in a country like India where pressures of social equity and access are constantly damaging the quality, why is it that television is still on the periphery of education and could not make its presence felt significantly and why could not it become a part of educational system in an organized manner? Why the perception of people in general about the television is not moving beyond "frivolity"? Why the teachers and students still are not motivated enough to demand educational television programmes as a part of teaching pedagogy? Why no pressure groups have emerged to force legislations in favour of educational television? People always tend to attribute the failure of television as means of education to the pressures from commercial television and the capitalist societies driven by commercialism. In today's commercial world educational television is not, sadly, seen as lucrative as the other forms of television like entertainment, sports and news channels.

One can understand the disinterest in educational television in the past, as very few channels were available, as well as possible, but to understand disinterest, particularly of the government, in educational television in 21st century, when digital revolution offers opportunities for running multiple channels on the same bandwidth, is hard to comprehend. Today we have hundreds of television channels beaming all sorts of programmes, the audience has got fragmented and each channel is catering to the needs of a relatively very small audience, creating its own niche to drive the add revenue from its share of audience. Yet people are not ready to invest in educational television, despite availability of the bandwidth and a relatively good share of serious audience. As the trend and preference of advertisers is fast moving from a general or mass audience to specific quality audience, who can be the potential buyers of their products, students and teachers, who constitute a significant size of the population, have still not caught the imagination of the commercial television.

Pulitzer Prize winner Thomas Friedman, in his book, *The World is Flat*[20], discusses and demonstrates with various examples that as the frontiers of human knowledge are pushed, the work at all the levels become more and more complex. It requires a lot of time and technique to recognize various complex patterns to solve the problems arising out of very simple things. Technology he believes has made the earth flat, making boundaries and frontiers of the countries irrelevant and creating equal opportunities of profit-making for all around the globe. It depends on the creative imagination and the ability of a person to be among the first to create products, communities and opportunities and that alone shall determine the profits that one can make from the new global market. Though knowledge as a product has a strong market in the form of students and teachers it still continues to be a vast wasteland. The policy-makers and planners also shy away from advocating proper investment in technology that could result in accelerating globalization of education and lead to democratization of educational resources. They base their arguments in consonance with contrarians who believe that investment in educational technology has not delivered the desired results and that the promise of academic learning through technology has gone unfulfilled. Again a Stanford University professor, Larry Cuban, in his book *Oversold and Underused*[21], while arguing that the results of investment in educational technology are not sufficient to warrant continued investment in technology cautions that the very introduction of information technology into educational institutions over the past two decades have neither achieved any transformation in teaching and learning nor has shown the desired productivity gains. He in fact advises that educators, academics and other stakeholders must critically re-examine reforms, assumptions and potential of the new technology before investing in it as a tool for education.

Notwithstanding the argument put forth by the contrarians, as it is not getting much support from the research, we in India must take the lead in investing in educational technology to make quality education available to all irrespective of their geographical location. But before that is done it makes sense to understand the scope of educational television from the perspective of our own academics and broadcasters, who constitute two important sections of the society directly related to use of television for education.

Present Study

In a country like India, which figures with the countries having lowest per capita investment for higher education, the implication of using television effectively for higher education are of a very high significance. India with one of the largest state owned higher education systems in the world comprising over 348 universities or deemed universities, 17,625 colleges, about 10 million students and 0.5 million teachers has only an enrolment ratio of 7%, which is far below than the world average of 23%. Even the average for developing countries, 11.3%, is higher than that of India. (Prakash : 2006)[22] Despite such a huge superstructure for higher education the total public spending on education in India is only 3.4 % of Gross National Product (GNP), this includes spending on primary, secondary and tertiary education. (Reddi : 2003)[23] With a meagre amount available for higher education and enrolment estimated at 15% by the end of Eleventh Plan, India seriously has to find a viable alternative to effectively increase equity and access without undermining the quality. One of the alternatives is to make use of new technology, particularly educational television, for taking quality education to the students. But before investing the precious resources in furthering the growth of educational television India will have to fully understand how to make the best use of the technology for education.

Television in conjunction with other technologies and the classroom teaching can make a difference in teaching and learning, but that can only happen when the use of television is done in a wise and balanced way. To further understand educational television from the perspective of broadcasters and academics and to find the feasibility and necessity of such a channel in India this researcher undertook a study based on in-depth interviews with broadcasters and academics across the country. The study was necessitated because the perceptions of broadcasters and academics have not yet been presented, as this researcher could not find any evidence or reference of any such study. The research on television in higher education in India as discussed in the literature review of this study is limited to utilization of ETV, needs assessment of the target group, the feasibility of certain programme genres, production techniques, media habits of the target group, impact of interactivity on learning, etc. The studies have been mostly done from the perspective of students and with limited response or participation of some teachers. No attempt has been made to understand the educational television from the standpoint or perspective of academics or broadcasters. It is important to understand various spheres of educational television from their perspective as they are the ones who are directly involved in use of television and/or the process of teaching and learning. The understanding of academics about the educational phenomena and that of the broadcasters about the nuances of television as a medium can be of great help to understand how this audio-visually powerful medium can be best utilized for the purpose of education. The study will also help to find alternative ways of making best use of educational television in a resource starved country like India.

This study is, therefore, an attempt to fill this valid void or gap in research pertaining to educational television and higher education, particularly with reference to UGC Countrywide Classroom. The research findings or ideas generated by the broadcasters and academics together with the structure, functioning and role of Consortium for Educational Communication (CEC) may help to draw a road map for television in higher education; which in turn will help provide quality education to a vast population of students across the country facing dearth of good teachers, laboratories and libraries.

The Objectives of the Study

The primary objectives of the study are :

(a) To find perception of broadcasters and academics about television as a medium of education in general and UGC Countrywide Classroom in particular.
(b) To understand the reasons whether or not UGC Countrywide Classroom has made or can make difference to education.
(c) To understand the type of content/programming that are best suited to help students achieve higher learning.
(d) To find an effective mode of delivery of Countrywide Classroom programmes on television for a better utilization.
(e) To find the role of academics and broadcasters in making Countrywide Classroom more effective.
(f) To study the possibility and feasibility of a dedicated higher educational channel at par with the commercial television.

(g) To suggest measures for improvement of UGC Countrywide Classroom.

Operational Definition of the Key Terms Used

As words and phrases have different meaning for different people and in different contexts it is always advisable to provide an "operational definition" of some of the key words that figure frequently and constitute the crux of a study. Some keywords used in this study that need to be provided operational definition are listed as under :

(i) *Broadcasters :* The Cambridge advanced learner's dictionary of English describes 'broadcaster' as "someone whose job is to speak on radio or television programmes". In essence and particularly in Indian perspective the word is most often also used for those who are in the broadcast industry as programme producers, directors, or transmission executives besides anchors and others. The word 'broadcaster' in the context of this study is limited to those who are involved in production and transmission of educational television programmes as producers, directors or managers of production centres and educational television channels.

(ii) *Educational Television :* The term 'Educational Television' refers to broadcasting of a myriad of television programmes for educating a community ranging from simple health, hygiene, family planning, agricultural practices, civic sense to highly technical, curriculum or non-curriculum based programmes meant for a general or specific audience. It also includes instructional programmes meant for school or college students in professional and non-professional courses and varieties of documentaries of general or specific interest. For the purpose of this study "educational television" refers to broadcast of educational television programmes in UGC countrywide classroom on DD or VYAS —the higher educational channel of UGC meant primarily for the students of higher education.

(iii) *Academics* : The word 'academic' or 'academician' in Cambridge advanced learner's dictionary of English means, "Someone who teaches in a college or who studies as part of their job". Academics are, therefore, all teachers in schools, colleges and universities, besides it include a whole lot of researchers and technocrats who undergo all types of studies to refine their research or technical tools. However, for the purpose of this study the definition of word 'Academics' is limited to the University and Senior College teachers who have made a significant contribution to knowledge especially in the field of education and communication. It also includes academic administrators like Principals and Directors of academic institutions.

Delimitation

The present study is limited to UGC Countrywide Classroom on Doordarshan and VYAS —the higher educational channel of UGC. Since the study is made with special reference to educational television in Kashmir, majority of the academics and broadcasters selected for the study are purposely taken from Kashmir valley, however some respondents from other parts of the country, who have made significant contribution towards use of television for education were also selected.

Method and Procedure of the Study

Notwithstanding the fact that there are various well-defined research methodologies that are increasingly being used by the social scientists allover the world, the fact remains that every study requires a unique method and procedure for collection of data that suits its universe and meets the objectives. Naturally, when the respondents are of high academic and administrative standing one has to design a research methodology to benefit from their expertise in a qualitative rather than quantitative manner. Again people of such a senior standing find it difficult to find time to fill a survey questionnaire but may easily consent for a one on one interview. In fact this researcher had a first hand experience of such a situation. About 30 questionnaires, which were made as a guideline for the "In-depth Interviews", were mailed to reputed broadcasters and academics of the country, which the researcher thought might provide useful prior information and guidance, did not get any response from almost all the respondents despite reminders. Only six respondents returned the questionnaires answering the questions very briefly. But two of those who did not respond to the questionnaire, later, were able to sit with the researcher for a long conversation lasting from one to three hours when requested for an "In-depth Interview". Further, since the opinions based on experience of the respondents are more important for this study, than the quantitative data which one may collect from a huge sample, qualitative method serves a better purpose. In view of these considerations this researcher chose to conduct "In-depth Interviews" with a select sample of academics and broadcasters to elicit their opinions about educational television and understand the subject from their perspective.

In-depth Interviews, also referred to as intensive interviews is a qualitative research technique accepted the world over. Wimmer and Dominick (1997) reported five "In-depth Interview" based studies, these include :

(a) Baldwin and Lewis (1972) studied "violence on television" with a small sample of Hollywood writers, producers and directors. The respondents were interviewed which lasted for 1 to 4 hours.

(b) Graber (1988) conducted in-depth interviews with 12 registered voters to understand their 'use of information media'.

(c) Swenson (1989) studied television news viewers using this technique. 'Classified advertisements in local newspapers' were issued by the researcher and 8 respondents, who met the requirements of study, were selected for the in-depth interviews.

(d) Priest (1992) used the method to 'interview people who had revealed highly intimate information about themselves' on a TV show.

(e) Pardun and Krugman (1994) studied 'the influence of architectural style of the home on television viewing' by interviewing 20 families, 10 living in traditional homes and 10 in transitional homes. (pp 101-102)[24]

In-depth Interviews are a hybrid of one on one interview approach and their success or failure depends on the rapport interviewer is able to make with the interview at the time of the interview. Some of the In-depth Interviews are highly yielding and may last for hours together yet some may fizzle out soon after they begin. This technique, owing to its laborious exercise, uses a very small sample size but allows a lengthy conversation and observation of non-verbal cues that are not otherwise possible. So the "In-depth Interviews" are always "customized to individual respondents" and most of the questions asked or raised during the interview evolve during the discussion. However, to make sure a comprehensive interview is conducted the interviewer always has a set of questions, pertaining to the specialization of the interviewee, with him which serves as an outer guideline or framework for the interview. The advantage of the in-depth interviews lie in the wealth of information generated during the interview, however, analysing the data poses a great challenge and requires a great skill on the part of the researcher. The validity and generalizability of in-depth studies remains a concern as the analysis of same data by two different researchers may yield different results. Again the in-built bias of the researcher and his own mannerism during the interview may influence the response of the interviewee. Nonetheless, it remains a unique technique that suits the requirements of the present study.

Sampling

A purposive sample of 20 respondents was selected for the study. But before the actual selection a small simple questionnaire (See Appendix IV) containing both open and close ended questions, was either mailed or personally handed over to 80 possible respondents. The list of 80 academics and broadcasters was drawn randomly seeking help of friends and colleagues and in some cases the academics and broadcasters suggested some names. Out of them only 37 questionnaires were received back from which 18 respondents were selected on the basis of their responses to some of the questions on the questionnaire. These questions were aimed to find out if the respondents were aware about the other educational channels like Gyandarshan, VYAS and EKLAVYA, and if they have seen some of these channels. The idea was also to find out their level of exposure and understanding of educational television.

Out of 37, a very good proportion of 28 were found fully aware about these channels and all of them had seen at least one of the channels. The other nine had not seen any of the channels and cited the reasons of either "channels were not available in their areas" or they "do not find enough time to watch television beyond news". The 28 respondents were graded on the basis of their exposure and understanding of various educational channels, with the respondent with higher exposure at the top and the persons with least exposure of ETV at the bottom of the list. From this list, 18 respondents were selected, 9 from the top and 9 from the bottom. Two more senior level persons with known contribution to education and television, who had not returned the questionnaires, were also added. Those selected included 9 Professors, 4 Progamme Producers, 3 Directors of media organizations, 3 senior educationists/consultants and one former education planner. Again out of 20, 11 selected were from Kashmir valley and the remaining 9 from outside the valley.

Collection of Data

For the conduct of interview date, time and venue was fixed with each selected respondent quite in advance. The interviews were conducted, mostly on schedule except a few which were rescheduled for one or the other reasons, either at the residence or in the office of the respondent. One interview was, however, conducted at a hotel. Each interview lasted from 2 to 4 hours. For the interview a detailed questionnaire was drawn as a guideline. Some of the questions from the questionnaire already given to the respondents prior to their selection were again listed. This was done for two reasons : One to reconfirm their responses and second to initiate the discussion. With the permission of the respondents all the interviews were recorded on a mini tape recorder, with the assurance that it will not be aired and is meant only to take notes. This enabled the researcher to concentrate more on the interviewee, without bothering to taking any written notes, which resulted in a better quality interview. The researcher also left his telephone number with the respondents, with a request to call him in case they wished to add anything new that may have occurred to them after the interview. But not a single respondent called after the interview.

The interviews recorded were transcribed resulting in a huge volume of responses spanning over 600 written pages. Some of the responses were brief and crisp but others were too elaborate and unwinding, with lots of relevant/irrelevant details, anecdotes and incidents.

Data Analysis and Interpretation

The analysis of the data was done in two stages. In the first stage, the quantitative data pertaining to the close ended questions was tabulated and analysed. In the second stage, qualitative data was loosely codified on the basis of uniformity or disuniformity in ideas. Some of the unique ideas and opinions expressed by the respondents were kept separately. The findings of the study are reported as under :

1. To begin with it was found that exposure to educational channels of the respondents was quite high. 28 out of 37 had seen at least one of the ETV channels *viz.* VYAS, Gyandarshan, EKLAVYA. 16 of them had seen all the three channels, 5 had seen only VYAS channel and 7 had seen only Gyandarshan. (Figure. 4.1) The other 9 who had not seen any of the Indian educational television channels had, however, seen some programmes on Discovery, National Geography, and History Channel. The reasons for not watching local educational channels were attributed either

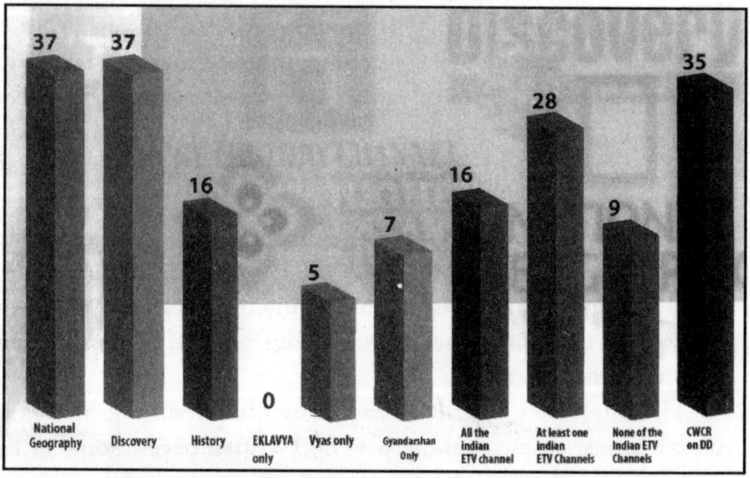

Figure 4.1 : Exposure to Education Television Channels.

to non-availability of these channels in their areas as cable does not carry them or they do not have enough time and motivation to watch these programmes. All the 37, however, had seen, at least once, some programme on Discovery or National Geography and 16 among them had also seen programmes on History channel. (Figure. 4.2) The reasons for higher viewership for Discovery, National Geographic and History channel are their easy availability through cable, exotic quality of their programmes, refuge from entertainment television and redundancy in News Channels. Most of the respondents revealed that whenever they have some time in the evenings after watching news or current affairs programmes, especially in late night hours, they enjoy watching programmes on these channels.

2. On a multiple choice option question, out of the 20 who watch or have watched some programmes on local educational television channels 18 feel that these channels are not given proper presentation and publicity, 15 said programmes generally are not of good quality, 16 have recommended that the channels shall be clubbed together for a quality educational channel catering to the needs of all

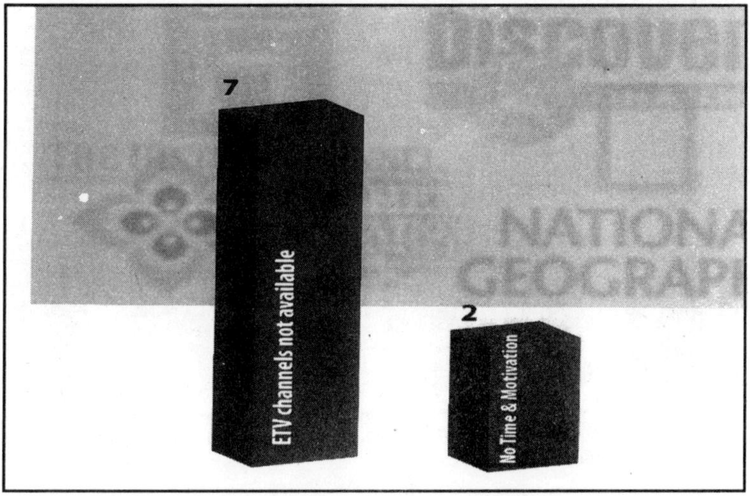

Figure 4.2 : Reasons for not viewing Indian Educational Television Channels

the students, 4, however, are satisfied, to a great extent, with the contribution these channels are making. (Figure. 4.3). But all of them are unanimous that the potential of these channels has remained underutilized and there is a dire need to refurbish these channels for the greater cause of education. When asked why they feel that the channels be clubbed into one, the respondents said that there are not enough programmes with any of these channels so they keep on endlessly repeating the programmes resulting in redundancy and repulsion. At present they can pool their resources for one good educational channel, which will have specified sections for every group of students and even teachers. This will enable them to have a whole lot of fresh programmes everyday, some of which, depending on demand, can be re-telecast. These channels at present are a good means to educate viewers but lack of professionalism, authority, control and absence of objectivity fail them to reach the target audience and keep on doing the damage in making their net worth realized. People can benefit from them more as source of information or education and less as knowledge.

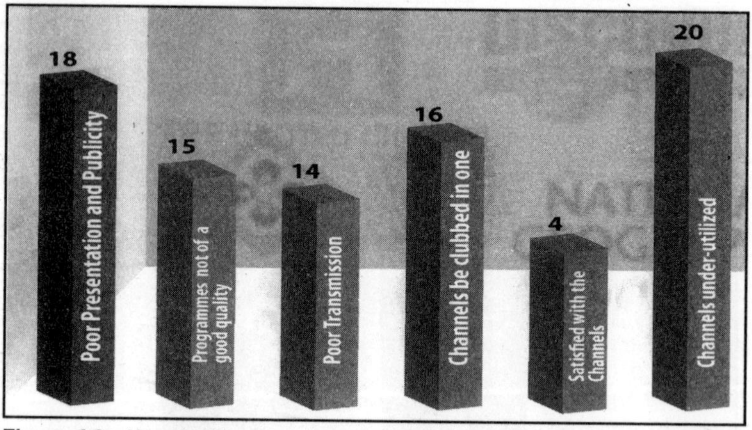

Figure 4.3 : How the Respondents feel about the Indian Educational Television Channels?

Most of the respondents felt sad for the under-utilization of these educational channels. Looking very optimistic one respondent felt that "the channels are coming up nicely and he mostly enjoys watching them". It is only a matter of time that the channels will approach and evolve innovative techniques in production and delivery that will distinguish them from mainstream entertainment channels.

It is then they will get a real punch to be understood as effective means of education. What is required is a continuous research into need assessment of the viewers, development of good quality programmes and a very strong feedback system to improve the programmes and evolve newer effective methods. On the whole these channels are a good effort in reaching out to students and teachers but the question of access is yet to be tackled. First the educational channel has to reach home or college television set, through terrestrial, cable or DTH, then automatically people will start watching them. As on today these programmes do not reach the target audience.

3. When the respondents were asked whether or not they agree with the statement, "Television is a very good medium of education". They were given five options ranging from

'strongly agree' to 'strongly disagree'. All the 20 respondents agreed with the statement, including 8 agreeing very strongly and 3 partially. None among them disagreed. (Figure 4.4)Those who partially agreed, when asked during the in-depth interview said that television by itself is neither good nor bad medium of education but it cannot be seen in isolation. To agree or disagree is related to how we use it. At present we are not able to use it to the advantage of education, which it is capable of, that is why despite its strength it remains only a medium neither good nor bad. The respondents in general cited various experiments that were conducted by scientists across the globe to determine the impact under various circumstances. The experiments most of the time yielded results if not higher but at least at par with the classroom teacher. Even under natural circumstances television with its audio-visual power makes things easy to understand and comprehend; that should be

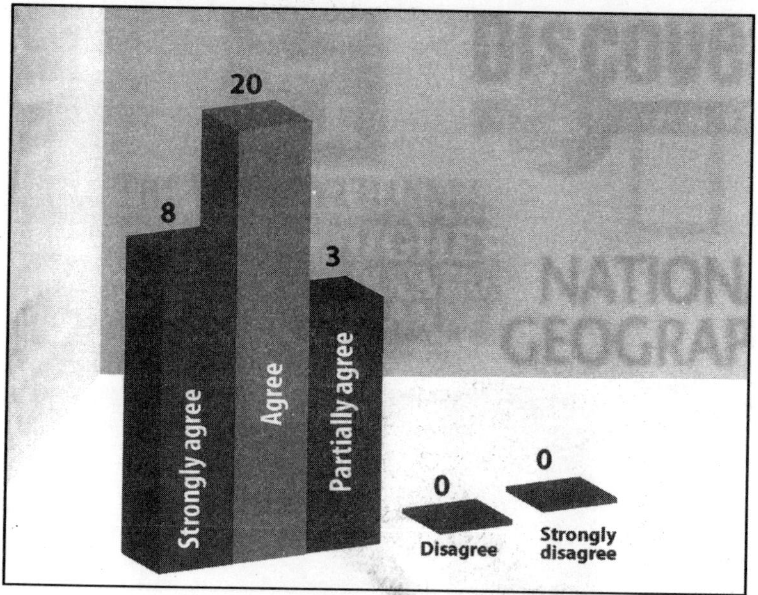

Figure 4.4 : Response to the statement, "Television is a very good medium of Education"

enough indicator to understand the potential this medium has in the field of education.

4. In response to question related to 'passivity theory', i.e., "television viewing is a passive activity, only 7 persons agreed, 4 including who partially agreed and the majority, i.e., 13 disagreed with the theory including 5 who strongly disagreed. (Figure 4.5) The reasons for disagreement with the theory are related to intent for which television is viewed. If watching television is purposeless and does not engage the attention of audience, that means no viewing has taken place; because viewing by very definition of the word "is an occasion for a special look on an exhibition or a film", said one respondent quoting dictionary meaning of the word. "It is like, said another respondent, "keeping a television set on while you are asleep, that does not constitute viewing". So either you view or you don't view, "a casual glance at the screen does not mean viewing". When reminded that active or passive viewing is related to the degree of attention that a television programme gets from its audience, most of the

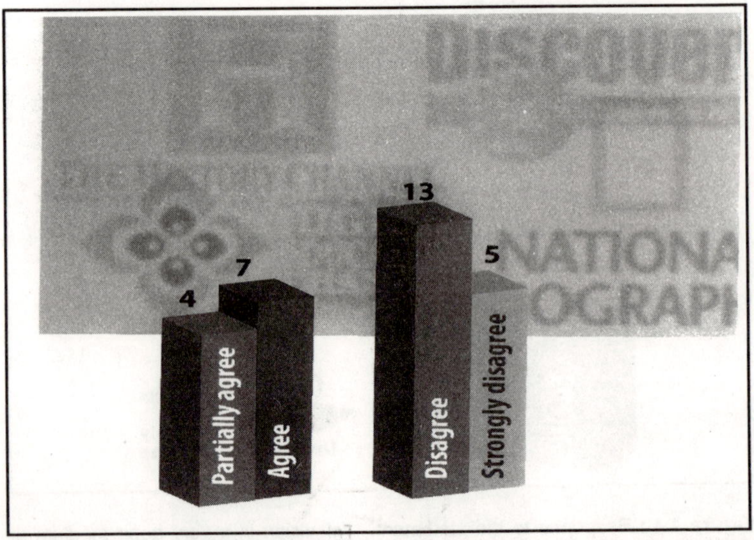

Figure 4.5 : Response to the Statement : "Television viewing is a Passive Activity".

respondents were quick to respond that it is related to how much attention a programme requires. "Viewing in relation to educational television cannot be 'passive viewing' it is to be seen with rapt attention for higher learning outcomes. It is again like a student in the classroom not paying enough attention to the teacher; the learning of such a student is bound to be shallow". Educational programmes are to be seen with seriousness for which proper viewing arrangements are to be made, a conducive atmosphere is to be created and the viewers must be given prior information about the programme. It is not seeing yet another television programme because here the intent is to learn.

5. With regard to potential of the medium for education, majority of the respondents, 13, said the potential of television for education is underutilized and 7 felt that it is not utilized at all. (Figure 4.6). Not a single respondent even remotely felt that the potential of television, at least in this country, is being exploited seriously for the purpose of education. There are some "half hearted efforts" in the form

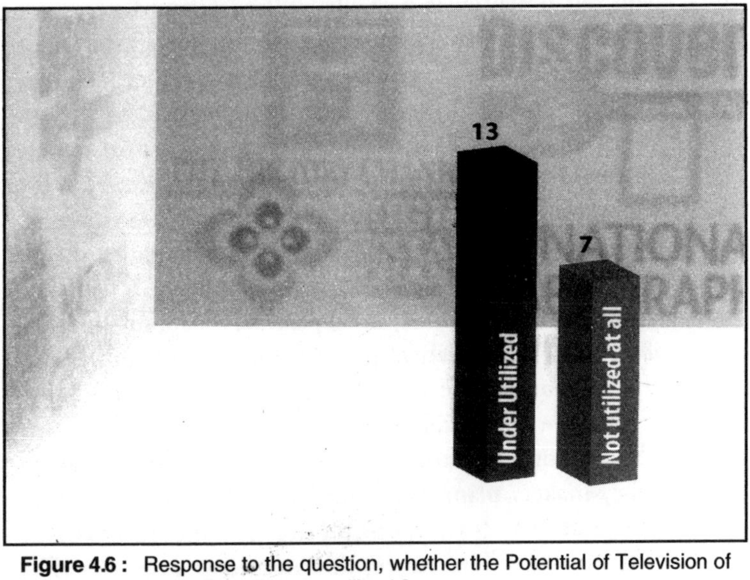

Figure 4.6 : Response to the question, whether the Potential of Television of Education has been utilized ?

of UGC countrywide classroom or Gyandarshan but any serious attempt involving all the stakeholders of "education for development" is yet to be seen. Televisions' potential has been used to the fullest by the commercial world in "creating artificial needs" and selling all sorts of "avoidable consumables" to one billion people in the country but its strong potential for "equalizing educational opportunities" among 10 million students of higher education has received almost no interest. The influence of "capitalistic mindset" that unfortunately afflicts the majority of our bureaucracy and "political bankruptcy" facing the nation for last 50 years has not allowed us to utilize television to the advantage of education. On one side "we take pride in having achieved a huge success by launching series of satellites in the skies, but on the ground we are yet to make electricity and drinking water available to the people" across the country. In the absence of electricity, especially in the rural areas of the country in general and Kashmir in particular, use of television for education is hard to think about. Among those who felt potential is partially utilized referred to use of television in carrying programmes for general education of the masses like health, hygiene, farming techniques and other socially and economically relevant programmes.

6. When asked, on a multiple option choice question, whom they hold responsible for underutilization of television for education, 11 hold broadcast agencies like DD, satellite and cable channels responsible as they ignore educational television programmes. While 8 hold students, 6 teachers, 7 programme producers, and 3 parents, 7 respondents hold all of them collectively responsible for the underutilization of educational television. Only two respondents felt none of them are responsible. 14 respondents, including the two who do not hold others responsible, hold administrators, policy-makers, planners and media managers of commercial organisations also responsible for the underutilisation. (Figure 4.7). The in-depth interviews revealed that

respondents on the whole felt that television in India has forgotten its social mandate and is blinded by the commercial considerations which take precedence on everything else. "The policy-makers of this developing country failed to understand the real value of education for development" and could not see the immense potential television offered for higher education in a resource scarce country. They did not encourage development of proper infrastructure for education in general and educational television in particular, because as they say, "education has been the last priority of policy-makers and planners". Development in the country is unfortunately seen in huge buildings, long flyovers, variety and number of automobiles, increasing consumption of utility goods, aeroplanes in the air and satellites in the skies. The "mindset of policy-makers regarding the use of television for educational purpose requires a change". They must try to lay down clear cut guidelines for the use of television for education and back it up with support from the government.

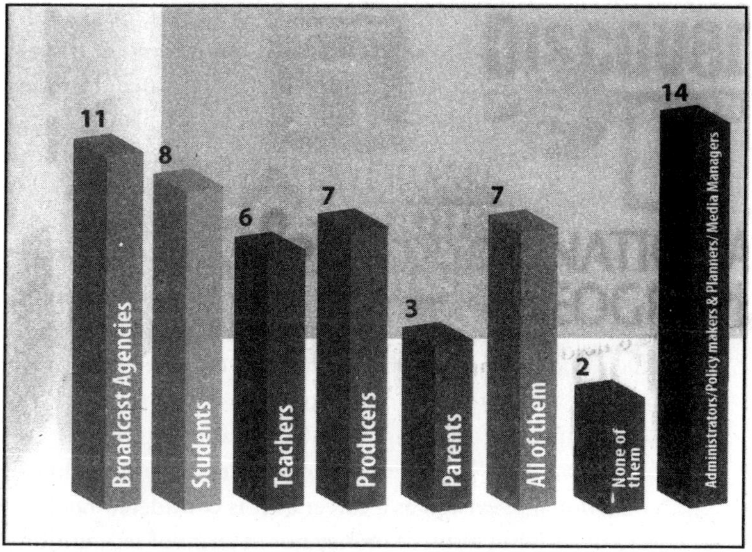

Figure 4.7 : Response to the question, who is responsible for the underutilization of television for education ?

The state broadcast agency, "Prasar Bharti, forgot its social mandate", thanks to DD mandarins who convinced the policy-makers and planners that DD can be a "huge revenue generator and blindfolded them with the short-term commercial gains" at the cost of long-term benefits of education. It is surprising that "DD, the so-called flagship of public broadcasting in India, has failed to establish a true dedicated educational channel" when it has the option of launching multiple channels. All the DD channels are filled with entertainment, news and sports programming. The social agenda on national network is limited to 2 or 3 hours of general educational programming concerning health or agriculture. "If national television DD could consider education a priority we must not blame the satellite and cable channels which in essence are commercial channels", yet we could have motivated them to at least carry some educational programmes in their schedule or create some channels for education in multi-channel approach. The overflow and unprecedented demand for entertainment has made the programme broadcasters shift their priorities. Changing priorities of broadcasters reduced educational programmes into mere time fillers. The programme producers at the same time cannot escape the blame. They have been "churning mediocre programme quality" not utilizing the real potential of television as a medium. While some of them simply "brought classroom on the screen", in an effort to sideline classroom teacher, others are swept away by the documentary format irrespective of the consideration whether or not it suits their objectives in an effective way. "Deglamourised treatment of programmes" further takes the punch away from educational programmes. The commitment of the majority of programme producers is seen as wanting. "The best in the country never thought of educational television as a career as it is considered neither very lucrative in terms of money nor in terms of recognition that other forms of television offer". The teachers and students are yet to understand the real value of television for education and their disinterest is rooted in non-availability of programmes in planned and organised manner on one hand and the age old teaching and evaluation practices on the other. Our higher educational system has not yet evolved on scientific lines as it is still "based on memorizing the chapters" and what in Kashmir we call "*gottafication*" of knowledge resources. Our examination system values you on the basis of how good you are at memorizing the chapters that were taught and not how good you have understood a concept.

This has resulted in "teaching pedagogy that lays more stress on memorizing rather than knowledge and skill transfer". Under the circumstances education through television is not seen of much help as it does not follow a set pattern of teaching and is caught in uncertainty due to infrastructural back-up. The parents could never inspire their children to see television for education. "The television is either damned by them as an evil destroying our social fabric or glorified as a great medium of entertainment and information". Very rarely are parents heard asking their children watch educational programmes on television. There was a consensus among the respondents that educational planners of the country have failed to sell the idea of using television for education and convince government to encourage the use of educational television at a mass level. Even the distance education or distance learning institutions are yet to capitalise on the potential of the medium in an effective manner. On the whole everyone in the society including programme makers, broadcasters, students, teachers and parents are equally responsible for underutilization of educational television for education.

7. While responses at six above held everyone responsible, though with varying degrees, for the plight of educational television in India as educational programmes could not be offered a proper platform from where they could have made

a significant contribution to education and equalized educational opportunities at national level, nonetheless the educational programmes of UGC Countrywide Classroom on national network of Doordarshan could not get many takers. As Admar Services (P) Ltd. reported a total of 22 million audiences for such programmes in 1997. This researcher, therefore, tried to find reasons in the failure of Countrywide Classroom programmes on DD, which probably is one of the reasons that forced DD to reduce the time slot for these programmes and push these programmes to insignificant timings. Ten probable or possible reasons were listed and placed before the respondents who were asked to arrange them in order of ranking from 1 to 10; with 1 as the most appropriate reason and the 10 as the least appropriate. Only nine out of 20 respondents provided ranking from 1 to 10. Five provided ranking from 1 to 5; 3 from 1 to 6 and 3 from 1 to 7. (Table 4.1). The responses were then tabulated in terms of frequency of a particular reason mentioned by the respondents at each ranking. (Table 4.2).

From a detailed study of the Table 4.2, the following conclusions emerge :

(a) that option *'c'* i.e., "inappropriate timings" of these programmes on Doordarshan is the first reason, with a frequency of 8, ranked by the respondents at No. 1, i.e. the most appropriate reason for educational television programmes not being watched by the target audience. This is followed by poor quality of programmes (option *'a'*), poor transmission of programmes (option *'b'*) and poor publicity of transmission schedule (option *'d'*) at top ranking.

(b) that option *'d'* i.e., "poor publicity of the transmission schedule" of the programmes, with a frequency of 6, is the second most appropriate reason ranked at number 2 followed again by "inappropriate timings (option *'c'*) at that ranking.

Table 4.8 : Rankings of the reasons, provided by the respondents, for non-viewing of the ETV programmes by the target audience. Respondents were asked to arrange the reasons from 1 to 10, with 1 as the most appropriate reason. 9 respondents provided ranking from 1-10; 3 from 1-7, 3 from 1-6 and 5 from 1-5.

Rankings

Respondents	a	b	c	d	e	f	g	h	i	j
20	6	1	5	2	3	4	8	10	7	9
19	x	1	3	4	5	2	x	x	x	x
18	3	4	1	2	6	7	9	8	10	5
17	6	7	1	2	3	5	8	9	4	10
16	x	x	2	1	3	5	4	x	x	6
15	2	3	1	4	5	x	x	x	x	x
14	1	x	2	3	7	4	x	6	5	x
13	5	4	2	1	3	6	8	7	9	10
12	x	7	1	3	5	6	4	x	x	2
11	x	2	3	1	4	x	x	x	x	5
10	1	5	4	2	x	3	x	x	x	x
9	5	4	2	1	6	3	7	8	10	9
8	6	5	1	4	7	2	8	3	9	10
7	6	1	2	4	3	5	7	10	9	8
6	1	7	4	3	8	5	2	9	10	6
5	5	4	1	3	7	x	x	x	6	2
4	1	3	2	4	9	6	7	10	8	5
3	3	x	1	4	x	5	x	x	x	2
2	2	1	3	4	x	x	x	6	x	5
1	4	6	1	2	x	x	x	5	x	3

Rankings

Table 4.9 : Frequency with which an option figures at a particular rank. Option "C" i.e. Inappropriate timing of the programmes on DD is the most appropriate reason for non-viewing of programmes by the target audience with a frequency of 8.

Options										
j	0	3	1	0	4	2	0	1	2	3
i	0	0	0	1	1	1	1	1	3	3
h	0	0	1	0	1	2	1	2	2	3
g	0	1	0	2	0	0	3	4	1	8
f	0	2	2	2	5	3	1	0	0	0
e	0	0	5	1	3	2	3	1	1	0
d	4	5	4	7	0	0	0	0	0	0
c	8	6	3	2	1	0	0	0	0	0
b	4	1	2	4	2	1	3	0	0	0
a	4	2	2	1	3	4	0	0	0	0
	1	2	3	4	5	6	7	8	9	10

Rankings

Note : Freguency stands for the number of respondents, who placed a particular option at a particular rank

(c) that at 3rd ranking, option '*e*' i.e., "tough competition from informational and entertainment programmes", with a frequency of 5 takes the top slot followed closely by "poor publicity of transmission schedule" (option '*d*') with a frequency of 4 and "inappropriate timings" of these programmes with a frequency of 3.

(d) that the fourth rank is again grabbed by option '*d*' i.e., "poor publicity of the transmission schedule" of the programmes, with a frequency of 7. followed by "poor transmission of the programmes (option '*b*') with a frequency of 4.

(e) that "invasion from cable" (i.e. option '*f*') only figures seriously at fifth ranking with a frequency of five.

(f) that the "one-way communication and lack of interaction" during telecast of these programmes (option '*g*') is ranked as the least appropriate reason, with a frequency of 8, for non-watching of educational television programmes on Doordarshan.

(g) that the other options, including too much content in the programmes (option '*h*'), less content—the students needs are not met (option '*i*') and the students are not motivated to see television for education" (option '*j*'), are the least mentioned reasons.

From the above it is very clear that "inappropriate timings", "poor publicity of transmission schedule", "poor quality of the programmes", "poor transmission of the programmes" and "tough competition from informational and entertainment programmes" are the top five reasons, in that order, for non-watching of educational programmes by the target audience. A perception that "lack of interactivity and one-way transmission" may be a strong reason for non-watching of educational television programmes could not get ranked in the top 5 reasons and in fact is the least appropriate reason. The respondents believe that, "interactivity helps in better understanding of the subjects but is not sufficient to warrant a high viewership or motivate students to watch educational television programmes in normal viewing conditions". Normally "students are late risers" so telecasting programmes in early morning hours becomes a very big hindrance. Even earlier when programmes were telecast during the midday time slot, students were mostly out in the colleges, where they do not have enough time as "the timetable does not permit it nor do the colleges have proper space, electricity and above all an environment that encourages television viewing". "College as the concept goes is a place where a teacher teaches in the class, laboratory or student reads on his own in the library". The television generally is not thought as a medium for education because that mindset is yet to be created, so viewing in colleges remains a problem.

The "best time for countrywide classroom programmes on DD was prime time", but since that cannot be made available for obvious commercial reasons most of the respondents favour "shifting of these programmes to 10 p.m. to 12 p.m. slot". The best alternative shall be to "launch a parallel terrestrial educational television channel" that can be viewed by people directly in cooperative manner with other partners like UGC/IGNOU/IITs/CIET, etc. This 24-hour channel with proper scheduling of programmes shall make a great difference in motivating students to see educational television programmes. "The mere availability of an educational television programme on appropriate time shall count for 50% of the solution to the problem". The unorganized and haphazard manners in which the programmes are telecast at present and poor publicity of transmission schedules deprive students to get information about the telecast of programmes. Some of the ETV programmes may be of great interest to the students and may motivate them to see programmes of their choice and relevance. So the respondents lay stress on publicity of transmission schedules.

Quality of programmes and transmission is a matter of

concern. "The quality of UGC Countrywide Classroom programmes has remained more or less stagnant and has not shown much of improvement in terms of approach and treatment". Innovative techniques of production and packaging of content shall be a constant effort to boost the quality. The reason why content load in a programme is not a concern for broadcasters and academics, as they were among the least appropriate reasons was a little baffling in the beginning. But in-depth interviews revealed that "load of content is secondary", to the other reasons at the top. Once the students get a proper time slot and information about the programme then "next essential matter of research shall be how much content load is required for whom." "We are yet at the first stage, the content load shall figure at the second stage". Proper "formative research" and "entry level test" are much accurate under normal viewing conditions which we are yet to achieve. The research on UGC countrywide classroom, across the country by UGC media centres, reveals a "general apathy about the reception of these programmes and most of the students are not even aware about any such venture". This is more because of "non-visibility of programmes on proper time slots" and "poor publicity of transmission schedules" rather than the content load. "Competition from informational and entertainment television is always there but that should not deter us". If educational programmes are telecast at prime time they will also find a good share of audience despite competition, "provided they are able to create a niche for themselves". Creating a niche audience at prime time for educational programmes comes only when we are there with the programmes. "With fragmentation of audience no channel today can claim to be catering to mass audience". Every channel has its own audience for every programme. So the educational television programmes shall also have theirs.

8. The best way to make effective use of television for education is a "constant effort and requires a holistic approach on part of planners, educationists, social scientists, media

professionals and above all teachers and students". While the "programmes need to be of high quality, research based, rich in content, sleek in presentation, interactive by nature, in tune with the latest demands and requirements" they at the same time require to be "relevant to the specific needs of groups of students". When asked to check (√) all the most relevant options, on a multiple choice option question, that shall help in making effective use of television for education, the respondents were not much divided.

13 respondents laid more emphasis on content then sleekness, 12 laid stress on enrichment type programmes while 8 favoured more syllabus oriented programmes, 12 again favoured involving experts and teachers of national and international repute in the design and production of programmes and 9 respondents stressed more of interactivity. (Figure 4.8).

The respondents generated a whole lot of ideas during indepth interviews ranging from types of programmes

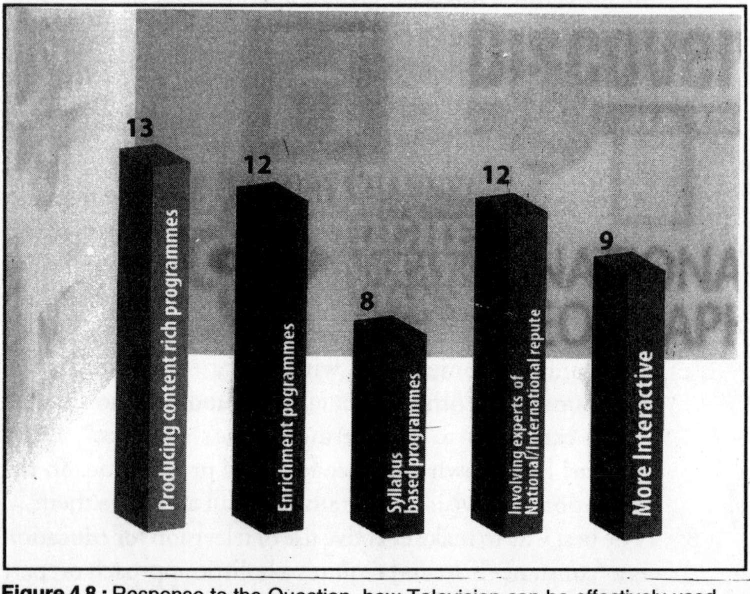

Figure 4.8 : Response to the Question, how Television can be effectively used for Education?

genres, packaging of capsules, introduction of new series, integration with syllabus, inbuilt interactivity on selected programmes with toll free numbers and use of new media. It emerged that special series on biographies, classics, historical events, monuments, inventions and discoveries, basic concepts in various subjects, places of interest, etc., shall be made alongside developing "syllabi oriented programmes in capsule form". The "syllabi oriented programmes need not be necessarily lecture" based they can use all the possible formats with lot of "visuals, graphics and animations" and each capsule shall cover at least one paper. "Instead of involving one or many experts individually they should be involved jointly or collectively" in the form of a group for the production of each capsule "so that the content is rich, up-to-date and uniform". Subject based "quiz competitions with good prize money" involving students at national level shall also be included to create an interest and involvement of the target groups in educational television. "Programmes on career guidance" with latest information shall be a constant feature and the "programmes that help students in preparing for competitive examinations" shall be made "in association with the leading agencies" of the country. Programmes from international agencies on "latest in science and technology" must be procured, re-edited or dubbed to suit our target audience and telecast on regular basis. This will "create a global window" for our students to see what is happening around the world. On the whole, a thorough scientific research is the key. "An innovative and effective treatment of apparently blunt subjects can prove gratifying and helpful". There is a "need to remove straits and make education television viewer friendly, no matter even if it means a timely departure from some worn out methods". As they say "seeing is believing", in certain cases television can prove more powerful than the original source of information.

9. The perceptions among teachers and students, as per numerous research reports by UGC media centres, vary

about the very nature of content of programmes. While a huge percentage among students and teachers are in favour of enrichment type programmes, the others feel they should be more syllabi based and yet a sizable percentage want a mix of both. But research is not very consistent in this regard. In fact, general perception is also not very clear. The majority of respondents of this study, 13 out of 20, favour a right mix of enrichment and curriculum based programmes, 4 are in favour of only enrichment type programmes and 3 categorically in favour of syllabi oriented programmes (Figure 4.9). While broadcasters in particular favour more enrichment type programmes which they feel are "more interesting and challenging" to produce but the academics seem to be more inclined towards "syllabi oriented programmes that help students pass examinations" and clear or brush up their confusions. This they also believe "will

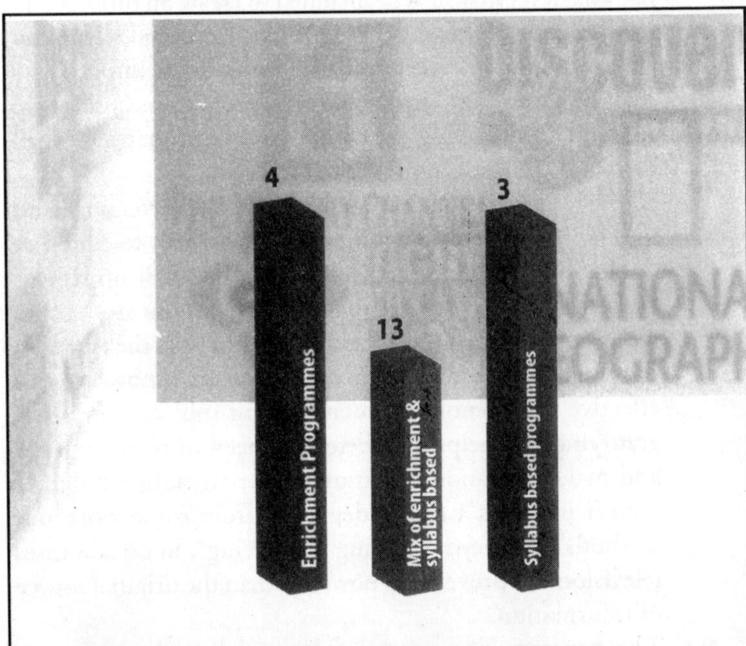

Figure 4.9 : Respondents Preference for the type of Programmes

take care of the dearth of good teachers in remote and rural areas" where they are in very short supply. This has "the advantage of making a good teacher in any subject available to students across the country". Those in favour of enrichment type programmes believe that, "in broadcast mode as of now we cannot achieve much success with the syllabi based programmes, because the limited time available to UGC countrywide classroom on DD cannot meet a huge requirement of programming based on syllabi. The time can best be utilized for enriching the knowledge of students by supplementing the classroom teaching. However, in case a 24-hour channel is made available for such a venture one can think of both the types of programmes.

The majority feeling that it should be a right mix of enrichment and syllabi oriented programming is based on "the supplementary and complementary approach" to educational television. While on one side the programmes should be serious enough and "directly relevant to the requirements of various courses taught" at the same time there must be enough to "what the appetite of students to know beyond classroom". The Countrywide Classroom credo states, "the idea is not to satiate but stimulate and broaden the mental horizons of the students". But even after over two decades it has neither been able to "satiate" the needs of students nor "stimulate" their imagination or creative faculties in a significant manner. The reasons for this are partly rooted in lack of clear and focused vision, in terms of type of programmes, for the countrywide classroom.

10. As UGC Countrywide Classroom on Doordarshan has failed to establish much rapport with the students and teachers, it could not make a significant contribution to teaching and learning process. Under the circumstances there were strong reasons being put forward to launch an exclusive channel for higher education. This resulted in launch of VYAS —the higher educational satellite channel by UGC in 2004. Research reveals that VYAS, after 4 years of operations, is yet to register its presence not to speak of

making a mark. Notwithstanding the failure of VYAS in making any worthwhile contribution to education voices are being raised to launch a terrestrial television channel exclusively for education. 18 out of the 20 respondents strongly favour the launch of such a channel in a cooperative form with other national agencies involved in production of educational television programmes; 2 however are skeptical about the prospects of such a channel at this stage and want that the "existing satellite channels dedicated to education shall be overhauled with a new look and made available to students and teachers through dish and cable" (Figure 4.10). The launch of terrestrial channel will take care of the question of access to educational television programmes which is a major concern at this time. "People are not convinced enough to buy a dish antenna, worth rupees four or five thousand, to receive VYAS" or other educational channels, nor are "cable operators ready to carry them on their bandwidth". The results are obvious, because people do not get to watch these channels.

11. The launch of a terrestrial educational channel "may be an

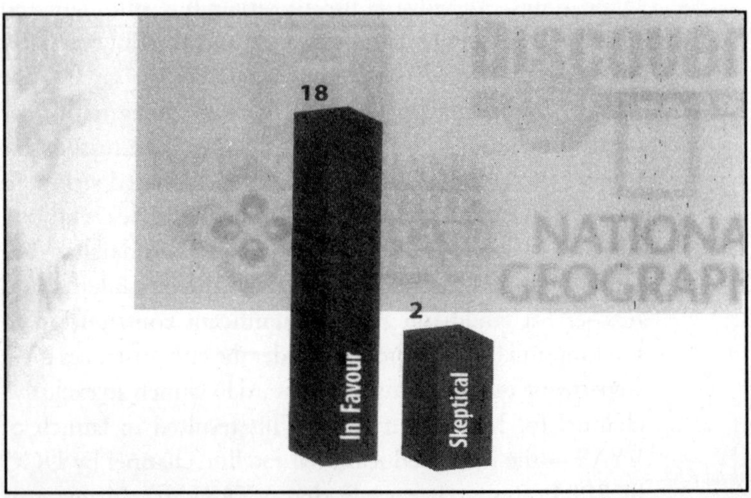

Figure 4.10 : Respondent's perception about the launch of an exclusive terrestrial educational television channel.

expensive proposition". Such a channel shall either have a solid financial support from government or shall be a self-financing endeavour. The possibility of an educational channel either in public-private partnership or in private sector depends on the economic viability of such a channel. 7 respondents feel that launch of a good educational channel may be economically viable and 9 feel it cannot be. Four respondents are not very sure about the economic feasibility of such a channel, as "no such serious feasibility survey or exercise has been conducted" as yet. One of them even felt he is "not competent to reply such a question" as it is a matter to be looked into and discussed by economists. (Figure 4.11). Those who support the economic viability of an educational channel mostly stress on "public-private partnership". They base their optimism in the "audience fragmentation", "falling audience share of major channels", "demand of a true educational channel" and the fact that "every channel has its own loyal audience". So if an educational channel is able to create its own niche market, which they strongly feel is possible, it shall also be a sought

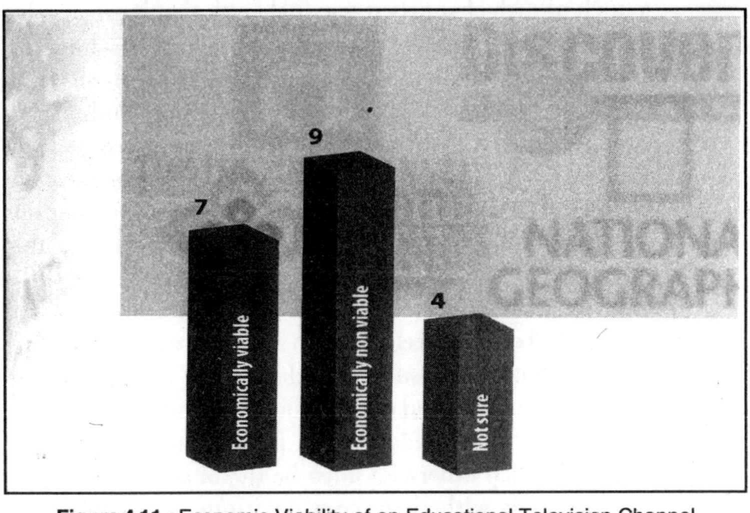

Figure 4.11 : Economic Viability of an Educational Television Channel

after channel by the advertisers and that will make it self-reliant.

12. As it is a known fact that advertisers are now increasingly looking for quality targets, who are the potential buyers of their products, no wonder then the companies dealing in stationery, publishing, apparels, boutiques, electronic gadgets, shoes, fashion designers, manufacturers of chewing gums, candies and chocolates, owners of private educational institutions, fast food giants and soft drink companies may want to put their advertisements on such a channel. This will ensure the economic viability of such a channel, if properly planned and executed. Private-public partnership is essential for such a venture. While the "involvement of experts from reputed educational institutions" in the country will ensure creation of quality academic content, the "expertise and experience of the private sector" will be a great help in packaging and marketing of the programmes. "The channel shall be treated as a business adventure with a social agenda like hundreds of successful corporations in the country". Even government can "encourage private entrepreneurship", with liberal financial assistance, for launch of such channels at regional level. Funds can also be raised by "special classes in career counselling, coaching for competitive examinations with e-content/print material back-up, discussion platforms for clearing doubts and conduct of trial or mock examinations for the registered students". One respondent feels that "education through entertainment" may be one of the ways to attract advertisements revenue and help channel survive in the private sector.

The pessimists about the economic viability of an educational channel feel that such a venture will take it away from the goal as pressures of industry will not allow it to take all the subjects and cater to the needs and requirements of the poors and needy located in far-flung areas of the country; which otherwise must be the objective of such a channel. It is with these considerations the viability of channel shall be examined. "Discovery" and "National

Geographic" may be economically viable but that is not the concept of educational channel that we are looking for. "For any channel to be economically viable two things are very important (a) Advertisement revenue; and/or (b) Pay channel viewership fee. As on date the educational channel may not be able to meet both the criteria".

13. So while economic feasibility still remains a big question educational channel shall have to look for financial support elsewhere. "Till now most of the educational endeavours were supported by the government, partially or fully, because it is considered a service to the quality of life and service cannot be expected to be financially viable". Like "Health" and "Army" are not economically viable for the state yet the government has to support them. The respondents during in-depth interviews stressed the "need of state finance for an educational channel". The government should "at least provide the initial funding and the channel over a period of time should achieve self-reliance". Majority of academics favour that "state must finance it, as a supporting activity for education". International aid agencies and institutions, like Ford Foundation, can also be approached for funding. Once an educational channel is able to establish itself on professional lines, with the help of "seed money" provided by any funding agency, it can "subsequently strive to achieve self-reliance through innovative and creative programming" that will be able to attract more audience and thus advertisement revenue. The possibilities of "collaboration with international agencies and educational television channels", like Public Broadcasting Service (PBS) of USA, must be explored to defray some of the production or equipment costs. The PBS in USA is receiving part of funding from general public in the form of donations; a similar effort can be made, involving NGOs in raising funds for the educational channel. "Whatever the source of funding, an educational television channel must have education as the only goal and all other measures shall only

serve as a means to achieve that goal". Like Doordarshan it must not be blindfolded with commercial or political considerations that will move it away from the real purpose.

14. New technologies offer a new opportunity for educational television. The respondents feel that "we must take the initiative to benefit from convergence of new technologies" and the growth and increasing penetration of these technologies in rural areas. The comfort and ease with which our young generation, the DIGITAL NATIVES, is making use of new technologies like multimedia cell phones and other electronic gadgets, even in rural areas, holds a promise for a bright future of the use of technology for education. While video streaming on mobile phones will help students receive educational television programmes anywhere, the GPRS and other web services on cell phones will provide them connectivity to sources of knowledge in electronic form. They at the same time can get in touch with the experts through phone, mail, blog or discussion platform to clear their doubts. What is required at present is to "have a multimedia approach for education". While a student or teacher is able to see an educational television programme through any of the available modes of transmission, he shall also be able to get a lot of reading material, exercises, etc., on the website of the educational television channel. This, some respondents feel, "can make virtual teaching and learning attractive for students and may even ultimately result in establishment of virtual institutions". This also brings "enormous advantage to distance mode of teaching". Currently most of the distance learning takes place with the help of reading material which is to be physically delivered to the students at distant places. This reading material most often never reaches the targets on time and also they do not always make much sense to the learner. "A multimedia approach using television and new media shall prove very useful to the learners and also cost-effective to organizations". The new technologies also offer a possibility of "launching

various local digital educational television channels", at a manageable cost, in various parts of the country. This will enable the broadcasters and academics "provide a local touch and flavour to the programmes" which may prove more beneficial as students can find it more relevant and related to their surroundings. The barriers on account of language and accent will also be removed to a great extent.

Respondents' Advice

Each interview concluded on a request to the respondents for advice to make better utilization of Educational Television. This evoked tremendous response and most of what has been enumerated above was echoed once again with much force and elaboration. However, some of the suggestions or advices made with unanimity or almost near unanimity can be summarised as :

Television till date has failed to come up to the expectations of students except for "entertaining them to the undesired extent". It could "help student community to compete at international level" by disseminating information catering to the needs of students at all levels. Quality need based educational television programmes, based or not based on syllabi, will help students understand basic concepts faster and prevent them from becoming "textbook worms". This will allow them greater "freedom to read books and publications other than the textbooks thus helping them enrich their knowledge". But the "programmes have to be attractive, visually appealing, innovatively treated and effectively transmitted". There is a need to benchmark software development process. Language has always been a huge barrier in understanding of programmes. While programmes in English language need to continue the language has to be simple and easy to comprehend. Also efforts should be made to "make programmes in regional languages as well".

A well planned and sustained effort is needed at all levels to effectively use television for teaching and learning. The element of interactivity should be increased so that process of teaching is not seen only one way but the teacher and the learner become partners in the whole process. The involvement of qualified, competent, motivated teachers in selection and screening of content relevant to various target groups and accreditation/validation of the programmes by experts at national level, before they are put on air, shall help benchmark the programmes and ensure quality. Telecast schedules must be widely circulated and teachers in every college and institution shall be involved in the process. The educational television programmes on tapes, CDs and DVDs must be kept available in libraries alongside the books. The cable operators should be impressed upon to carry educational television channels on prime bands/frequencies. Educational television should also be brought under "must carry" legislation.

What is most important is the change of mindset of the people. The mindset is to be changed. "Let people be motivated to see these programmes for a month, they will themselves feel what the programmes have done to them". "There is a need to have a separate set of advices for all the concerned. The planners and policy-makers should design policies that ensure uniformity in education at all levels". The "broadcasters must gear up for marketing knowledge" as India is expected to emerge as a knowledge superpower by 2020. "The teachers and students must draw the enormous benefits from educational potential of television" and ensure its proper use in teaching and learning methodologies. "Parents must themselves devote time to watch educational television programmes to inspire and encourage their children".

Educational television "must encourage experimentation, projection of divergent, conflicting views", "flexibility in the format", "technical and technological support", "exploring the knowledge beyond the prescribed outlines of the syllabi and provide perfection in all possible genres available". To conclude the only advice that can be offered to one and all is to give importance to educational television and utilize its potential to the benefit of society. That is the only way to realize the tremendous potential of television in the field of education.

Television on the whole is seen by the respondents as a very effective medium for education but its potential for education remains underutilized. This is due to general apathy towards educational television in which everyone has played its role. The half-hearted measures for using television for education has not served any worthwhile purpose so far. Television together with new technologies can bring huge dividends for distance learners, bring them face to face with the teachers across the country and make learning seamless, borderless besides making anywhere, anytime learning possible. The possible economic viability of educational television channels may help broadcasters understand and overcome the commercial considerations which kept them away so far, and may also result in establishment of certain quality educational channels in the private sector or in public-private partnership. This may also infuse new vigour and enthusiasm in programme producers, academics, students and parents to make best use of technology. What is most important is the change of mindset of everyone, with regard to television for education. One can only expect a complete change and transformation in the mindset of policy-makers, planners, managers, broadcasters, academics, students and people in general to effectively utilize the potential of television for equalizing educational opportunities for all irrespective of their location.

References

1. Brian Groombridge. *Television and the People.* (Middlesex England: Penguin Books Ltd., 1972), p. 7.
2. Williams, P.A.; E.H. Haertel; G.D. Haertel.; & H.J. Walberg. "The impact of leisure time television on school learning: A research synthesis". *American Educational Research Journal,* Vol. 19, (1982): pp. 19-50.
3. Blosser, B.J. "Television reading and oral language development: The case of Hispanic child". *Journal of the National Association for Bilingual Education,* Vol. 13, (1988): pp. 21-42.
4. Scarborough, H.S. "Prediction of reading disability from familial and individual differences". *Journal of Educational Psychology,* Vol. 81, (1989): pp.101-108.
5. Razel, Micha. "The complex model of television viewing and educational achievement". *The Journal of Educational Research,* Vol. 94 No. 6, (2001): pp. 371-379
6. St. Peters, M.; M. Fitch; A.C. Huston; J.C. Wright; & D.J. Eakins, "Television and Families: What do young children watch with their parents ?" *Child Development,* Vol. 62 (1991): pp. 1409-1423.
7. Comstock,G. *Television and the American Child.* (San Diego: Academic Press, 1991), p. 107.
8. Winn, M. (1985). *The Plug-in-Drug* (rev. ed), New York. Viking, in Robert Coonrad. "Television goes to school : The impact of video on students learning in formal education". (New York: A report by EDC's centre for children and technology, 2004): p. 5.

9. Anderson, J.A. "Television literacy and the critical viewer", in J Brayant and D.R. Anderson, (Eds.) *Children's Understanding of Television.* (New York: Academic Press, 1983).
10. Kozma, R.B. "Learning with media". *Review of Educational Research.* Vol 61, No. 2 (1991): pp. 179-211.
11. Peter Black, 'Bad News' Listener, 18th April, 1968, in Brian Bridegroom. *Television and the People.* (Middlesex England: Penguin Books Ltd, 1972), p. 18.
12. Kozma (1991): *ibid.*, p. 185.
13. Wiman and Miechenry (1969). in Robert Coonrad. (2004) : *ibid.*, p.6.
14. Salomon, G. "Television watching and mental effort: A social psychological view". (1983), in J. Brayant and D.R. Anderson, (Eds.) (1983). *Children's Understanding of Television.* (New York: Academic Press, 1983).
15. Flood, J. and D. Lapp. "Television and Reading: Refocusing the Debate". *The Reading Teacher*, Vol. 49, issue 2 (1995): pp 160-164.
16. Wright, J.C. & A.C.Huston. "Effects of educational television viewing of lower income preschoolers, on academic skills, school readiness, and school adjustment one to three years later". (1995). in Robert Coonrad. (2004): *ibid.*, p.8.
17. Levin, H.M. "Cost effectiveness and educational policy". *Educational Evaluation and Policy Analysis*, Vol. 10 No 1, pp. 51-69 (Spring 1988): p. 62
18. Thompson, F.T. & W. P. Austin. "Television viewing and academic achievements revisited". *Education. Chula Vista*, CA Vol. 124, No. 1, 194-202. (Fall, 2003): p. 197.
19. Chu, G.C. and W. Schramm. "Learning from Television : What the research says". In Robert Coonrad. (2004) : *ibid.*, p. 11.
20. Friedman, Thomas L. *The World is Flat: A Brief History of the Twenty-first Century.* (Farrar: Straus and Giroux, 2005).
21. Cuban, Larry. *Oversold and Underused: Computers in the Classroom.* (Harvard University Press, 2001).
22. Prakash, P, Jt. Secretary, UGC., Power Point Presentation. (New Delhi: University Grants Commission, 2006).
23. Reddi, Usha Vyasulu. *Educational Broadcasting in the Commonwealth: With Special Reference to Educational Television.* (New Delhi: COL-CEMCA 2003): p. 3.
24. Wimmer, R.D. and J. R. Dominick. *Mass Media Research : An Introduction.* (Wadsworth Publishing Company, 1997), pp. 101-102.

Chapter-5

The New Paradigm

"Technology Blended Education" – A New Paradigm of Educational Television for Higher Education in the Twenty-first Century

Introduction

The revolution of information and communication technologies, increasing use of satellites for information and communication, packaging and delivery of knowledge in electronic formats, the convergence of media technologies and above all the high penetration of electronic gadgets like cell phones, computers and television sets offer enormous opportunities for higher education. Educational content generation in 'e-form' has gained importance world over especially in developed and emerging countries. For country like India with vast geographical areas, huge rural population, limited resources for higher education, which are mostly confined to bigger cities, the growth and development of information and communication technologies promise a great relief.

The former President of India, Dr. A. P. J. Abdul Kalam, identifies India's human resource base as one of its greatest core competencies, in a book titled *India 2020 : A Vision for the New Millennium*[1], where he predicts that India will become a developed country by 2020. He advocates that Indians at all the skill levels can excel in knowledge-based services, if given the right training and are placed in intellectually challenging environments. A small minority of the scientists and engineers, primarily those who graduate from the IITs, IIMs and other elite institutes in India, have figured out on their own how to become world-class knowledge workers and thought leaders. But the advantage remains with these chosen few who create a universe of their own. The crux of the challenge is to find the way to train what Dr Abdul Kalam calls the "ordinary Indian engineers and scientists" to achieve a similar level of competence that would gain them the global recognition as being world class. This can be made possible by judicious use of technology for teaching and training to create a workforce for generation of educational and technical software that can be used within the country for overall development of the nation and marketed globally for boasting the economy.

Thanks to the passing of "Information Technology Act, 2000" by the Government of India, that gives legal recognition to and regulates transactions through new technology, the Indian software companies have the potential of creating educational and informational software that can be marketed globally and we can hope, aspire and work towards becoming global leaders. The vast English educated population, especially in the urban India, comes as a natural advantage. Though the population explosion of India is a matter of great concern for the policy-makers and commoners alike, and it requires to be checked, but at the same time it provides a unique opportunity in the form of human resource. It gives the country the strength of numbers, which no other country can match; at least in numbers. "The sheer numbers are mind boggling —the IT industry will have potential worth $200 billion by 2010" (p. 7). More than the revenue that it will generate, what is more important for the country is the potential of the industry in employment generation. It is estimated that "for every crore of rupees invested in IT enabled industry over 200 jobs can be created" (p. 7). If India taps the potential, providing over a million jobs every year through IT enabled services for the next 10 years it will create an "untold prosperity to every corner of the country; it will also create an advantage that other countries will find tough to match" (p. 7). (Vittal and Mahalingam: 2001)[2]

The time, thus, is opportune for us to make the use of technology in the field of education or else we may miss yet another revolution sweeping the world as we missed the earlier revolutions. Till now the communication technologies, be that radio, TV, or the new technologies like computers and internet, were mostly used for entertainment or at best for information but its use for education has been minimal. With the growth and convergence of technologies the realization, world over, is to make the best use of new information and communication technologies in the field of education. This has resulted, basically, from two concepts that are still developing :

(a) the emergence of "knowledge societies", and
(b) the "knowledge based economy".

For the development of a knowledge based society the University Grants Commission (UGC) of India is reported to have drawn a strategy for the development of higher education in twenty-first century with the following vision :

> "*The scope and demand for higher education is increasing and the new paradigm in higher education involves creation of intellect (and that means promotion of global standards in institutions of higher education) of world standards and also training of skilled human power at a mass level without compromising on quality (and that means making quality as an integral part of working of institutions of higher education.)*"
>
> (Sharma : 2004, p. 1)[3]

The vision clearly states quality at par, if not better than, the world standards, as a hallmark for growth of higher education. The ground realities on the other hand present a horrible picture of higher education in terms of quality. Even quantitatively we are not better. In a population of over one billion the enrolment for tertiary education in 1996 was reported as only 7% (Reddi : 2003)[4] expected to cross 10% by the end of Tenth Plan and 15% during Eleventh Plan (Prakash : 2006).[5] Scholars believe that Indians are able and willing to learn the necessary analytic and interpersonal skills needed to achieve thorough leadership qualities in the knowledge economy. It is believed that the future economies of the world shall be "knowledge driven" rather than commodity driven or in other words knowledge is going to be the most expensive commodity in the near future to drive the economies of nations. This is substantiated by the fact that education is fast turning "borderless" and "seamless" and most of the authenticated and validated educational content on the internet is paid. Educational institutions of repute are fast extending their reach at global level and online courses are being offered internationally making use of all kinds of technologies. These courses are attracting a huge response, even in developing countries, given to their flexibility, relevance and suitability for the students, keeping in view their constraints and requirements and increasing acceptability of these courses and degrees by the multinational companies.

The excessive dependence of today's youth on the internet and online sources is an indicator that educational content in electronic format is going to be in great demand in the years to come. The demand will be much higher when the "*digital natives*" —the today's children, grow into teens. Even the "*digital migrants*" —including the present youth, adults and the older generations, are increasingly becoming dependent, for knowledge resources, on information and communication technology.

Today, as stated above, knowledge knows no boundaries, thanks to the revolution in communication and information technology. The students have access to resources of knowledge across the globe. Most of the static knowledge has already been put together and packaged in e-form and is available on the internet. But in the archeology of knowledge all knowledge is provisional. What is permanent is the quest for knowledge. Having known certain knowable things, there is a huge universe of knowledge which till now could not be the province of a human being.

With this fundamental concept of provisional and permanent knowledge, or what in web terminology is usually referred to as 'static' and 'dynamic' knowledge there is a whole universe of knowledge that remains unexplored and that is what is going to be one of the driving forces of the economy of any modern society. The other important factor is going to be the packaging of knowledge and marketing of the same at global level.

For exploration and packaging of knowledge technology is already in place. While for exploration of the hidden knowledge the countries like India may not have enough resources but for packaging and transmission of existing knowledge no such limitations exist. In fact in the field of knowledge packaging, the ICT has created a level playing field between the east and the west; irrespective of our geographical location the latest information and communication technologies are available round the globe. The educational institutions, across the world, today are investing liberally in creating an ICT environment in their campuses. Computers have become the classrooms of new age. Older methods are fast replaced by new ones and the change is being nicely negotiated by the proponents of IT revolution. The entire process of teaching and learning is going digital. Amidst all this, it cannot be possible for any one to keep a distance from modern electronic gadgets and machines or shy away from use of technology for education.

Realising the importance and significance of ICT for development particularly for education the central government has taken some positive Steps to promote creation of solid infrastructure and networking across the country. These include exemption or subsidy on sales tax, VAT, State entry tax on IT sector, reduction in custom and excise duties on optical fibre, IT hardware, set top boxes, internet devices; duty exemption on TV sets for distance education, extension education and research programmes; allowing laying of fibre optic cable around national and State highways, roads; establishment of private universities and technical institutions; allowing the use of satellites, Ku band and Ka band for education; and encourage e-governance to improve transparency, accountability and efficiency at all levels. The easy affordability of IT gadgets with falling prices and the ever-increasing penetration of electronic equipments even in the rural areas of the country have given credence to the thought that this revolution can slowly but surely make a huge difference to India at global level. On the other hand with advancement of technology, the possibility of reaching to masses would further increase. The television technology together with the new media, internet and web technology shall be able to take quality education to students and teachers at any time and at any place through a high bandwidth fibre optic cable or a satellite connection.

The technological revolution has made the duty of a teacher relatively tougher and comparatively more demanding than before. Today students have access to sources of information across the globe and virtual teaching is the order of the day. The learning through internet has resulted in the creation of global learning communities. Number of people from across the globe, working on same or similar educational or scientific problem, are able to come together and share their knowledge and innovations with their global partners in the community. The cliché is that everything is available on the internet. Click a button, hundreds and thousands of pages from across the globe are loaded on any topic. Overwhelming data and content on almost every subject is available on the internet and at times one finds it hard to synthesize the information in a meaningful way. But the problem with the internet is that most of the information available is not properly authenticated, as anybody from anywhere can load anything on Internet. Internet in a way can safely be referred as 'garbage in' and 'garbage out'. The authenticity and reliability of information freely available on the internet makes it a poor source of reliable information. What can be termed as really authentic and reliable material on the internet is not mostly free. Some of such materials are priced too exorbitantly that students and teachers in developing countries are hardly able to make use of them. The increasing demand of educational material on internet is bound to cause a cascading effect on the prices of these 'commodities' making it very difficult for people, even in developed countries to make use of these resources. This will again give a fillip to information "have's" and "have not's".

To make the best use of the information on the internet, the sea of information, available through different sources, need to be properly synthesized and doled out in discrete units to avoid confusion of choice and requirement. This is where the need for the development and generation of content in electronic form or e-form by the authentic sources is felt. And this is where the university and college teachers have an important role to play. But unfortunately majority of college and university teachers are not showing much interest in the use of modern Information and Communication Technology for education; despite the fact that the concept of information highways and superhighways have already been achieved and the IT has become the leading technology in the world with direct bearing on all spheres of life with education being no exception.

Going back to the idea of Information highways, the expression can be traced to the computers communicating through the telecommunication network. If people can talk to each other through communication networks, so should the computers. This resulted in creation of "Local Area Networks (LAN)" initially which later expanded into "Wide Area Netwok (WAN)" and finally resulted in an explosive growth of internet. Today people across the globe communicate using various audiovisual, and written modes of communication, interact with each other in real time. No matter where you are, you stay connected with your home and office.

The growth and revolution, that internet brought brings us back to the "Wave Theory" of Alvin Tofler (1980).[6] Tofler, while describing the new information and communication technology, writes :

> "we are now witnessing the Third Wave, the age of computers and information technology. The smoking chimneys of factories are thus being replaced by environment friendly and knowledge intensive technologies." (p. 221)

An analysis of emerging national and global scenario makes us strongly believe that the world has become a "global village", the technology is in place and India is poised at a critical mass to launch an information and education revolution, through nation-wide 'national information highway'. Unfortunately, when the "borderless" and "seamless" education in the current era, with the use of information highways, are making waves across the world, the mindset of Indian teachers and students is finding it difficult to accept the hard reality. The closed mindset is partially due to technophobia that majority of the teachers harbour and mostly due to non-availability of electronic gadgets, lack of power supply and above all will to learn the new technology. Despite growth their still exist a huge gap between the teachers and the technology.

To bridge the gap between technology and the teachers

government is pumping liberal grants in educational institutions to equip them with the latest technologies of Information and Communication. Use of technology for education across India is visible as most of the educational institutions are in the process of establishing ICT networks and laboratories, number of dedicated educational broadcast services like Gyandarshan, EKLAVYA, VYAS etc., are operational, a dedicated satellite for education EDUSAT has been launched and a number of educational software production centres have been established across the country. UGC alone has established 17 media centres, i.e., Educational Multimedia Research Centres (EMMRCs) in select Universities in the country. These centres, earlier called Audio Visual Research Centres and Educational Media Research Centres, are engaged in production of educational television programmes and documentaries.

With the paradigm shift in technology the nomenclature of these centres also changed and that changed their nature of work. Now the centres are also actively engaged in production of syllabus based video lectures with multimedia inputs, development of Learning Object Repository (LOR), e-content and multimedia generation and off late Virtual Classroom operations through EDUSAT. The centres are equipped with broadcast quality television and video equipment including digital cameras, Linear and Non-Linear editing suites, and state of art multimedia set ups. The centres are linked through EDUSAT for delivery of content in the form of live lectures from experts followed by a two-way audio-video interaction. The centres have so far produced over 17,000 educational television documentaries and programmes in 49 subjects (CEC : 2006)[7] ; over 500 educational multimedia and thousands of Short Learning Objects (SLO) for the Learning Object Repository (LOR). The programmes are made with the help of university teachers and academics for the benefit of vast student community living in distant areas, where good teachers, laboratories and libraries are a rare commodity.

As these media centres (EMMRCs) are located in the universities, their contact with academic staff is direct. This offers greater opportunity for production of quality, content rich, educational programmes and interactive multimedia e-content. Besides these centres several universities, have started Multimedia Education Departments, some of which can also be engaged in development of educational multimedia. Additionally many institutions like IITs have created infrastructure for production and development of content in various forms.

Under the given circumstances, when resources are limited and demand is more, when expertise and facilities are few and the enrolment in higher education is on rise, when quantitative expansion is taking place in the absence of a matching qualitative growth of educational institutions, media centres like EMMRCs can make a big difference in equalizing educational opportunities with the help of information and communication technologies. Today India has one of the biggest higher education system in the world, with over 348 universities, deemed to be universities/institutions, over 15,640 colleges, about 10 million students and about half a million teachers (Prakash : 2006).[8] Though the quality of many Indian institutions is recognized and compared at par with many institutions of higher learning at global level, yet India has failed to create a university that can figure among the 100 top universities in the world. While the gigantic higher education system looks very impressive, nonetheless enrolment of 7% in higher education is too meagre when compared to global average of 30%. The Indian higher education system, like other developing countries is facing enormous problems of equity in terms of access to quality education and equitable distribution of knowledge resources. The best institutions, teachers, infrastructural facilities, libraries and laboratories are located in cities and major towns. These institutions historically have been consuming the major chunk of the budget set aside for education, leaving thousands of other educational institutions, elsewhere in the country with meagre resources, thus poor infrastructure and a scanty manpower that can hardly impart education not to speak of quality education.

While globalization has stimulated the demand in quality education and created a demand for quantity, it has developed a situation allowing foreign universities to market their degrees in this country. So the Indian educational system is going through a very tough but interesting phase. While equitable distribution of resources for inclusive growth of higher education is a matter of concern, competition from institutions from outside has thrown up new challenge. Under the circumstances only clever and innovative integration of information and communication technologies, in an open and flexible academic structure would help the country to address the question of equity, access and quality. Given the Indian experience of over two decades, in using television for higher education, it may not be difficult to take advantage of new technologies to address the new challenges.

The EMMRCs in this regard are in fact making a humble contribution in "liberating education from the confines of classroom" and taking quality education to the doorsteps of students irrespective of their location. The results are heartening. Students, though a small percentage, have benefited a lot from the educational content packaged by EMMRCs in the form of ETV documentaries/programmes, e-content, multimedia and Learning Objects. The research indicates the experience of using technology for teaching and learning has been quite enriching for both, students and teachers.

The UGC in collaboration with ISRO has also established over 60 Satellite Interactive Terminals (SITs) throughout the country, for Virtual Classroom operations through EDUSAT. The establishment of Virtual Classrooms has made virtual teaching at national level a real experience for our students and scholars. Attending lectures of some of the renowned academics of India, interacting with classmates and experts from different subjects, who necessarily do not sit shoulder to shoulder in the same room but are connected through EDUSAT, have added a new dimension to the academic environment. The best teachers available in the country are able to reach a vast heterogeneous community of students through virtual classroom and share expertise at the national level. Introduction of *Lectures on Demand* by EMMRC Srinagar in May 2007, have made virtual classrooms learner-centric and need-based. Owing to the success of lectures on demand the UGC on September 5, 2007, the Teacher's Day, dedicated the 'Lectures on Demand' to the nation. The sharing of resources at national level, through virtual classrooms, has become easier and a single expert of any speciality is available to the students throughout the country on any given moment without actually leaving his city. Virtual teaching in a country like India, where resources are always scanty, is the most cost-effective, time and money-wise, way of reaching more and more students across the country. This also overtakes the inconvenience of travelling to share one's expertise. As Tofler makes us believe homes in modern age shall turn into "electronic cottages" and people will move electronically then physically, the experts of knowledge also shall commute huge distances virtually.

The educational television programmes produced by EMMRCs are repeatedly telecast from various television channels of Doordarshan, DD Bharti, Gyandarshan, and VYAS —the higher educational TV channel of UGC. While DD telecasts these programmes at odd hours that do not suit the majority of students, the other satellite channels are hardly available to the students. The cable operators are reluctant to carry these channels as they believe 'there are no takers for such programmes.' The teachers generally are indifferent to educational television and do not see or encourage students to benefit from these programmes. The result of these programmes, of critical academic importance, remain inaccessible for the students who are not able to benefit from these programmes. "While the growth of the electronic media of radio and TV in terms of reach, popularity and variety has been phenomenal, there has not been a corresponding growth in their education related usage. Lack of publicity about the contents and timings of the programmes, inability of one's electronic equipments to receive the signals and lack of interactive nature of their programmes have contributed to the under-utilization of these educational media." (Arulchelvan and Vishwanathan : 2006).[9] The underutilization, due to general apathy towards educational television, restrains the educational outcome of the initiatives by UGC-CEC and the media centres. Otherwise research is supportive of enhanced educational outcomes due to exposure to the educational television programmes. As research has made us believe that students did significantly better when they viewed the lessons that demonstrated planned visual continuity, contained visual reinforcement and had been the result of a team approach to make effective use of the television medium.

The endeavour of UGC to make use of technology for education is making good strides and promises the potential of bridging the gap between the teachers and technology in packaging authentic and reliable knowledge and disseminating the same among the students in an easy and effective way. This will also pave the way in creating a vibrant knowledge society that may become a viable source of economy in the years to come. But technology in itself is no magic wand. Just because the arrival of a new sophisticated technology pulls your mouth wide open, does not necessarily mean the gadget will succeed in the real marketplace. The television history is littered with lots of good ideas that never went anywhere. While the device itself may be perfectly functional and effective and idea and intentions for its use for the education are noble, there is no guarantee that it will achieve the desired goals if teachers and producers, academics and broadcasters remain indifferent.

The creation of quality educational videos or e-content with broadcast quality equipment of high value is expensive, and the high end system normally yield the best product, yet quality work can be delivered with relatively inferior mid range or low end equipment also. If creative producers and willing teachers are ready to invest intelligence and care in their productions, the calibre of their equipment becomes secondary. Need of the hour is to pool our resources at all levels and try make use of technology that is available for the growth of education. This requires a paradigm shift in teaching and learning on one hand and the use of technology on the other. The role of technology for holistic and inclusive education under the new paradigm can be classified into two distinct, yet interlinked areas :

(a) *For Content Generation :* For centuries teachers have been generating educational content by writing books, essay and articles. The changing scenario under new paradigm expects teachers to also generate content in various electronic forms (e-form). Currently the teachers at international level are engaged in generating content in the following e-forms :

- Production of ETV programmes/enrichment documentaries.
- Production of Educational Radio Programmes.
- Production of Multimedia, e-content.
- Creation of Reusable Learning Objects and Development of Learning Object Repositories (LOR).
- Development and management of educational websites.

The generation of content in e-form is a teamwork involving media persons, web/instructional designers and teachers. The role of teachers here is very crucial and central. To involve teachers, workshops for capacity building in content generation are being conducted. The e-content is generated using various kinds of software stressing on interactive and 'adaptive learning'.

(b) *For Dissemination :* From talk and chalk approach or simple telecast of educational television programmes on a television channel, we are gradually moving to dissemination of knowledge using newer and multiple forms. The content generated in e-form is being disseminated through various means of communications using new technology. In India the following modes, at present are used :

1. Telecasting of programmes on various television channels like Doordarshan, VYAS —the higher education channel of UGC, Gyandarshan of IGNOU, Regional TV and Local cable networks;
2. Broadcasting of programmes on AIR stations, Gyanvani and a few FM Radio Stations;
3. Virtual Classroom operations through EDUSAT;
4. Distribution or sale of cassettes/CDs/DVDs/Audio Tapes; and
5. Broadband services for access to rich media sources through internet and Video Streaming for web-based learning.

Generation of quality educational e-content and its efficient distribution across the country, involving various modes of communication, is resulting in a paradigm shift in packaging and dissemination of knowledge and shall very soon affect the teaching and learning process. The teacher and student both shall undergo a transformation for making the process of knowledge transfer a more enriching and rewarding experience.

The New Paradigm

The new paradigm of education, where technology is seen as a partner, shall be of great help in effective distance learning in the following manner :

1. Extends the reach of a teacher beyond classroom and college; making good libraries, laboratories, and experts available to students living in distant areas;
2. Facilitates easy simulations and virtual experimentations at a low cost which can also be repeated any number of times;
3. Student friendly —study anytime, anywhere and any style (asynchronous learning);
4. Authenticated and validated information will be made available to the students in discrete units making it easy for them to access and assimilate knowledge; and
5. Create a knowledge society that may help us emerge as global leaders to embrace "the knowledge-based economy".

In the new paradigm the focus shall be more on e-content development alongside the production of educational television programmes. While the educational television programmes through television and live lectures on specific subjects are disseminated to the students through various means, the e-content on the same topics shall be made available freely using all the available means of communication. This together with the involvement of teachers in distant colleges shall create a healthy learning environment in these institutions. The availability of quality e-content and multimedia will provide additional material in many forms to satiate the urge of students in getting more knowledge on the subject.

For the development of e-content Consortium for Educational Communication (CEC) New Delhi proposes a detailed methodology (CEC 2006).[10] The salient features of the methodology can be briefly summarized as under :

1. The Approach

The methodology proposes a multilayered approach. Knowledge shall be packaged in all the possible forms of media, the same shall be disseminated using all the available means of transmission including telecast through VYAS, video streaming for web-based learning, EDUSAT for live lectures/interaction and internet for creating a learning community. The teachers shall be involved in packaging of knowledge resources with the help of media centre staff. The packaging of knowledge shall be done in the following forms :

(a) Creation of Instructional design based E-content/ Multimedia modules;
(b) Developing Learning Object Repository;
(c) Production of Educational Video Programmes with multimedia inputs; and
(d) Live lectures-cum-demonstrations with graphic inputs through EDUSAT.

The knowledge thus packaged shall be made available to students through EDUSAT network for "synchronous" or "asynchronous" learning. The former shall be during the live lectures utilizing EDUSAT/VYAS Channels for telecast/simulcast and interaction of students with expert through EDUSAT. The live cast can be either by "a single teacher" or "more than one teacher" using multimedia inputs. It can also be "resource based teaching" using prerecorded lectures, demonst-rations followed by interaction. For "asynchronous" learning, that shall be "anytime anywhere learning", the packaged material, "e-content modules, LOR and Video on Demand" shall be kept available on the server at CEC for the use of students through EDUSAT or internet.

The project shall begin with focusing on providing required skills to teachers in the area of "script writing", "voice-over", and "visualization" taking into account the specific needs of teachers in different subject areas. Each subject requires a special treatment depending on the nature of the very subject to keep the "basic content intact" and at the same time make it "more understandable and exciting with the new medium for the learners". The teachers in association with the nearest media centre shall then produce or develop educational content and package it in various forms.

2. The Quality Assurance and Authentication

For quality assurance, which is paramount for any serious educational endeavour, strict quality control measures are proposed to be taken to ensure the "correctness of facts, free from prejudice and bias", with stress on latest information, and to see if it is "attractive for teachers and students".

The quality assurance of e-content in various developed countries is done by processing the content through two stages namely "alfa" version and "beta" version. This method checks the quality at several stages ranging from "content development, content vetting, peer group preview, content acquisition, identification and grading" to assure the quality of e-content. This is important as the "e-content quality has to be assured for granules, modules as well as the entire courseware". The evaluation of the content for "beta" version includes, "evaluation and the impact of programme on the viewer's browsers. This helps in refinement of e-content. For proper assessment and accreditation of the e-content CEC envisages to constitute a "joint group of CEC and NAAC" i.e National Assessment and Accreditation Council, of India to work out proper "parameters of quality assurance of e-content". The content developed shall thus be properly evaluated and assessed with the help of experts and certified by CEC before it is telecast or webcast.

3. The Distribution

The distribution of the content across the country shall be through various available means of communication with stress on television and web-based learning. In addition to telecast of programmes on various channels, viz., VYAS, Døordarshan, EDUSAT network, and live lectures and interaction through EDUSAT, CEC is planning to keep the content available on computer server for streaming through internet or EDUSAT network. The CDs/DVs of the packaged content shall also be made available to colleges and universities to develop proper e-content libraries.

The consortium for educational communication (CEC) believes and hopes that, "this will provide an opportunity to teachers to learn and acquire skills required under the new paradigm of teaching profession. It would also provide an opportunity to students and teachers throughout the country to know the queries of students and responses given by the experts thereby enabling them to benefit from countrywide virtual classroom". (CEC : 2006)[11]

With the initial success of Virtual Classroom operations through EDUSAT, we can optimistically conclude that the Virtual Classrooms, together with other means of dissemination and the convergence of technology, promises free flow of e-content for the use of students irrespective of their location. Additionally UGC Information Network (INFONET), that connects colleges and universities across the country, can facilitate free flow of information or knowledge resources, course wares and the reference material. With increasing use of cell phones and the mobile telephony the possibilities of distributing educational content are becoming more easy and speedy. This would enhance the academic infrastructure in each classroom virtually, irrespective of its location, to improve teaching learning process in an equitable manner. The paradigm shift from traditional to e-learning as an integral part of the teaching and learning process has resulted in the concept of "borderless" and "seamless" education. The concept is fast seen turning into reality and eventually giving rise to the establishment of "Virtual Universities". For the best results a massive exercise, involving teachers, technocrats, media professionals and institutions of higher learning, is required to be taken at the earliest to develop and distribute knowledge resources, in a fast and proficient manner, among the students, scholars and teachers.

Issues and Concerns

While technology and teachers together with other players are making a significant contribution in the generation and dissemination of authentic knowledge resources for creation of a credible and vibrant knowledge society there are some serious issues and concerns that need attention.

For development of quality educational software in the form of Multimedia it is essential to create a trained manpower in every subject. Thus there is a dire need of training of teachers and multimedia staff in methodology and the practice of e-content development at par with the international standards. But the motivation level of teachers to use new technology for content generation at present is very low. One of the reasons for this is that it does not count for their growth. The workshops conducted for capacity building need to be weighed at par with refresher or orientation courses and the content generated need to be valued at par with the publications. Or these can be made as additional requirements for personal promotion schemes.

Though the costs are coming down, the availability of technology especially in rural India is still a problem. The visibility of VYAS/ Gyandarshan is a matter of concern. The Internet connectivity is still trying to overcome the teething troubles. The return path of EDUSAT for virtual classroom operations is not very clear. Broadband is still a luxury. In some rural areas there is acute shortage of power making the use of new technology very difficult and uncertain.

The mechanism for quality and standards for content generation are yet to be developed. Though CEC-UGC proposed a model Educational Effectiveness Standards of e-contents (EESeC) the same is yet to be adopted. At international level content generators are advising compliance to 'Shareable Content Object Reference Model' (SCORM). It is important to set the standards for e-content at the earliest so that the authenticity and validity of the content is guaranteed.

Motivation of students at present is also low but is showing a steady increase and is bound to increase manifold in the coming years. This optimism is rooted in two reasons : one the easy availability of valuable e-content free of cost or at a very low cost; and the second the arrival of 'digital natives' —the present young generation who are more technology savvy. Distribution of educational software remains a concern but future holds a promise as the new digital world is offering launch of multiple educational channels; that can be easily available to people in different broadcast and non-broadcast ways. It is also required to give a wide publicity to the educational endeavours taken under the new paradigm as most of the end users are not yet aware about the availability of storehouse of knowledge in the form of educational television programmes, multimedia, etc.

Conclusion

The involvement of academicians in content generation in 'e-form' will help to create an authentic and credible platform where the specialists and experts in various fields of education can put authentic information for the use of students and researchers. The content thus produced will not be only highly valuable, authentic and easily available, it will make the whole process of teaching and learning an enriching and entertaining experience. Fortunately, there is enough talent available in this part of the globe but what is required is a little bit of motivation and exposure to new technology. That said teachers need not be web junkies but saying 'No' to technology at this stage is just unavoidable.

It is neither possible nor advisable to digitalize the whole intellectual world so that teachers become instructors and students amateurs of an automobile workshop. Though the use of technology in education indeed is very fascinating and rewarding but a fine balance between mind and machine is to be struck. To meet this challenge, we will have to make use of all we have — mind and the machine both. Human stuff coupled with a technological support can make the job possible for us. Not relying purely on the mechanics of the process, we will try to hone human skills, spot genius wherever we see and tap the potential to the fullest. That is to expand the very horizon of education to socialize the institution of knowledge and institutionalize the content generation in e-form. The very process must not be seen as a plain exercise of teaching and learning but a vibrant interaction where everyone inspires everyone else. We need to conquer distances so that the barriers disappear and ideas travel freely transcending territories. Our modest attempt will be to realize the dream of universalizing quality education. So far we have dreamt, now is the time to do. Use of technology for teaching and learning should be made a national movement. The efforts shall be made to involve all— the media persons, the ICT persons, teachers and students. Together we can create a knowledge society that may drive the economy of our nation and make us a knowledge superpower.

The new paradigm for educational television in higher education envisages blending the technology with teaching using a multimedia approach rather than simple broadcast of programmes. While quality educational programmes, both enrichment and syllabus based, shall be telecast using all the possible modes of transmission, there shall be enough flexibility for students to access them as and when they feel. The telecast again shall not be made in isolation they shall be integrated with the classroom involving teachers and the institutions. The e-content back-up, with constant upgradation of learning resources, shall be easily accessible on the websites with vibrant discussion platforms and blogs. This is how the technology blended education shall result in creation of a vibrant knowledge society under the new paradigm of educational television.

References

1. Kalam, A.P.J. Abdul and Y.S. Rajan. *India 2020: A Vision for the New Millennium.* (New Delhi: Penguin, 2003).
2. Vittal, N. and S. Mahalingam. *Information Technology—India's Tomorrow.* (New Delhi: Manas Publications 2001), p.7.
3. Sharma, G.D., "E-Content Development—An approach paper", (New Delhi: Consortium for Educational Communication, Unpublished, 2004), p.1.
4. Reddi , Usha Vyasulu. "*Educational Broadcasting in the Commonwealth*" (New Delhi: COL-CEMCA, 2003): p. 3.
5. Prakash, P. Jt. Secretary, UGC. Power Point Presentation (New Delhi: University Grants Commission, 2006).

6. Toffler, Alvin. *The Third Wave : The Classic Study of Tomorrow.* (New York: William Morrow, 1980), p. 221.
7. Consortium for Educational Communication. *CEC Annual Report 2005-06,* (New Delhi: CEC 2006) : p.22.
8. Prakash, P. (2006), *ibid.*, PPT.
9. Arulchelvan, S. and D. Vishwanathan. "Pattern of usage of various electronic media by higher education students". *International Journal of Education and Development using Information and Communication Technology* (IJEDICT), Vol. 2, Issue 4. (2006): p. 100.
10. CEC Annual Report (2006): *ibid.*, Annexure, p.3.
11. CEC Annual Report (2006): *ibid.*, p.3, Annexure-V.

Chapter 6

Educational Television–Kashmir Scenario

A Profile of Television and Educational Television in the Kashmir Valley.

History and Growth

Jammu & Kashmir State was among the earliest to have a television broadcasting station in India. Only a few months after the launch of second Doordarshan station at Bombay the third Doordarshan station was launched, on 26th January, 1973 at Srinagar in the Kashmir valley (Raina, 1997).[1] Doordarshan Srinagar started telecasting programmes for four hours a day in the evening. On Sundays there was an additional two-hour transmission in the morning hours. The programmes mostly in Urdu and Kashmiri consisted of general interest programmes, news bulletins and programmes targeted on special audience like women, children, health, agriculture, etc. Doordarshan Srinagar also transmitted two weekly educational programmes on general science for the primary schools and one weekly enrichment type programme for the university students. Under community viewing scheme, 218 schools in and around Srinagar city were provided with television sets. (CIET : 1984)[2]

Keeping pace with Doordarshan stations in other parts of the country DD Srinagar also started colour transmission and joined the national network of Doordarshan with the telecast of programmes from Delhi Doordarshan from 15th August, 1982. This was made possible with the launch of INSAT-1(A) which linked all the Doordarshan stations in a national network and allowed people to get direct reception from satellite through specially designed dish antenna. The transmission time, therefore, was shared between the programmes telecast on the national network and the programmes produced locally.

In 2003, "DD Kashir", the Kashmiri language satellite channel supported by Doordarshan studios in Srinagar, Jammu and Leh, was launched. Initially, the channel used to telecast programmes for fourteen and half hours daily but the channel has now become a 24-hour channel. DD Kashir which was supposed to cater to the needs and requirements of local population keeping in view the regional aspirations and tastes sadly has majority of imported programmes including a variety of programmes entertainment serials, infotainment programmes, news and current affairs programmes, social and cultural programmes and a huge film and film based programmes as its major content. The channel also has some special audience programmes in Gojri, Pahari, Ladakhi, Dogri, Sheena, Balti, Pushtu, Bhadarwahi and Punjabi languages. There are hardly any serious educational television programmes seen on Doordarshan Srinagar or DD Kashir except some soft educational programmes catering to general audience. These include *Butrat*, a programme for farmers that has been on the air since the inception of the Doordarshan Srinagar, telecast 5 days a week; *Krishi Darshan*, another farmers' programme, mostly imported from other DD stations from 2006, 5 days a week including live phone in programme; two children's programmes a week, *Shagufay* in Urdu and *Bamen* in Kashmiri; and two youth programmes *Shaheen* and *Yawun*, covering issues concerning the youth. The DD also has two online programmes like health programme "Doctor on line" and a programme based on public grievances "Hello DD". Under educational programme category the DD Srinagar telecasts a one hour programme *"Sitaroon Say Aagey"* on first and third Sunday of the month. The programme is targeted on youth in general. On second and fourth Sunday of an hour long educational programme, "Tele-class Room", is telecast for the students of 9th and 10th standard. DD Srinagar time-table from 1977 to 1994 shows a regular ETV slot. The perusal of fixed point chart of DD Srinagar from 1977 to 1995, as published by Raina (1997)[3], does not show any local educational television programmes except higher education programmes of UGC countrywide classroom from 1984 onwards.

Today Doordarshan's main channel is available to 94.8 per cent of the population and DD Kashir is available to 77 per cent of the population of the valley. The channels with such a wide reach could have been effectively used for education in Kashmir. Especially for higher education it would have been of great help, as the colleges in rural areas of the valley are experiencing shortage of competent and experienced teachers, have very limited infrastructure and almost no libraries. But as is happening elsewhere Doordarshan here also does not recognize its role in the field of education.

The DD Kashir channel in particular could have played an important role in carrying educational television programmes rather than retelecasting the programmes of other channels or carrying the programmes of the main DD Srinagar channel in a simulcast mode. The channel which was supposed to be a non-propagandist in essence actually aims at integrating the people of the State with the rest of the country. The integration could have been better achieved by including educational television programmes rather than the bombardment of film and film based entertainment programmes that are otherwise also available to the audience in Kashmir. The Kashir Channel as it is today does not serve any useful purpose and remains grossly underutilized.

Cable Channels and DTH Service

The nineties of the last century saw cable and private DTH services grow in Srinagar city and some urban areas reducing the viewership of Doordarshan and providing endless entertainment, news and sports channels to people. In first few years of the current century local cable television channels also started their operations in Srinagar. These channels because of dearth of programming bombarded audience with latest feature films and film songs most of which are pirated without caring for the copyright violations. They created a niche for themselves in the local market and gradually started news and some other local programmes including local music and current affairs programming.

The cable programmes are mostly produced using low end consumer quality equipment. Nonetheless these channels, five in Srinagar city alone, because of their local touch and latest film based programmes have created a good audience base for themselves. Today the cable operators are running multiple channels but most of the channels carry only entertainment programmes based on "Bollywood" films. Like other parts of the country the cable operators in the valley are also not interested in carrying the educational television channels nor do these channels cablecast any educational television programmes. The efforts of EMMRC Srinagar to convince cable operators to carry the educational channels or at least the programmes produced by the centre did not yield any positive results. One cable operator offered to telecast the EMMRC Srinagar programmes and pay a nominal royalty to the centre withdrew after two months because of his inability to pay the royalty. The vast potential of cable for educational television in Kashmir, therefore, remain underutilized.

Contribution of EMMRC

The Educational Multimedia Research Centre (EMMRC), Srinagar (formerly Audio Visual Research Centre), sanctioned in 1987, is one among the 17 media centres, established by UGC allover India. EMMRC, an autonomous centre of the University of Kashmir, was established primarily for production of educational television programmes for UGC countrywide classroom. Over the period of time as the centre grew and policies at UGC evolved to incorporate the growing demands of student community, owing to the revolution in information and communication technologies, the objectives of EMMRC also widened to accommodate the new ideas. Currently the objectives of the centre are :

(a) Production of Educational Television Programmes;
(b) Production of Syllabus Based Video Lectures with multimedia inputs;
(c) Development of Educational Multimedia and e-content generation;

(d) Development of Learning Object Repository (LOR).
(e) Conduct research to improve the overall quality of the programmes; and
(f) Conduct Virtual Classroom operation through EDUSAT Network.

The centre became fully operational and functional in 1992; and started making educational television documentaries, involving university and college teachers, as a regular feature. By the end of December 2010, the centre had produced over 500 educational television programmes covering a wide range of subjects. The programmes produced at the centre are forwarded to the Consortium for Educational Communication (CEC) New Delhi, for transmission in UGC countrywide classroom. These programmes were regularly telecast in the UGC countrywide classroom over Doordarshan National Network, *VYAS*—the higher educational channel of UGC and Gyandarshan. Some of the programmes of the centre are even shown on DD Bharti. The ETV programmes produced at the centre have bagged eight national level awards, in various video competitions organized by CEC/UGC. The centre has produced educational television programmes, syllabus oriented and enrichment type, in various subject areas as per the distribution shown in Figure 6.1. Out of the 340 programmes produced by the centre up to December 2007, 199 are lectures or discussions based directly related to the syllabus and the remaining 141 are enrichment type in various other formats.

For the production of television programmes the centre has created a television studio with basic broadcast quality equipment including Betacam and XDCam Cameras, linear and non-linear editing suites, graphic and multimedia platform, microphones, lights and projection systems including monitors, television sets and a multimedia projector. The centre has facilities for both indoor and outdoor shooting.

Educational television research at the centre is one of the major activities and EMMRC has done eight research studies on educational television in Kashmir. In fact the research conducted by the centre is the only research source on educational television available in the valley. The centre also participated in National Talk Back experiment

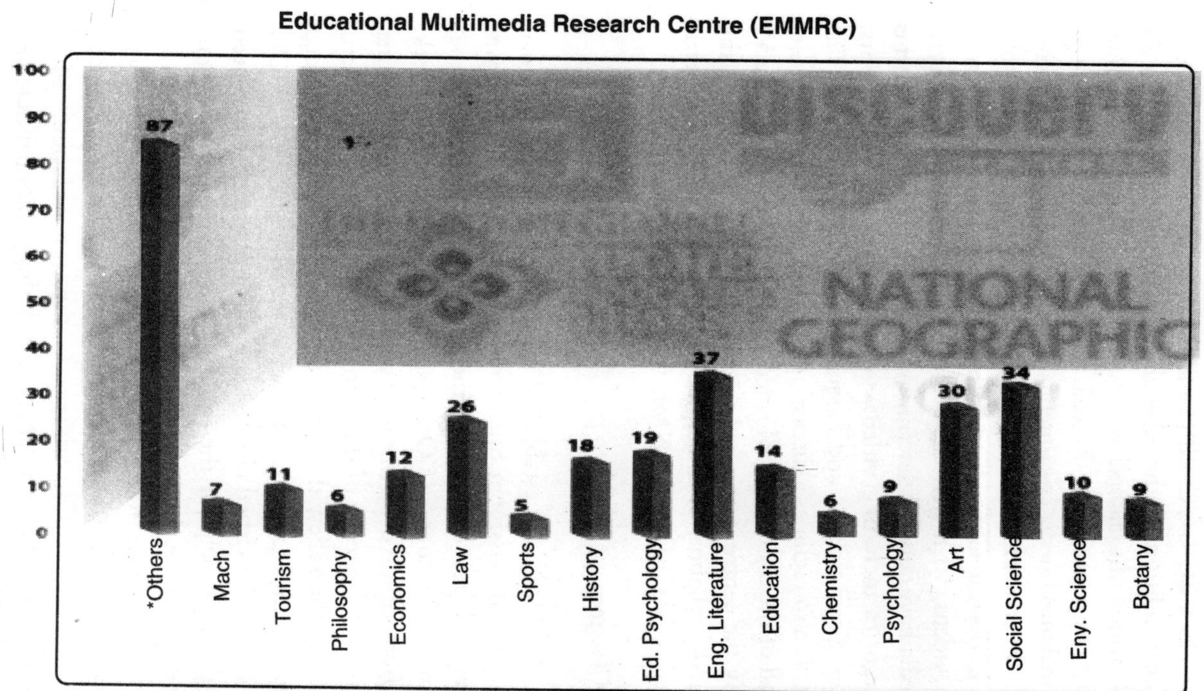

Figure. 6.1 : Subject-wise Production of Educational Television Programmes by EMMRC, Srinagar up to December. 2007

* **Note :** Others include Fisheries, Medicine, Science, Agriculture, Zoology, Geology, Remote Sensing, etc.

conducted by CEC-UGC, ISRO and Doordarshan in 1995. Due to precarious conditions in the valley during that period, owing to the political turmoil, the talkback was conducted by the centre at Jammu.

Since the year 2005, the centre started the development of educational multimedia / e-content and Learning Objects Repository (LORs). The centre has developed 32 e-content/Multimedia modules and 65 LORs for CEC-UGC. While LORs are simple one to 2 minutes videos, with written text, explaining the basic concepts, multimedia have detailed description of the subject in various forms and categories including videos, graphics, animations, contents, references, glossary, quiz, and Frequently asked questions; etc. The multimedia also includes a discussion platform and allows complete download of the content once loaded on the web. (See Appendix V) Currently the centre is engaged in creating e-content covering the UGC model syllabus for undergraduates in Botany. The project is supported by MHRD under NME-ICT project.

Virtual Classroom

In 2005, EMMRC also established a Satellite Interactive Terminal (SIT) for virtual classroom operations at national level which was ranked as number one among the top ten most active virtual classrooms in the country. On regular basis, 4 or 5 days a week, students from various departments of the university, attend the lectures in the Virtual Classroom of the centre and interact with the experts from outside the valley, through a two-way live audio and video interaction. From May 2007, the centre started "LECTURES ON DEMAND" in the virtual classroom, which has made it more need based and a great help for the students. On the request of various teaching departments 'Lectures on Demand' are organized in virtual form involving experts from various parts of the country, on different topics benefiting our students and teachers from Law, Commerce, Arabic, Sociology, Chemistry, Computer Science, Mass Communication, Home Sciences, Psychology, Library Science, Management, Hindi, Physical Education, etc. The "Lecture on Demand" that was started by the centre became very popular allover the country and was dedicated to the nation by the Chairman UGC on September 5, 2007.

Workshops and on-line Courses

The centre conducted three 21 days workshops on Capacity Building Programme on Multimedia and e-content Development in collaboration with CEC, New Delhi through EDUSAT and trained 42 teachers from the affiliated colleges and the university departments. By the end of workshop, each participant developed one e-content module and two LORs. A workshop on adaptive learning conducted at CEC was also extended to the centre through EDUSAT and 22 students and scholars from the university attended the workshop. As CEC started online course the centre enrolled students for various part time online courses which included :

1. e-scripting — an online course on script writing for television/films;
2. On-line course in Marketing Communication and Salesmanship (19th February to 5th April, 2007);
3. On-line course in Digital Library and Information Science (24th February to 17th April, 2007);
4. On-line course in Editing for Films and Television (26th February to 19th April, 2007); and
5. Two On-line workshops in Remote Sensing. (29th January to April, 2007) and (September 2007 to January 2008).

Utilization of ETV in Kashmir

The developmental and limited educational television programmes telecast on Doordarshan in Kashmir on the whole remains underutilized. The UGC countrywide classroom programmes telecast on the national network of Doordarshan and carried by Doordarshan Srinagar also remain underutilized in the valley. There are two reasons for this :

1. In the urban areas the high penetration of cable and private DTH services like DishTV and TATAsky etc., has seriously affected the viewership of Doordarshan; and
2. The acute power shortage in the valley, particularly in the rural areas, where power remains cutoff for almost 12 hours everyday, people are not able to watch most of the telecasts.

The above two reasons have resulted in underutilization of television programmes in general and educational television programmes in particular. Doordarshan at Srinagar has no special provision for telecast of educational programmes meant for UG or PG students. It only carries the countrywide classroom programmes that are telecast at the national network. DD Kashmir a 24-hour channel does not have a single educational television slot. The main channel of Doordarshan, however, does telecast some poorly conceived and produced school television programmes in the day time but their utility remains a matter of concern. In the day time the students are mostly out in the school and the schools invariably in the valley have neither television sets nor the electricity supply. Some schools have television sets but no space for viewing of programmes, and if by chance some school has a functional television set, it is used for anything other than education, as the teachers here also are caught in the same mindset as is seen elsewhere in the country.

Gyandarshan bouquet including VYAS channel are hardly visible in the valley. Though the regional centre of Indira Gandhi Open University (IGNOU) at Srinagar with an enrolment of 30,000 students for various courses has the facility to receive the Gyandarshan channels, but very few students are seen to use the facility. Similarly, EMMRC at the University has installed a special dish antenna to receive Gyandarshan and VYAS channels but the telecast is seen mostly by their own staff only. It has been observed that Gyandarshan and VYAS channels are not generally seen in the valley as they are not freely available. Neither cable operators carry them nor people aware about these channels so that they can install a dish antenna or ask the cable operator to provide the channels. Ignorance and indifference of academia towards these otherwise useful educational channels is inexplicable. But again this is nothing new in Kashmir because the case is almost similar in most parts of the country.

Research reveals that educational television programmes of UGC countrywide classroom have a very little audience. Jan Salima (1997)[4] conducted a survey in six colleges, located in three districts of the valley, viz., Srinagar, Baramulla and Kupwara to ascertain the needs assessments of the students, utilization of Countrywide Classroom programmes, constraints in viewing of programmes and viewing pattern of the students. The three districts were selected to incorporate a sample of urban, semi-urban and rural students. The study reported a higher percentage of viewership for Countrywide Classroom in urban areas (40%), followed by semi-urban areas (38%) and lowest in the rural areas (20%). Though a good proportion of students watch these programmes but none of them watch the programmes frequently (3 to 4 days a week) or daily. The students want to watch the programmes only in the evenings because in the day time they are busy in the college. Though 90 per cent students feel that CWCR programmes are very useful still most of them do not watch or are not able to watch them. The reasons for not watching the CWCR included "inconvenient timings", "non-availability of television sets", "non-availability of electricity" especially in the rural areas, "programmes not very interesting" and the students are "not aware about these telecasts".

Another research study, Jan Salima (2007)[5], reported that though 47.75% of the respondents have seen some UGC CWCR programmes on Doordarshan, they are yet to see "VYAS-channel" as it is neither available in the colleges nor it is being shown by the cable operators. Even after two years in operation a majority of them have heard the name of the channel for the first time. The study further revealed that while majority of the students, 52 per cent, want to see programmes of general nature including a mixture of enrichment and syllabus oriented, 41.75% want pure enrichment type programmes, 23.25 per cent want pure syllabus oriented programmes. The teachers are divided in their opinion, with equal number 45.5%, for enrichment and syllabus based programmes. The use of multimedia, i.e., visuals, graphics and animations, the majority said, make the programmes more interesting. The study also revealed that none of the colleges have facility for receiving VYAS-Channel nor is the college administration in any college aware about such a channel, some of them have, however, heard about the Gyandarshan.

EDUSAT Experience in the Valley

EDUSAT marked its presence in Kashmir with the establishment of a Satellite Interactive Terminal (SIT), also called Virtual classroom, on the national beam, at Educational Multimedia Research Centre, University of Kashmir. The virtual classroom provided an opportunity for the students and scholars of the university, and a sizable number of them benefited from the expertise and scholarship of experts from outside the State using two-way audio and video conferences and also shared their knowledge with the students and academics across the country. For a landlocked place like Srinagar with limited facilities and expertise available for higher education EDUSAT brings in a lot of hope. Though the EDUSAT experience at EMMRC is heartening in terms of the response that it has received, it is still in infancy and trying to overcome the teething problems of transmission and acceptance by the academia. Another SIT in Kashmir, on the national beam, is provided at Government Degree College (boys) Baramulla. The college initially showed some enthusiasm, even conducted one multimedia workshop using the EDUSAT facility, but over a period of time it was observed that the SIT at Baramulla college is not being put to much use and the facility remains grossly underutilized.

Indian Space Research Organisation (ISRO) also provided a regional beam on EDUSAT for use in higher education in Kashmir. Under the regional beam 21 undergraduate colleges, 25 Higher Secondary Schools and District Institutes of Educational Technology (DIET), 11 Industrial Training Institutes (ITI) of the valley are connected into a regional network with the hub at Degree College for Women, Maulana Azad Road, Srinagar. Each college appointed a nodal officer for the EDUSAT project. The nodal officers were trained in the EDUSAT Operations. But despite pumping in a lot of money in creating the facility and network it could not be made operational in real sense. The regional beam, therefore, remains totally underutilized. Not a single session, other than the experimental sessions, has been conducted using the EDUSAT regional network.

Implications of using ETV and New Technologies for Higher Education in Kashmir

In a resource starved place like Kashmir, with a huge enrolment of over 50,000 in higher education and only a skeletal teaching staff available in the 28 affiliated colleges of the University of Kashmir, located in various parts of the valley, the use of technology for education cannot be overemphasized. As per the statistics available in 2005, University of Kashmir had 51,998 students enrolled for various undergraduate course in the affiliated colleges, 11,381 enrolled for B.Ed courses, 4,175 students for PG courses at the main campus and various postgraduate centres located in the colleges. (Handbook : 2005).[6] Besides thousands of students are enrolled for various professional and semi-professional courses conducted by various professional colleges and other Universities and deemed Universities in the valley.

To cater to the needs of such a huge student population the State requires enormous resources to create quality infrastructure and employ competent manpower. At present the State government manages to spare a meagre 46.86 crore (Budget : 2007-08) for higher education most of which is spent on the salary of staff and construction of new buildings. The result is that most of the institutions of higher education in the valley do not have a quality infrastructure for teaching. Most of the colleges are understaffed with ill-equipped laboratories and libraries. Majority of the faculty in the colleges is inexperienced as most of them are working on contractual basis on a meagre consolidated salary.

In such a situation technology could be of great help in making up some of the deficiencies in the system and helping students reach quality sources of education in a very cost-effective manner. But it requires a collective effort on the part of the broadcasters, academics, planners and the students. Today, when we have technology in place it should not be difficult to help to take the best teachers anywhere to the students in any part of the valley. A single teacher from one college can teach students across the valley by taking a class through EDUSAT network. The lectures can also be recoded, embellished with graphics and other multimedia inputs and telecast on DD Kashir, local cable channels or transported to the colleges in the form of tapes, CDs and DVDs. The interaction of the students can be organized using the EDUSAT network. Interactive multimedia and e-content can be developed, utilizing the services of best teachers and the same can be made available to the students through internet or in the CDs and DVDs. The colleges in the valley can also invest a little money, Rs. 3,000 to Rs. 5,000 to install a dish antenna to receive Gyandarshan and VYAS Channels and encourage students to watch these programmes.

A judicious use of technology together with educational television and the teacher shall help in removing the imbalance between the urban and rural colleges considerably and make the best in any subject from any college available to all the students throughout the State.

References

1. Raina, Rajinder Singh, eds. *Srinagar Doordarshan*: *24 years*, (Srinagar : Doordarshan Kendra, 1997), Preface
2. CIET, *History and Development of ETV in India : A Report.* Mimeographed (New Delhi : NCERT, 1984).
3. Raina, Rajinder Singh, eds. (1997) *ibid.*, pp. 201-257.
4. Jan Salima, *UGC Countrywide Classroom : A Feedback Study on Kashmir* (Srinagar : Audio Visual Research Centre, University of Kashmir, 1997).
5. Jan Salima, *Regional Report on VYAS Channel* (Srinagar, Educational Multimedia Research Centre, University of Kashmir, 2007).
6. Handbook of University Statistics, 7th Edition. (Srinagar : The University of Kashmir, 2005).

Chapter 7

Educational TV Synthesis

The Conclusions and Recommendations

The general perception of broadcasters and academics is that the policy-makers and planners have a closed mindset about use of television for education. There perception is more rooted in the ground realities rather than the policies on paper. Realizing the importance of the use of technology for education, "the National Policy for Education" as far back as 1986 emphasized the use of new technology in formal and non-formal education. The policy paper on education, as quoted by Gandhi (1995)[1] states :

> "Modern communication technologies have the potential to bypass several stages and sequences in the process of development encountered in earlier decades. Both the constraints of time and distance at once became manageable. In order to avoid structural dualism modern educational technology must reach out to the most distant areas and most deprived sections of beneficiaries simultaneously with the areas of comparative affluence and ready availability". (p. 132)

Contrary to the above, the modern technologies of communication particularly television and radio have made the least contribution in taking education to distant and deprived learners. As Dr. Abdul Waheed Khan, former Vice Chancellor, Indira Gandhi National Open University (IGNOU), observes that :

> "Education occupies the lowest rank in the ladder of priorities in AIR and Doordarshan. The working group

> of software for Doordarshan observed that only 14 per cent of television time is being used for developmental programmes as against 21 per cent devoted to films and film based programmes. This clearly indicates that the powerful medium is not properly used for developmental efforts in the field of education, agriculture, health, family planning, etc." (IGNOU : 2000, p. 37)[2]

The irony is that the infrastructural facilities and technologies are more ubiquitous in cities and towns rather than in the villages and distant areas. So the benefit which the use of technology could have provided to the distance learners in rural areas, as was envisaged in national policy for education, could not reach them and these facilities again remained available to those who otherwise also had not much resource deficiencies when compared with their rural counterparts. What is required, therefore, is to create and develop a solid technological infrastructure, in terms of information and communication technologies particular availability of educational television backed by interactivity and e-content, in educational institutions in rural areas that will enable the students and teachers to access and benefit from rich educational resources available in the cities and towns. It is also required to make serious efforts to launch an effective and easily accessible "Educational Television Channel" that is available to students anywhere. There must be a conscious, systematic and planned effort to organise activities involving teachers, students, academics and media professionals for the efficient use of educational television and new communication technologies. The planning should be done keeping in mind the social, economic, political and cultural realities of the country and various regions besides the needs of the beneficiaries. It is also essential for planning to be consistent with the goals and process of education.

Use of new information and communication technology together with the convergence of media and ever increasing mobile telephony bring an added advantage for educational television which requires to be tapped to make teaching and learning through technology an enriching experience. With regard to use of new technologies people generally are skeptical in the beginning and once they start using the technology they understand its merits and feel confident in its use. Khan & Sharma (1993)[3] reported a teacher having said that :

> "I was highly skeptical at first but now that I have a say in the planning of programmes that we use, I feel ETV has become necessary. It represents another teacher on my team and brings experiences into my classroom, I ordinarily cannot get my hands on." (p. 51).

Again another parent is reported to have said that :

> "I am glad it is finally being used in the classroom. Why, when I think of our living room just before dinner time — the youngsters glued to the television screen ! That kind of interest should be incorporated into our classrooms."
>
> (p. 52).

The availability of a true educational television channel that breaks the jinx of mediocrity afflicting the present educational television channels shall be sufficient to convince people change their mindset about use of television for education and shatter their skepticism about its success. The economic viability of educational channel, owing to fragmentation of audience and preference of advertising companies for quality audience, may help educational channels override the competition of commercial television and who knows in near future we may have many private entrepreneurs launching educational channels. There is also a strong possibility of public-private partnership which needs to be explored in the wider interest of quality education in a resource starved country like India.

The success of an educational television channel primarily can be determined on the basis of its easy accessibility, wide publicity of its programmes, relevance of its programmes to the target audience, Quality of content, visual attractiveness of the programme design, packaging of knowledge rather information, interactivity, participatory approach and involvement of teachers, students and parents. The present scenario of educational television in India, on the basis of these parameters, is pathetic and dismal. On the other hand India, owing to a huge quantitative growth of higher education with not much quality support due to resource crunch, has to look for alternatives to reach students with quality education. The launch of an effective higher educational television may be the only cost-effective way of reaching students scattered allover the country. Best teacher in any subject somewhere can be made available to students everywhere. Further distance learners shall find such a channel more useful than the reading material that is provided to them.

With television penetration on the increase at a rapid pace, and broadcasting techniques showing a considerable improvement and flexibility Waghmare (1992)[4] visualized the future of television as :

> "Television can be one of the truly significant aids to good instruction. It can be to the classroom teacher what the pigment, canvas and brushes are to the artist...a combination of elements that can be used to create daubs or masterpieces. Television is here. It is now up to the educators to provide the guidance and assistance necessary to bring its vast educational potentialities to fruition. The danger of misuse, as well as the values of potential goods, are the responsibility and concern of the teaching profession. Much talent and money will be devoted (to the) in developing television as a sheer entertainment medium. Whether or not its educational potentialities as fall by wayside will be determined largely by the energy and imagination with which educators test and use television while it is still in its formative stages. Education can utilize television to open wider horizons and bring knowledge to our future citizens...." (p. 55)

The credo of UGC countrywide classroom made a pledge to reach a vast majority of students, particularly in rural areas through television. "The idea" credo said, "is not to satiate but stimulate the imagination of students and broaden their mental horizons." But after over sixteen years neither television has been used the way Waghmare thought it can be nor did UGC countrywide classroom make any significant difference to teaching and learning despite being in service for more than two decades.

The potential of television for education continues to remain underutilized; even today when it is required the most to address the issues of access and equity without undermining the quality of education; particularly higher education. For better utilization of educational television programmes, which is a dire requirement for quality higher education in India, it is important to facilitate the access to these programmes to a vast majority of students living in far flung areas of the country. But mere telecast of the educational television programmes may not be enough to achieve the desired goals, it is essential to use a multi-pronged strategy involving academics, experts, researchers, programme producers, web designers and above all students and teachers to create a research based interactive Educational Television Channel and use it together with new information and communication technology to take quality education to the door steps of learners.

Conclusion

The present study is an effort to study the educational television in India, particularly with reference to use of television in higher education with a special reference to educational television in the Kashmir valley. The study traces the origin and growth of television and educational television around the globe. It reveals, though the television across the globe and particularly in India was introduced as a medium of education, it is now seen more as a medium of information and entertainment relegating its mandate for education to the "back burner". This is primarily attributed to the pressures and temptations of the commercial world. The revenue generation potential of commercial television has blinded the imagination of policy-makers and planners making television a source of endless entertainment. The use of television for formal education in general in India is minimal and for the higher education it is limited to the half-backed efforts by IGNOU in the form of GYANDARSHAN and UGC Countrywide Classroom and VYAS. The literature survey reveals that television has a strong potential as a medium of education but the potential has remained grossly underutilized. Under experimental conditions use of television for education has demonstrated the learning outcomes, invariably, at par with the classroom teaching. It also reveals that various techniques and technologies used for dissemination of educational content through television had a significant impact on the students. The literature survey reveals though UGC countrywide classroom was a humble attempt to satiate the educational and enrichment needs of the students but no serious effort has been made to study the countrywide classroom from the perspective of overall perception of academics and broadcasters. The study of UGC countrywide classroom is still limited to the in-house studies mostly catering to the utilization of ETV programmes by the students. This researcher, therefore, studied the educational television particularly the UGC countrywide classroom from the perspective of broadcasters and academics. For this purpose detailed in-depth interviews were conducted with a select group of broadcasters and academic. The study reveals that television, owing to its versatile audio visual nature, has a strong potential as medium of education but its potential has remained grossly underutilized due to various reasons. The reasons include poor publicity of programmes, poor quality of programmes, poor transmission and above all the half-hearted efforts of the broadcasters and academics. Based on the findings of this research, together with the opportunities provided by the revolution of information and communication technologies sweeping the country, this study provides a new paradigm of educational television. The new paradigm shall help in equalizing the educational opportunities across the country and in making quality education available to all irrespective of their location. The study also reveals the dismal presence of educational television in the Kashmir valley, where in addition to the other factors non-availability of electricity for most of the time adds to non-viewing of the educational television programmes by the students.

To wind up the following conclusions can be drawn on the basis of the present study and the related literature on educational television:

- Television is a very powerful medium that holds a strong potential for education but that potential remains underutilized due to general apathy facing Educational Television in India.

- The commercial agenda of the state owned television, Doordarshan, has put its social agenda on the back-burner resulting in pushing the educational programmes to insignificant time slots.
- Educational television in India in general is facing a complete apathy. Educational channels like Gyandarshan, EKLAVYA, VYAS are underutilized and have failed to make any mark. UGC countrywide classroom on Doordarshan was just ritualistic.
- Policy-makers, planners, broadcasters, academics, teachers, students and parents are equally responsible for underutilization of educational television in general and UGC countrywide classroom programmes on Doordarshan in particular.
- Inaccessibility of educational television channels, poor quality of the educational television programmes, general misperception about television, lack of proper infrastructure for viewing in colleges, failure to properly publicise the transmission schedules and unorganised and haphazard management of the "Educational Television Channels" contribute significantly to their underutilization.
- Television viewing is not necessarily passive in nature; viewing can be both active and passive depending on the purpose and interest for which television viewing takes place. However, the fact remains that nature of viewing is directly related to learning outcomes. Passive the viewing shallower the learning and active the viewing much deeper the learning. For better results Educational Television requires a more active and involved viewing.
- While educational television programmes based on syllabi shall make best teachers in any subject available to all across the country and help students in better understanding of their course material, the enrichment programmes shall serve to broaden their mental horizons. The easy availability of additional reading material on dedicated educational website shall fill their appetite for more information on a particular subject.

- As they say "seeing is believing", Educational television, because of its unparallel and most versatile audio-visual potential, shall help students in easy understanding of certain complicated concepts and problems, that too in a much better way as compared to classroom teaching.
- Educational television is marked by lack of coordination and seriousness among the educational institutions and broadçast agencies, poor publicity of programmes and transmission schedules and overall negligence by government and society in general.
- The rapid growth of new technologies offers a new hope in integrating Educational Television with new media to make learning through television more interactive, productive and gratifying. The technological developments, growth of ICT and increasing penetration of electronic gadgets in rural areas of the country, are a positive indicator for the growth and success of educational television. This is also resulting in a "new paradigm of educational television".
- The role of teachers in "new paradigm" shall remain central, the technology shall only facilitate teaching and learning more effectively. Television or technology as an active partner alongside the teacher shall make classroom teaching dynamic and versatile. At the same time educational television technology will be of a great help to independent distance learners.
- To address issue of access and equity without compromising the quality in higher education, Educational Television together with new technologies can play an important role provided a serious and sustained effort is made by academics and broadcasters with solid financial support either from government or from private funding agencies. Such an effort shall be based on research and shall include all the sections of society including teachers, students and parents.
- There is a strong need for an effective educational television channel for higher education to equalize and democratize the educational opportunities across the country.

- For establishment of educational television channel on professional lines an all-inclusive multi-pronged approach, based on research must be adopted so that everyone, particularly teachers and students, are involved in making it a success.
- The economic viability of an educational television channel in private sector is seen a distant possibility as the cost-effectiveness of such venture is yet to be ascertained. Nonetheless, there are indicators that such a channel may be economically viable with proper planning and marketing. This requires further investigation and analysis involving economists and people from commercial television.
- Possibilities of launching an educational television channel in public-private partnership do exist, but in such a case we must not allow commercial temptations overtake the cause of education.
- The new paradigm of educational television for higher education is required to be drawn in consultation with academics, broadcasters, planners and policy-makers. This will help take quality education to the doorsteps of students in a cost-effective manner, create a knowledge society and help India to achieve the dream of emerging as a knowledge superpower.

Recommendations

The tremendous growth of information and communication technology and convergence of media shall facilitate the establishment of an educational television channel in a cost-effective manner. The indicators with regard to the possible economic viability of an educational channel shall prompt the policy-makers and planners to jump on the idea of launch of a true educational channel. The channel must not be only visible and accessible everywhere, it must have the seriousness that suits teaching and learning keeping in view the requirements of students.

Under the given circumstances, therefore, the University Grants

Commission must take a lead in converting the existing Countrywide Classroom or Vyas Channel into a full-fledged terrestrial educational television channel and redesign it, as per the requirements under "new paradigm", to cater to the demands of a vast majority of students scattered across the country. To make such an endeavour succeed with a difference, on the bases of the findings of this study, the following recommendations are offered :

(a) University Grants Commission (UGC) taking advantage of Consortium for Educational Communication (CEC) and Educational Multimedia Research Centres (EMMRCs) located at various universities and educational institutions, must pool all its resources to launch a professional terrestrial Educational Television Channel using all the modern means of technology. Channel must telecast a mix of enrichment and syllabus oriented programmes catering to needs of all the undergraduate and postgraduate students in all the streams. The programmes of the channel shall be simultaneously multicast, through video streaming, for viewing through web browser or mobile phones. The programmes shall also be kept available on the computer server for Video on Demand (VOD) for anywhere, anytime viewing.

(b) The channel must ensure involvement of academics and broadcasters for production of high quality educational television programmes rich in content, pleasing in appearance and innovative in treatment. The programmes both enrichment and syllabus oriented, must be visually rich and aesthetically pleasing to attract and hold the attention of target groups. Each programme should involve a battery of subject experts to ensure the content is processed properly, in tune with the requirements of the primary target group, before it is made into a programme. For syllabus oriented programmes in particular a group of teachers must be involved in integrating the content of a television programme into the stream of classroom instructions, other group of experts shall be involved in evaluating the quality of the content keeping in view the requirements of the target group, the content shall then be converted into a television programme by the producer in association with the experts. At each stage during the production the programme must be evaluated by many experts and researchers till the final version is prepared that is complete in all respects.

(c) The channel must make full use of the latest technology in packaging of educational material in multimedia format and keep the same available for specific target audience on a website. Creation of multimedia and e-content is necessitated by the "New Paradigm of Educational Television" which holds the promise to make it more effective and meaningful. Multimedia or e-content shall be developed for each educational television programme, enrichment or syllabi oriented, that is telecast on the channel.

(d) For the development of multimedia and e-content multimedia teams must be created at each centre involving college and university teachers and other experts from various disciplines. Such teams shall be created in each subject and the best teachers in the country should be brought together for the purpose. The teachers must also be provided training to design and develop e-content in their respective subjects independently. For accreditation and validation of e-content Consortium for Educational Communication must evolve a standard mechanism and each e-content module developed shall be properly evaluated before it is put on the website for use of the students. The website should be quite dynamic supporting "blogs" and discussion platforms.

(e) The educational television programmes and multimedia in various subjects shall be also made available to all the educational institutions, particularly those in rural and remote areas, and the institutions be encouraged to establish e-Content and Educational Television Programme libraries and create space in the form of kiosks in the educational institutions for easy viewing of the programmes. The educational television programmes and multimedia can even be issued to the students, like books, for viewing at home.

(f) The educational television channel, it is desired, shall be a co-operative venture involving broadcast agencies, production centres, educational institutions of repute, international collaborators and even private entrepreneurs for planning, production, marketing and delivery.

(g) The colleges must create infrastructural facilities for viewing of programmes of the educational television channel, interacting with experts through satellite/telephone or some other available communication technology, and accessing of reading and other academic material on the dedicated websites.

(h) The programmes and transmission schedules shall be given wide publicity involving all the possible forms of mass media, besides sending e-mails to specific groups of students and teachers. The Consortium for Educational Communication should encourage and facilitate creation of students study groups in the form of learning communities across the country. Written content in the form of booklets, brochures, pamphlets, flyers, posters, etc., must be mailed to the educational institutions for distribution or display a day before the programme is telecast. The telecast must be integrated with the timetable and the teacher concerned must facilitate the viewing helping students what to look for in the programme and involve them in a discussion after the programme is over.

(i) Interactivity, as far as possible, should be integrated into the programme and subject experts shall be available to the students on given date and time for replying questions and removing doubts of students. Given the enormous effort required to facilitate a live interaction for every programme, live interaction can be need based for rest of the programmes it can take place through e-mails, discussion platforms or 'blogs'.

(j) Monitoring and evaluation of each telecast shall be done scientifically, involving reputed researchers and research organizations. The research findings and constant feedback shall become the guiding principle in evolving the educational television channel in tune with the requirements and needs of the target audience. Formative and summative research of each programme shall become a routine affair to ensure the programmes are designed to make teaching and learning an enriching experience.

(k) The government must be convinced to issue or move a legislation that forces cable and DTH operators to carry the Educational Channel on its primary band. Legislation may not be enough it must be forced using all the available means within the Constitution including fine and cancellation of franchise on the complaint of residents of any area. This will ensure the availability of the educational channel in cable and DTH areas. In non-cable and non-DTH homes people shall be able to see the programmes through terrestrial channel.

(l) The policy-makers and planners must also encourage study of economic viability of educational television channels. If found cost-effective and economically viable establishment of educational television channels in private or public-private partnership at national and regional level must be encouraged and supported. Even reputed educational institutions in the country must be allowed to launch educational television Channels.

The Last Word

This study was an effort to investigate and analyze the present scenario of educational television in India in general and UGC countrywide classroom in particular. The study established beyond doubt the pathetic state of affairs of educational television despite the fact television has a strong potential in equalizing educational opportunities in India. Educational Television has much more to offer for teaching and learning especially when we are experiencing a total technological revolution in information and communication technologies. The policy-makers, planners, broadcasters, academics, parents and students must harness the benefits of Educational Television and technological innovations for overall development of the society. The study of this kind, it is hoped, must find immediate application for achieving excellence in quality teaching across the country, irrespective of geographical location of an institution or a student, thus liberalizing, democratizing and equalizing educational opportunities for one and all.

The application of the findings of this study provides a solution for reaching distance learners in a much better and effective way. The "New Paradigm for Educational Television" for higher education discussed in detail in the Chapter Five, envisages the use of television for higher education in conjugation with other ICT based new technologies to take quality education to the doorsteps of students across the country in a much economical and effective way. The new paradigm shall bring in seriousness among the students and teachers and help them benefit from the academic resources scattered around the country. The expertise and the technology hitherto available in the metropolitan and other major cities of India shall reach the education seekers around the country with much ease. This will also help in paving way in achieving the equity without undermining the quality of education. In a country like India, owing to the scarcity of resources for education, it is important to make use of television for higher education together with the new information and communication technologies for the quality growth of higher education that will eventually lead to creation of a vibrant knowledge society.

References

1. Gandhi, V. P. *Media and Communications Today, Vol., 2*, (New Delhi: Kanishka Publishers, 1995). p. 132
2. Khan, Abdul Waheed. "Vice Chancellor's Report". (New Delhi, IGNOU 2000), p. 37
3. Khan, M.I. & S.R.Sharma. *Instructional Technology –Media and Theory.* (Delhi: Kanishka Publishers, 1993). p. 51-52.
4. Waghmare, S.K. *Audio-Visual Education.* (New Delhi: Metropolitan Book Co. Pvt. Ltd. 1992), p. 55.

APPENDICES

APPENDIX I

VYAS-Channel Schedule for March 2008

	Time	*Saturday, 1st March, 2008*
Env Sc.	0530/1130	• A Story of an Urban Zoo. 7
	1730/2330	• Eco Friendly Farming
	0600/1200	• Weeds — The Biological Invaders
	1800/0000	• Environment Impact Analysis
	1630/1230	• Perspective on Mt. Tourism - 1
	1830/0030	• Amal Varsha
	0700/1300	• Energy and Environment - 1
	1900/0100	• Corals
Communication/ Info. Sc.	0730/1330	• Technical Writing - 1
	1930/0130	
	0800/1400	• How Communication Works -1
	2000/0200	• Strokes from Past - C . T. Sarwati
	0830/1430	• Principles of Advertising - 1
	2030/0230	• Reporting
	0900/1500	• Basics of Library Science
	2100/0300	• Melody out of Tune
Anthro / Medical Sc.	0930/1530	• Totopara - A Distant Dreamland - 1
	2130/0330	• Feeling Good - 3 (Deafness)
	1000/1600	• Bronchial Asthma
	2200/0400	
	1030/1630	• Why Cancer?
	2230/0430	• Chain Reactions
	1100/1700	• Changing the Face of Future
	2300/0500	• Safe Motherhood: Causes of Maternal Mortality

Appendix-I (contd...)

	Sunday, 2nd March, 2008
Music, Art /Cul.	• Performing Arts - Kathak - IV - II • Museums and Museology • Tabla - Sangeet ka Atal Sathi -5 • The House Boat • Performing Arts - Theatre Arts - T 5.1.2
Technology	• Earthquake Engineering for Common Man • Control System - 3 • Application of Technology Tools through Multimedia • Optical Fibre Communication - 3 • Data Structure - 3 • High Voltage Electrical Engineering • Recent Innovations in Short and Medium Span Bridges - 3
Career Watch	• Disha-Travel and Tourism • The Encounters • Quiz Show - 12 • Strange Artistry • Young Entrepreneurs - Computer Maintenance • Engineering • Swamim Itihaas Se Swamim Bhavishya Ki Ore - 1 • Sports Karma - Batting Techniques: Defensive batting

	Time	• *Monday, 3rd March, 2008*
Fine Arts	0530/1130 1730/2330	• Kathak - Shloka
	0600/1200	• Khalid Tyabji on the Fool
	1800/0000	• Mharo Rajasthan
	0630/1230	• Weaving Dreams in Silence
	1830/0030	• Dance Depicts Life
	0700/1300 1900/0100	• An Introduction to Kathakali
Maths	0730/1330	• Geometry: Transformation Geometry - 1
	1930/0130	• Parallels in Geometry
	0800/1400 2000/0200	• The Field of Quotients of an Integral (Dr. Sunder Lal)
	0830/1430	• Slicing-n-cubes
	2030/0230	• Origins of Geometry
	0900/1500 2100/0300	• Polynomial Rings (Dr. Sunder Lal)
Geography	0930/1530	• The Story of a Map - 1
	2130/0330	• Twinning
	1000/1600 2200/0400	• Human Impact on Natural System - II
	1030/1630	• Mizoram - 2
	2230/0430	• Remote Sensing in Natural Resources Inventory - 1
	1100/1700 2300/0500	• India in the World

Appendix-I (contd...)

	Tuesday, 4th March, 2008
History	• Ek Khoobsurat Shahar - Bhopal • Protect Heritage • Socio-cultural Development in Mughal Period: Major Characteristics of Mughal Paintings (S. P. Verma) • Egypt and its Monuments • History Writes itself • Socio-Cultural Development in Mughai Period: Main Features of Rajput Paintings (S. P. Verma)
Eco./Comm.	• Advertising and Sales Promotion - 4.9.5 • Dividend Policy - I (Dr. Ramji Narayan) • Six Sigma - 3 Quality Improvement • Advertising and Sales Promotion - 4.9.6 • Theory of Cost - II (K. Roy Choudhary)
Zoology/Biology	• Insect Migration • Muggermuch (Crocodile) • Insect of Mangroves • Pearis of Enterprises • Light and Vision • Kitchen Zoo • Hanuman Langoors in their Habitat • Where Bees and Butterflies Visit?

	Time	*Wednesday : 5th March, 2008*
Home Sc.	0530/1130 1730/2330	• Hotel Management - Food Production-2
	0600/1200 1800/0000	• Prenatal Development (Dr. P. Chandra)
	0630/1230	• Environmental Friendly Detergent
	1830/0030	• Cockroaches
	0700/1300	• Nutritional Deprivation and Its Effect (Dr. P. Chandra)
	1900/0100	• Diet and Cancer
Pol. Sc.	0730/1330	• Sociological School of Jurisprudence
	1930/0130	• Edu Arena - Evolution of Indian Administration - Mughal Administration - 2
	0800/1400 2000/0200	• Marxist Concept (Moh. Siddique)
	0830/1430 2030/0230	• Liberty, Equality and Fraternity
	0900/1500 2100/0300	• Elite (Prof. Ali Ashraf)
Botany/ Agricul.	0930/1530	• Khejri - The Lifeline
	2130/0330	• Orchids of India - Boat Orchid, Cymbidium Iridiodes
	1000/1600	• Prickly Poppy
	2200/0400	• Mulberry
	1030/1630	• Thar Marusthal : Places, People and Plants - 2
	2230/0430	• Tulsi
	1100/1700	• Pushpraj Gulab
	2300/0500	• Mushroom Production

Appendix-I (contd...)

	Thursday 6th March, 2008
Sociology	• Contraception - Tomorrow • Once, I was a Soldier • Measures of Central Tendency - III (Prof. K. Radhakrishnamurthy) • Siskiyan Lena Ek Hunar - Himru • Shodhayatra - 6 • Ladki Naai Sadi Ki • Measures of Dispersion - I (Prof. K. Radhakrishnamurthy)
Physics	• Temperature Measurements • Gama Ray Burst • Experiments and Observations (Prof. J.V. Narlikar) • The Physics of Music - 2 The String Instrument • Laws of Motion - I • Symmetry (Prof. A.D. Gangal)
Lang./Lit.	• Language : Teaching and Learning • Vemana • Stylist - 2 : Verbal and Visual • Shakespearean Tragedy : Life Kaleidoscope - 2 • Understanding Orientation • Sentence Rhetoric - Cumulative Sentences

	Time	*Friday : 7th March, 2008*
Chemistry	0530/1130	• Oxidation Potentials - 1
	1730/2330	• Gravimetric Estimation of Barium
	0600/1200 1800/0000	• Liquid Vapour Equilibrium - 1 : Fractional Distillation
	0630/1230	• Lead - The Deadly Pollutant
	1830/0030	• Chroma Recovery and Reuse
	0700/1300	• Phase Diagram - Two Component
	1900/0100	• System - Solid, Liquid System
Psycho.	0730/1330	• Coping with Stress - 5 : Accepting Responsibility
	1930/0130	• As good as Anyone : Visually Impaired not Handicapped.
	0800/1400 2000/0200	• Affective Disorders : Menia and Depression (Dr. Usha Ram)
	0830/1430	• Visual Impairment - Mobility
	2030/0230	• Don't Worry be Happy - The Nature of Worry
	0900/1500 2100/0300	• Schizophrenia (Dr. Usha Ram)
Education	0930/1530 2130/0330	• Tyohaar : Shiksha Ka Ek Anoupcharik Sadhan
	1000/1600	• Integral Pedagogy Process-2 : Context
	2200/0400	• They Can Also Do It - Education for All
	1030/1630	• A Culture of Science - A Lecture by Prof. Jayant Narlikar
	2230/0430	• Education Technology - 4
	1100/1700	• Khoj Prashikshan Pratimaan - 8
	2300/0500	• Khoj Prashikshan Pratimaan - 9

Appendix-I (contd...)

	Saturday, 8th March, 2008
Env. Sc.	• Modern Society Plastics and Recycling
	• Water in Life
	• Biomass Fuel Use and Health Hazards - 1
	• Perspectives on Mt. Tourism - 2
	• Biomass Gastification - I
	• Energy and Environment - 2
	• Wealth of Waste - Microbial and Worm Composting
Communication/Info. Sc.	• Technical Writing - 2
	• How Communication Works - 2
	• Definition and Types of Communication
	• Principles of Advertising - 2
	• Space Communication - An Overview - I
Anthro/Medical Sc.	• Totopara - A Distant Dreamland - II
	• Feeling Good - 4 (Kidney Transplant)
	• Safe Motherland - How to Achieve it?
	• Ear Discharge - Don't Take it Easy
	• Fitness : The Essence of Success
	• Infertility
	• The Healing Touch
	• Science of Twins

	Time	*Sunday, 9th March, 2008*
Music. Art/Cul.	0530/1130	• Performing Arts - Kathak - IV - III
	1730/2330	
	0600/1200	• Jageshwar Shrine - 1
	1800/0000	• Qutub Shahi Architecture
	0630/1230	• Tabla - Sangeet Ka Atal Sathi - 6
	1830/0030	• Mosque Architecture
	0700/1300	• Theatre Architecture - Japanese Nai Theatre
	1900/0100	• Miracles of Prayer
Technology	0730/1330	• Another Bhagirath
	1930/0130	• Telephone - Probing an Everyday Technology
	0800/1400	• Micro Hydro Power Plant - 1
	2000/0200	• Micro Hydro Power Plant - 2
	0830/1430	• Extending Edges of Technology
	2030/0230	• Blending Beauty : Crystal Art
	0900/1500	• Recent Innovations in Short and Medium Span Bridges - 4
	2100/0300	
Career Watch	0930/1530	• Disha - Courier and Cargo
	2130/0330	• Citizen's Identity - Passport
	1000/1600	• Vocational Eduation
	2200/0400	
	1030/1630	• Young Entrepreneurs - Home Tuitions and Coaching Centres
	2230/0430	• Fisheries Aquarium
	1100/1700	• Swarnim Itihaas Se Swarnim Bhavishya Ki Ore - 2
	2300/0500	• Sports Karma - Stroke Playing

Appendix-I (contd...)

	Monday, 10th March, 2008
Fine Arts	• Kathak - Gat Bhava
	• Creativity - G. M. Sheikh
	• Popular Cartoonists - Election Indian Style
	• The Dawn After - 1
	• Puppetry and Communication : The Living Art
	• Lasya Kala - Bharathnatyam Kuchipudi
Maths	• The Search For Primes
	• The Ambiguity of Randomness
	• The Polynomial Ring Q (x) (Dr. Sunder Lal)
	• A Question of Proof
	• First Step : Arvind Thiagarajah
	• Construction with Straight edge (Dr. Sunder Lal)
Geography	• The Gambler's Ruin
	• Story of Map - 2, From Clay to Computers
	• Management of Water Resources
	• Scope of Economic Geography
	• Remote Sensing in Natural Resources Inventory - 2
	• Approaches to Economics Geography

	Time	*Tuesday, 11th March, 2008*
History	0530/1130	• Orissa ke Mandir
	1730/2330	• Early Chalukyan Temples - Aihole
	0600/1200	• Kingdoms of Yadavas, Kakaityas, Hoysalas and Pandias (T.K.
	1800/0000	Venkatsubrahmanian)
	0630/1230	• What is History?
	1830/0030	• Indian Historiography - 1
	0700/1300	• Vijayanagar : State and Policy (T.K. Venkatsubramanian)
	1900/0100	
Eco./Comm.	0730/1330	• Advertising and Sales Promotion-
	1930/0130	Advertising Message - 2.5.2
	0800/1400	• Dividend Policy - II (Dr. Ramji Narayan)
	2000/0200	
	0830/1430	• Krya Vyavahar Evam Krya Prernayen - I
	2030/0230	• Advertising and Sales Promotion - Time Management
	0900/1500	• Theory of cost - III (K. Roy Choudhary)
	2100/0300	
Zoology/Biology	0930/1530	• Crocodiles - 1
	2130/0330	• BMI - Body Mass Index
	1000/1600	• Receptors and Sense Organs - 1
	2200/0400	• Serpentine Senses
	1030/1630	• Role of Genomics and Proteonics in Drug Development
	2230/0430	
	1100/1700	• Applications of Bioinformatics to Biotechnology
	2300/0500	

Appendix-I (contd...)

	Wednesday, 12th March, 2008
Home Sc.	• Hotel Management-3 : Food and Beverage Services • Childcare (Dr. P. Chandra) • Bitter Fruits - Effects of Pesticides on Human Health • Bridging the Calorie Gap - Weaning Foods • Domiciliary Management of illness in Children (Dr. P. Chandra) • Sweets of Bengal - Sitabhaja and Mihidana
Pol. Sc.	• Edu. Arena - Evolution of Indian Administration - British Administration - 1 • Anarchist and Gandhian View (Prof. Ali Ashraf) • Changing Priority of Information Foreign Policy • Fascism (Prof. Ali Ashraf)
Botany/Agricul.	• Floriculture • Phalon ka Raja : Aam • Agroforestry for Dryland Farming - Agribiotech : I • Botanical Pesticides - Agribiotech - II • Kamal - Bharat Ka Rashtriya Pushp • Satyanashi • Afat Bhari Jhaariyan • The Rubber Tree - 1 : Hevea Brasiliensis

	Time	*Thursday, 13th March, 2008*
Sociology	0530/1130 1730/2330	• Dance Theory - Changing Lives Through Movement
	0600/1200	• Measures of Dispersion - II (Prof. K. Radhakrishnamurthy)
	1800/0000	• Youth Hostel - A Home Away From Home
	0630/1230	• Poverty - Changing Scenario
	1830/0030	• Nightmare - World of Child Labour
	0700/1300	• Analysis of Attributes - I (Prof. K. Radhakrishnamurthy)
	1900/0100	
Physics	0730/1330	• Simple Experiments in Electromagnetism
	1930/0130	• My Teacher : Birefringence or Double Refraction
	0800/1400	• Symmetry of Physical Laws (Prof. A.D. Gangal)
	2000/0200	
	0830/1430	• Physics of Music-3 Deriving Music Mathematically
	2030/0230	• Control Systems
	0900/1500 2100/0300	• Cartesian Vectors and Orthogonal Transformations (Prof. A.D. Gangal)
Lang./Lit.	0930/1530	• Language Grammar Meaning
	2130/0330	• Rhetorical - Language
	1000/1600	• Kavita, Geet aur Gazal : Kya Kehte Hain Neeraj
	2200/0400	• Mansikta Ek Vyangkaar Ki - Ashok Chakradhar
	1030/1630	• Music Images in Tagore's Literature
	2230/0430	
	1100/1700	• Modern Ghazal ki Shakhsiat - Dr. Bashir Badra
	2300/0500	• Sentence Rhetoric - Periodic Sentences

Appendix-I (contd...)

	Friday, 14th March, 2008
Chemistry	• Oxidation Potential - 2
	• Preparation of Aspirin
	• Liquid Vapour Equilibrium - 2 Non Ideal Liquid Mixture
	• Diamond - A Gem of a Mineral
	• Application of Acid Base Titration
Psycho.	• World Through Sounds
	• Supersititious?? Me??
	• Personality Disorders (Dr. Usha Ram)
	• The Human Mind - A Divided Mind
	• Don't Worry Be Happy - How to be Happy?
	• Disorders of Childhood and Adolescence (Dr. Usha Ram)
Education	• Speak So That We May Hear
	• Creation - India For The World
	• Integral Pedagogy Process - 3 : Experience
	• Mass Literacy - The Third Eye
	• Safalta Ka Mantra - Team Bhavana
	• Khoj Prashikshan Pratimaan - 10
	• A Career Oriented Graduation

	Time	*Saturday, 15th March, 2008*
Env. Sc.	0530/1130	• Food for Plants : Exploring Eden
	1730/2330	• Thar Registaan - Jeevan Vividhta
	0600/1200	• Plastic Baba
	1800/0000	• Sandesh Ek Log Anek
	0630/1230	• Role of Energy Management Centre in Improving Energy Efficiency
	1830/0030	• Biomass Gastification - II
	0700/1300	• Management Control Energy - 1
	1900/0100	• Green Worrier : Maruti Chitampalli - 1
Communication/ Info. Sc.	0730/1330	• Hansi - Tu Dhanya hai
	1930/0130	• Care The Greens
	0800/1400	• How Communication Works - 3
	2000/0200	• Non-Verbal Communication
	0830/1430	• Leather Puppets - A Native Silver Screen
	2030/0230	• Story Telling
	0900/1500	• Elements of Space Communication - II
	2100/0300	
Anthro/Medical Sc.	0930/1530	• The Samanthas - An Anthropovision
	2130/0330	• Feeling Good - 5 (Obesity)
	1000/1600	• Genetic Markers and DNA
	2200/0400	
	1030/1630	• Leprosy or Hansen's Disease
	2230/0430	
	1100/1700	• Dance Therapy : Changing Lives Through Movement
	2300/0500	

Appendix-I (contd...)

	Sunday, 16th March, 2008
Music. Art/Cul.	• Performing Arts - Kathak - IV
	• Melody Out of Tune
	• Jageshwar Shrine - 2
	• Architecture of Manipur
	• Tabla - Sangeet ka Atal Sathi - 7
	• In Search of Architectural Roots
	• East West Rhythms
Technology	• Learnig Through Computers
	• The Art of Screen Printing
	• Non Point Pollution - Searching A Solution
	• Radio Frequency - Management
	• Shaktiheen Power Loom
	• Recent Innovations in Short and Medium Span Bridges - 5
Career Watch	• Raah - MCA
	• Career Update - Hotel Management
	• Foreign Language as a Career
	• Career Update - Landscape Designing
	• Young Entrepreneurs - Tailoring
	• Creativity - Sculptures
	• Swamim Itihaas Se Swamim Bhavishya ki Ore - 3
	• Golden Sitter - A Profile

	Time	*Monday, 17th March, 2008*
Fine Arts	0530/1130	• Bunakari Ka Chamatkar - Ikat
	1730/2330	• Popular Cartoonists : Sandeep Adhwaryu
	0600/1200	• Sharddha Evam Aastha Ka Mahaparva
	1800/0000	– Singhaspha
		• Popular Cartoonists : Rajendra Puri
		• Thappattam
	0630/1230	• The Dawn After - 2
	1830/0030	• Puppetry and Communication : The Living Form
	0700/1300	• Kalakshetra – Spirit of India Heritage
	1900/0100	
Maths	0730/1330	• Surreal Numbers
	1930/0130	• Gamber's Ruin
		• Triumph of the Spirit
	0800/1400	• Sub. Groups : Operation on Sub Groups
	2000/0100	(Dr. Ramji Lal)
	0830/1430	• Karein - Milman Theorem
	2030/0230	• From Farm to Home
	0900/1500	• Operation on the Set of Sub Groups (Dr. Ramji Lal)
	2100/0300	
Geography	0930/1530	• Mount Vesuvius
	2130/0330	• Fault Plane Solutions
	1000/1600	• Rivers of India
	2200/0400	
	1030/1630	• Glaciers - I
	2230/0430	
	1100/1700	• Climate - I
	2300/0500	• The Ozone Hole

Appendix-I (contd...)

	Tuesday, 18th March, 2008
History	• The Lakes of Bhopal • Hazarat Bal Shrine • Vijaynagar : Society and Economy (T.K. Venkatsubramanian) • Indian Historiography - 2 • Aurangabad - The Gateway of Cultural India • Brahmins (B. Sheikh Ali)
Eco./Comm.	• Advertising and Sales Promotion : Personal Selling Skills • Financing of Small Scate Industries (Dr. Ramji Narayan) • Aay Arjan Evam Vipanan Kriyaen • Internal and External Economics of Scale (Prof. V.K. Anand)
Zoology/Biology	• Crocodiles - 2 • Images of Bats • Receptors and Sense Organs - 2 • Chick Embryo Culture in Vitro • Insects of Mangroves • Rabies - 1

	Time	*Wednesday, 19th March, 2008*
Home Sc.	0530/1130 1730/2330	• Hotel Management - The Art of Bread Making
	0600/1200	• Mental Development During Infancy (Dr. Mrs. N. Jaya)
	1800/0000	• Nutrition and Immunology
	0630/1230	• Human Immune System - My Defence
	1830/0030	• Shackled Motherhood
	0700/1300	• Children with Hearing Impaired (Dr. Mrs. N. Jaya)
	1900/0100	• Sweet of Bengal - Langcha
Pol. Sc.	0730/1330	• Edu Arena - Evolution of Indian Administration - British Administration - 2
	1930/0130	• Siddh Kshetra : Bawangaja
	0800/1400 2000/0100	• Theory of Separation of Power (Prof. M. N. Meenai)
	0830/1430 2030/0230	• Karl Marx's Philosophy of Man
	0900/1500 2100/0300	• Parliamentary and Presidential Forms of Government (Prof. M.N. Meenai)
Botany/Agricul.	0930/1530	• Mangroves of Sunderbans
	2130/0330	• Modern Nursery Practices
	1000/1600	• Bacillus Thuringensis - Agribiotech - III
	2200/0400	• Castor Wilt Management : Agribiotech - IV
	1030/1630	• Weeds – The biological invaders — Parthenium Hysteropharus
	2230/0430	• Carrot Weeds
	1100/1700	• El Sensor Cactus
	2300/0500	• The Rubber Tree - 2

Appendix-I (contd...)

	Thursday, 20th March, 2008
Sociology	• Women of Japan-From Kyokikumama to Derukagi • Yet Another Plight of Women – Widowhood • Analysis of Attributes - II (Prof. K. Radhakrishnamurthy) • Scheduled Castes Development - 1 • Poverty - Dimensions • On Errors of Survey Research (Prof. K. Radhakrishnamurthy)
Physics	• Gravitational Waves and Black Holes • Yantra Mandir : The Temple of Instruments • Vector Algebra - I (Prof. A.D. Gangal) • The Electro Magnetic Spectrum • Angular Momentum - 1 • Atmospheric Electricity • Vector Algebra - II (Prof. A.D. Gangal)
Lang./Lit.	• Task and Gender - 1 • Sentence Rhetoric - Question • Reflections of an Author • Fool in King Lear • The Poetry of Jayantha Mahapatra • The Tragedy of Hamlet • Chaman Nahal – The Man and His Work

	Time	*Friday, 21st March, 2008*
Chemistry	0530/1130	• Exciting World of Hydrogels-1 : An Introduction
	1730/2330	• Polymer – A Scenario of Origin
	0600/1200 1800/0000	• Liquid Liquid Equilibrium–Phase Equilibrium
	0630/1230	• Phase Diagram – Two Component
	1830/0030	System – Condensed Phase Diagram
	0700/1300	• Froth, Foam and Clean : What Soap Does?
	1900/0100	• Catalysis and Mechanism of Reaction - 1
Psycho.	0730/1330	• Coping with Stress–5 : Accepting Responsibility
	1930/0130	• As Good As Anyone : Visually Impaired not Handicapped
	0800/1400 2000/0200	• Behaviour Therapy (Dr. Usha Ram)
	0830/1430	• Visual Impairment - Limitations of Blindness
	2030/0230	• Don't Worry be Happy – 4 : How to Reduce Worry
	0900/1500 2100/0300	• Community Mental Health (Dr. Usha Ram)
Education	0930/1530	• Nature of Teaching
	2130/0330	• In Conversation with Sato - Kunio
	1000/1600	• Integral Pedagogy Process - 4 : Reflection
	2200/0400	• The Overhead Projector
	1030/1630	• Supporting Higher Education for Equity and Quality
	2230/0430	• Orchids of India : Lady's Slipper
	1100/1700 2300/0500	• English Grammar – Application of Figures of Speech of Poetry

Appendix-I (contd...)

	Saturday, 22nd March, 2008
Env. Sc.	• Exploring Eden : Madhuka • Environment Protection and Youth • God's Elephant • Hidden in the mist • Lakes in Tears • Management Control Energy - 2 • Green Worrier : Maruti Chitampalli - 2
Communication/Info. Sc.	• Some People Dream • Creation : India For The World • Development Communication - I • Technology Communication • Role of Mass Media and Popular Culture - I
Anthro/Medical Sc.	• In Communication with Sato Kuno • Feeling Good - 6 (Ayurvedic Medicine) • Function of Kidney and Physiology of Urine Formation • Fossil Evidence of Human Evolution : 2:4:1 • Haemoglobin : Structure and Blood Coagulation

	Time	*Sunday, 23rd March, 2008*
Music. Art/Cul.	0530/1130	• Baluchari Saree : The Best from the East
	1730/2330	• Khatamband
	0600/1200	• Raag Ranjan - Raag Charukishi
	1800/0000	
	0630/1230	• Tabla Sangeet Ka Atal Sathi - 8
	1830/0030	• Frozen in time - Glass sculpture
	0700/1300	• The Melody of Indian Notes : The Rarer The Sweeter
	1900/0100	• Malhaar Mahotsava – Dhulia Malhar - I
Technology	0730/1330	• Efficient Structural forms - I
	1930/0130	• Microwave Cooking
	0800/1400	• Searching the Frontiers - I
	2000/0200	• Pause and Ponder - Chemical Heart Beat
	0830/1430	• Courseware
	2030/0230	• Pause and Ponder - Chemical and Bio Luminescence
	0900/1500	• Recent Innovations in Short and Medium Span Bridges - 6
	2100/0300	• Wheel of Fortune
Career Watch	0930/1530	• Karate - The Combat Game
	2130/0330	• Electronic Books
	1000/1600	• Grooming The Grand Master
	2200/0400	• Career Update – Bio Informatics
	1030/1630	• Swarnim Itihaas Se Swarnim Bhavishya Ki Ore - 4
	2230/0430	• Career Update – Interior Designing
	1100/1700	• Fine Arts
	2300/0500	• Sports Karma – Hockey

Appendix-I (contd...)

	Monday, 24th March, 2008
Fine Arts	• Pena • Sandesh Ek Log Anek • Sampon Ka Khiladi • Special Effects in Photography • Indian Miniature Paintings • Grips Theatre
Maths	• Mathemajik • Algebra - Set of Functions • Correspondence Theorem (Dr. Ramji Lal) • Introduction to Calculus • Chemical Clock Reaction • Sub Group Generated by a Sub Set Cyclic Group (Dr. Ramji Lal)
Geography	• Rain, Rain Come Again • Electromagnetic Radiation • Climate - II • Sandesh Pani Ka • Glaciers - II • Soils of India

	Time	*Tuesday, 25th March, 2008*
History	0530/1130	• An Eternal Beautiful City : Bhopal
	1730/2330	• Stranger in Home Land
	0600/1200 1800/0000	• Shahis of Bijapur (B. Sheikh Ali)
	0630/1230	• Indian Historiography - 2
	1830/0030	• Non-Violence - Gandhi's View
	0700/1300 1900/0100	• The Marathas in South (T.K. Venkatsubramanian)
Eco./Comm.	0730/1330	• Organisational Behaviour - 1
	1930/0130	• Understanding WTO - I
	0800/1400 2000/0200	• Capital Market (Dr. Ramji Narayan)
	0830/1430 2030/0230	• Six Sigma
	0900/1500 2100/0300	• Determination of Supply : Elasticity of Supply (Prof. K. Roy Choudhary)
Zoology/Biology	0930/1530	• Month Ahead April, '08
	2130/0330	• Insect Migration
	1000/1600	• The Mammalian Heart - I
	2200/0400	• The Untrodden Niches
	1030/1630	• Saving the Sea Turtles
	2230/0430	• Fresh Water Aqua Culture - Learning to Grow with Fish - 1
	1100/1700 2300/0500	• Animal Sciences - Mastitis

Appendix-I (contd...)

	Wednesday, 26th March, 2008
Home. Sc.	• Flame of the Forest : Palash
	• Whenever You See Colours
	• Education of the Hearing Impaired (Dr. Mrs. N. Jaya)
	• Agriculture - 1 Home Grown Food
	• Vitamin D - Sunshine Asset
	• Heredity and Environment (Ms. N. S. Rohini)
Pol. Sc.	• Power - 1
	• Unitary and Federal System of Government (Prof. M.N. Menai)
	• Equality - 1
	• Liberty (Prof. M.N. Menai)
Botany/Agricul.	• The Lichens
	• Roots of Gold – The Chlorophylum
	• Joint Forest Mangement
	• Countryside Chronicle - 1
	• Apple Saga
	• Grainage - The Heart of Silk
	• Pushpa Krishi
	• Sahjan

	Time	*Thursday, 27th March, 2008*
Sociology	0530/1130	• Ek Gaon Aisa Bhi - Shani Shingna Pur
	1730/2330	• The Little Working Hands
	0600/1200	• Formulation of the Problems (Prof. B.K.B. Nayar)
	1800/0000	• Scheduled Castes Development - 2
	0630/1230	• Introduction to Sociology
	1830/0030	
	0700/1300	• Hypothesis (Prof. B.K.B. Nayar)
	1900/0100	
Physics	0730/1330	• Recent Trends in Cosmology
	1930/0130	• Megnetic Reversals
	0800/1400	• Vector Algebra - III (Prof. A.D. Gangal)
	2000/0200	
	0830/1430	• Angular Momentum - 2
	2030/0230	• Prof. Walter Kohn on Condensed Matter Physics
	0900/1500	• Additional Vector Concepts (Prof. A.D. Gangal)
	2100/0300	
Lang./Lit.	0930/1530	• Task and Gender - 2
	2130/0330	• Jab Uthe Hazaron Haath
	1000/1600	• Introduction to Sanskrit
	2200/0400	• Well Versed Poets in First Person - R. Rajarao
	1030/1630	• A Discussion on the Satire of Jonathan Swift (Gulliver's Travels)
	2230/0430	
	1100/1700	• Arms and the Man - 1
	2300/0500	• For they Stayed on

Appendix-I (contd...)

	Friday, 28th March, 2008
Chemistry	• Chemfun : Salt Hydrolysis • Glory of Glass • Rate of Chemical Reaction Depends Upon - Effect of Catalyst Applicaton of Electrical Conductivity Measurement in Solution • Exciting World of Hydrogels - 2 • Unusual Oxidation States • FRP – An Insight (Fibre Reinforced Plastic)
Psycho.	• Coping with Stress – 6 : Distancing and Selt Control • A World beyond Braile • Nature of Development (Prof. F. Tarapore) • Understanding Human Design • Don't Worry be Happy–5 : Worry Thinking is the Cause • Development and Related Concepts (Prof. F. Tarapore)
Education	• On Reaching the Parents : Optimum Development of the Individual • Shaping Young Minds • Integral Pedagogy Process-5 : Action and Evaluation • People's Organization from the Perspective of Self Reliance - 1 • A Unique Institute Yadavindra College of Engineering • Learning To Be • Strange Artistry

	Time	*Saturday, 29th March, 2008*
Env. Sc.	0530/1130	• Greening the Mining
	1730/2330	• Wild Life - In Communion with Nature
	0600/1200	• Eco-system – Predator and Prey Relationship
	1800/0000	• Why Conserve Wild Animals?
	0630/1230	• Symphony in Green
	1830/0030	
	0700/1300	• Broken Hearth
	1900/0100	
Communication/ Info. Sc.	0730/1330	• Pictorial Composition
	1930/0130	
	0800/1400	• Development Communication - II
	2000/0200	
	0830/1430	• Books Forever
	2030/0230	• Newspaper
	0900/1500	• Role of Mass Media and Popular
	2100/0300	Culture - II
Anthro./Medical Sc.	0930/1530	• The Riverine Gypsies
	2130/0330	• Feeling Good - 7 (Orthopaedics)
	1000/1600	• Blood Grouping
	2200/0400	
	1030/1630	• Fossil Evidence of Human Evolution : 2:4:2
	2230/0430	
	1100/1700	• Biology of Cancer
	2300/0500	

Appendix-I (contd...)

	Sunday, 30th March, 2008
Music Art./Cul.	• Melodious Encounters • Kathak - 1 : A Journey through History • Freedom of Expression in Art • Chavang Kut – An Autumn Festival • Raag Ranjan – Raag Bilas Khani Todi • Parampara Ki Tutati Kadi – Chirawa Khyal - 2 • Glimpses of Karnataka - II
Technology	• From Abstract to Concrete -1, Resolving Urban Issues • Wooden Imprints : Block Printing • Month Ahead April, '08 • Joys Micro Hydroelectrical Generator • Networks • Vigyan Rail : Science Museum on Wheels • The Queen of Stones - 1 • Microwave Antenna - I
Career Watch	• Uddan - III (Khanpan) • Bharatmuni's Natya Shastra • Quiz Show - III • Modelling as a Career • Japanese Languages as a Career - 1 • Masters in Business Management • Fitness Training as Careers

	Time	*Monday, 31st March, 2008*
Fine Arts	0530/1130 1730/2330	• Moibung • Popular Cartoonists - G.B. Trudeau
	0600/1200 1800/0000	• The Story of Indian Painting : Rajasthani Miniatures
	0630/1230	• Study of Indian Art History
	1830/0030	• Folklore Indian Context
	0700/1300	• Agni - A Dance Drama
	1900/0100	• Maand - An Echo of Ethos - 1
Maths	0730/1330	• Dissection of Some Triangles
	1930/0130	• Fermat's Last Theorem
	0800/1400 2000/0200	• Order of an Element of a Group (Dr. Ramji Lal)
	0830/1430	• Solving Integers in Equations - $ax^2 + by^2 + cz^2 = o$
	2030/0230	• Statistics for Microlevel planning
	0900/1500 2100/0300	• Coset Decomposition of Language Theorem (Dr. Ramji Lal)
Geography	0930/1530	• Month Ahead April, '08
	2130/0330	• Introduction to Seismology I
	1000/1600	• Irrigation
	2200/0400	• Preserving History
	1030/1630	• Seismic Waves and their Properties
	2230/0430	• Use and Scarcity of Water
	1100/1700 2300/0500	• Forest Wealth

Appendix -II

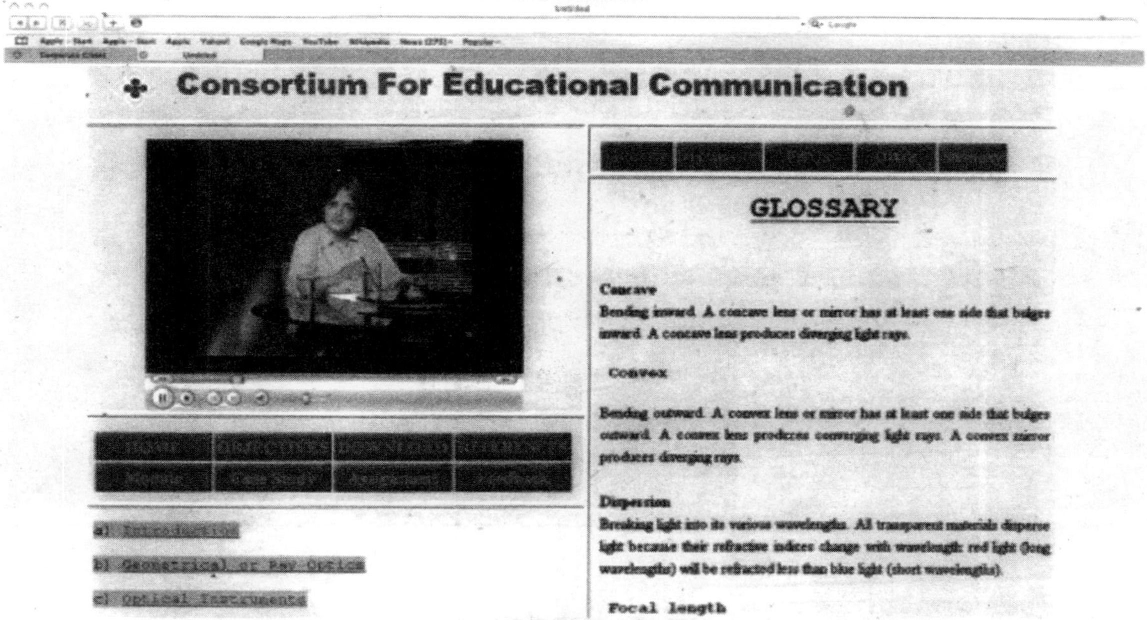

E-content template, used by Consortium for Education Communication (CEC), New Delhi.

Appendix -III

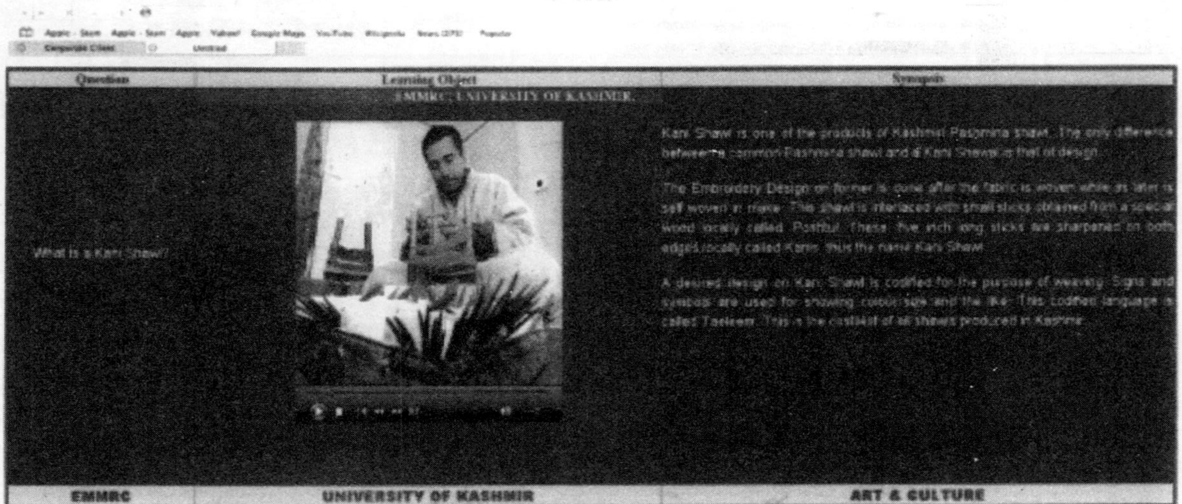

Learning object Repository (LOR) template used by Consortium for Educational Communication, New Delhi.

APPENDIX IV

Questionnaire

Name

Designation

Name of the Organisation

Address

1. Have you seen any of the educational television Channels?

   (a) VYAS —The higher educational channel of UGC
   (b) Gyandarshan of IGNOU
   (c) EKLAVYA of IITs
   (d) UGC Countrywide Classroom Programmes on DD
   (e) All of the above
   (f) None of the above
   (g) Any other please specify...........

2. If you have not seen any of the above channels, please state which of the following do you think are the reasons ?

   (a) Not interested in ETV programmes
   (b) The programmes are boring
   (c) Not aware about the ETV Channels
   (d) Not available in our area
   (e) Does not feel watching television for education
   (f) Any other (Please Specify).....................................
   ....

3. If you have seen how do you feel about these ETV channels:

   (a) They are going on nicely and I enjoy watching them
   (b) The programmes are not up to the mark
   (c) The transmission quality is poor
   (d) The channels are not given proper professional presentation
   (e) The channels should be clubbed together for one ETV Channel
   (f) The channels are underutilized
   (g) Any other, please specify

4. "Television is a very good medium of Education".

   (a) Strongly agree
   (b) Agree
   (c) Partially agree
   (d) Disagree
   (e) Strongly Disagree

5. 'Television viewing is a passive activity', therefore, television cannot be called a good medium of education :

   (a) Strongly agree
   (b) Agree
   (c) Partially agree
   (d) Disagree
   (e) Strongly Disagree

6. The potential of television, as a medium of education is :

   (a) Fully utilized
   (b) Partially utilized
   (c) Not utilized at all

   If television is underutilized or not utilized for education, who in your opinion is responsible. (Tick all those who appear relevant to you)

(a) The programme makers
(b) The programme telecasters
(c) Students
(d) Teachers
(e) Parents
(f) All of the above
(g) None of the above
(h) Any other

If the answer is not 'f' then please elaborate how do you think they are responsible?

7. ETV programmes are not being watched by the target audience because of :
(Please arrange in order of ranking 1-10, one is the most appropriate)

(a) Poor quality of programmes
(b) Poor transmission of programmes
(c) Inappropriate timings
(d) Poor publicity of transmission schedules
(e) Tough competition from informational and entertainment programmes
(f) Invasion of the cable
(g) One-way communication /Lack of interaction
(h) Too much content in the programmes
(i) Less content —The student needs are not met
(j) The students are not motivated to see TV for education

8. Television can effectively be used for education by :
Please Check (√) all you find relevant.

(a) making it more interactive,
(b) making more syllabi oriented programmes
(c) involving experts/teachers of national international repute

(d) Making programmes that are visually rich and sleek
(e) Laying more emphasis on content than the sleekness
(f) Making more enrichment type Programmes
(g) Any Other Specify....................

9. How do you think television can effectively be used for education ?

10. Some people believe educational television should broadcast enrichment type of programmes, others feel it can be used better for syllabi oriented programming. What do you think about it ?

11. How can we make better use of "IDIOT BOX" as a tool of Education ?

12. Do you think an educational television channel will be useful to the students and teachers ?

13. What is the future of television as medium of communication, can it be economically viable to run an exclusive educational channel in private sector, if yes how ?

14. If it is not going to be economically viable then how do you think should an educational television channel be financed and made available to the students.

15. How do you feel about educational channels like Gyandarshan of IGNOU, VYAS —The higher educational channel of CEC/UGC, EKLAVYA of IITs ?

16. How can an educational channel be made useful for education ?

17. What are the reasons we have not yet been able to think of television as a partner in education ?

18. Do you see a role for technology and television in higher education in India ?

19. What is the future and scope of ETV in India ?

20. What are the major problems facing educational television in India ?

21. What advice will you offer to educational planners, policy-makers, broadcasters, students, teachers and the parents for better utilization of TV as a medium of education ?

Appendix -V

E-Content Template of EMMRC, Srinagar

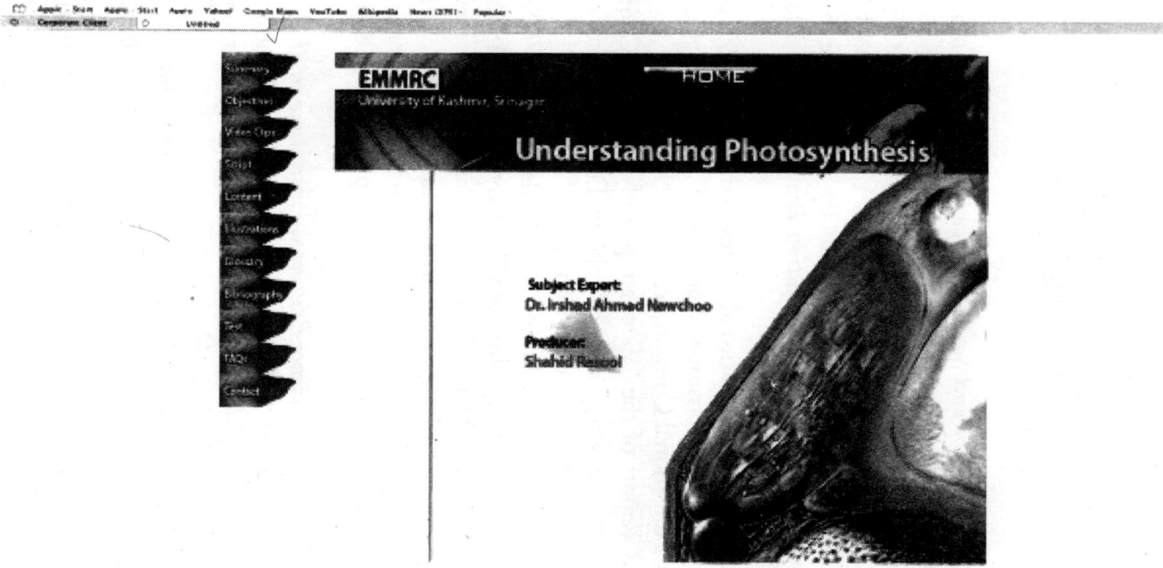

E-content template, generated at Educational Multimedia Research Centre, University of Kashmir, Srinagar.

Bibliography

Aaliya, A. *Television and Social Change.* Srinagar : Computer City, 2000.

Abramson, Jeffrey B., Christopher Arterton, and Gary Orren, (eds.) *The Electronic Commonwealth.* New York: Basic Books, 1988.

Acker, S. "Viewers perception of velocity and distance in televised events". *Human Communication Research.* 9, 4. 1983 : 335-348.

ADMAR Report of National "Viewership Study 97 on UGC Countrywide Classroom Programmes". New Delhi: Consortium for Educational Communication, 1997.

ADMAR Report of the "Viewership study on UGC Countrywide Classroom Programmes". New Delhi: Consortium for Educational Communication, 1993.

Agarwal, Binod, C. and Arbind Sinha (eds.) *SITE to INSAT.* New Delhi : Concept Publishing Company Pvt. Ltd., 1986.

Aggarwal B.C. and M.R. Malek. *Television in Kheda.* New Delhi: Concept Publishing Company Pvt. Ltd., 1986.

Aggarwal, Binod C. *SITE Social Evaluation : Results, Experiences, and Implications.* Ahmedabad : Space Application Centre ISRO, 1981.

Aghi, M.B. *Impact of Science Education Programme on SITE Children of Rajasthan.* Ahmedabad : Space Application Centre, 1977.

Agrawal, C. Binod. *Television Comes to Village : An Evaluation of SITE.* Bangalore : ISRO, 1978.

Akutsu, Y. "An analysis of factors related to use of school television at the elementary level". *The Japanese Journal of Radio-TV Education.* 1971: 69-80.

Anderson, C.M. "In Search of a Visual Rhetoric of Instructional Television". *AV Communication Review.* 20, 1972 : 43-63.

Anderson, D.R. and Levin, S.R. Young children's attention to "Sesame Street", *Child Development,* 47, 1976, 806-811.

Archer, W. "Delivering university-level communication programs at a distance : Benefits, costs and disruptions. *Canadian Journal of Educational Communication.* 24, 1999: 369-383.

Arnheim, R. *Art and Visual Perception.* Berkeley: University of California Press, 1974.

Arulchelvan, S. and D. Vishwanathan. "Pattern of usage of various electronic media by higher education students". *International Journal of Education and Development using Information and Communication Technology (IJEDICT)*, 2, 4, 2006: 100-118.

Bagdikian, Ben. *Media Monopoly.* Boston: Beacon, 1987.

Baggaley, J.P. and S. W. Duck. *Dynamics of Television.* Farnborough : Saxon House, 1976.

Baker, R.A., and Hansford, B. Evaluation of a cross-campus interactive video teaching trial. *Distance Education.* 11, 2, 1990, 286-307.

Ball, S. and G.A. Bogatz. *The First Year of 'Sesame Street': An Evaluation.* Princeton, N.J.: Educational Testing Service, 1970.

Barcus, Earl. *Images of Life on Children's Television.* New York : Praeger, 1983.

Barnouw, Erik. *Tube of Plenty : The Evolution of American Television,* 2nd ed. New York : Oxford University Press, 1990.

Batės, A. W. *Television, Learning and Distance Education.* Milton Keynes, UK: The Open University, Institute of Educational Technology, 1987.

——, "Towards a better Theoretical Framework for studying learning from Educational Television". *Instructional Science,* 9, 1980 : 393-415.

——, *Technology, Open Learning and Distance Education.* London : Routledge, 1995.

Bayline, L. "Mass Media and Children : A study of exposure habits and cognitive effects". *Psychological Monograph,* 73. Whole No. 471 1950.

Behera, S.C. *Educational Television Programmes : Impact on Teachers Competency.* New Delhi: Deep & Deep Publications, 1991.

Belson, W.A. *The Impact of Television.* Melbourne : Cheshire, 1967.

Berger, Arthur Asa. *Media USA.* New York : Longman, 1991.

Berman, Ronald. *How Television sees its Audience.* New York : Sage Publications, 1987.

Bernard, R.M. and G. O. Coldevin. "Effects of recap strategies on television news recall and retention". *Journal of Broadcasting and Electronic Media*, 29, 4. 1985: 407-419.

Berry, C. "A dual effect of pictorial enrichment in learning from television News: Gunter's date revisited". *Journal of Educational Television*, 9, 3. 1983: 171-174.

Berry, Gordon, and Joy Asamen. *Children and Television.* Newbury Park, Calif: Sage Publications, 1993.

Beville, Hugh. *Audience Ratings: Radio, Television, Cable.* Hillsdale, N J: Lawrence Erlbaum, 1988.

Bhaskaran, P. and I. Patel. *SITE for Children: Morning Feedback.* Mimeographed, Ahmedabad: Space Applications Centre, 1977.

Blosser, B.J. "Television reading and oral language development : The case of Hispanic child". *Journal of the National Association for Bilingual Education.* 13, 1988: 21-42.

Boverie, P.; W.G Murrell; C.A Lowe; R.H Zettl; and C. H. Gunawardena. *Live versus Taped: New Perspective in Satellite Based Programming for Primary Grades.* Albuquerque : University of Mexico, 1997.

Brand, Stewart. *The Media Lab: Inventing the Future at MIT.* London: Penguin Books, 1988.

Branscomb, Anne. *Who Owns Information: From Privacy to Public Access.* New York : Basic Books, Harper Collins, 1994.

Brayant, J., and D.R. Anderson (Eds.). *Children's Understanding of Television.* New York: Academic Press, 1983.

Brian Groombridge. Television and the People. Middlesex England : Penguin Books Ltd., 1972.

Brock, P.A. *Educational Technology in the Classroom.* Engelwood Cliffs, NJ: Educational Technology Publications, 1994.

Brody, E.W. *Communication Tomorrow : New Audience, New Technologies, New Media.* New York : Praeger, 1990.

Bryant, Jennings. *Television and the America Family.* Hillsdale, N.J.: Lawrence Erlbaum, 1990.

Cantor Muriel G. *Prime Time Television.* California : Sage Publications, 1980

Carnegie Commission USA. *Report on Educational Television in USA.* New York: Carnegie Corporation, 1967.

CEC, "Consortium for Educational Communication". *Project Report.* New Delhi : Consortium for Educational Communication, 1993.

Chandra, R. and K. Karnik. *Planning for Satellite Broadcasting : The Indian Instructional Television Experiment*. Paris: UNESCO, 1976.

Childers, P. and J. Ross. "The relationship between Television and student's achievement". *Journal of Educational Research*, 66, 1973: 317-319.

Choat, E.; H. Griffin; and D. Hobart. "Educational TV and the curriculum for children up to the age of seven years". *British Journal of Educational Technology*, 17, 3, London Council of Educational Technology. October, 1986: 53-66.

Chu, G.C. and W. Schramm. *Learning from Television : What the Research Says*. Stanford, CA: Institute for Communication Research, 1967.

Clark, W.J. *Off Children and Television.* Cincinnati OH : Xavier University, 1951.

Coffin, T.E. "Television's Impact on Society". *American Psychlogist.* 10, 1955: 630-641.

Coldevin, G. "Experimentation in TV presentation strategies II: Effectiveness of Full Screen *vs.* Corner Screen, symbol establishment background visuals". *Educational Broadcasting International.* 23, 1978 : 289-303.

——, "Spaced, massed and summary treatments as review strategies, for ITV production". *AV Communication Review.* 23, 1975 : 289-303.

Comstock, George; Steven Chaffee; Natan Katzman; Maxwell Mccombs; and Donald Roberts, *Television and Human Behaviour.* New York: Columbia University Press, 1978.

Comstock, G. *Television and the American Child.* San Diago: Academic Press, 1991.

Conrad, Peter. *Television : The Medium and its Manner.* Boston: Routledge and Kegan Paul, 1982.

Consortium for Educational Communication. *Annual Report 2005-06.* New Delhi : CEC, 2006.

Corporation for Public Broadcasting. *Strategies for Public Television in a Multi-Channel Environment.* Washington, D.C., PB, 1991.

Cronbach, L.J. "Beyond the two disciplines of Scientific Psychology." *American Psychologist.* 1975. 116-127.

Cuban, Larry. *Oversold and Underused : Computers in the Classroom.* Harvard University Press, 2001.

Czitrom, Daniel J. *Media and the American Mind : From Morse to McLuhan.* Chapel Hill : University of North Carolina Press, 1982.

D. R. Olson, (Ed.). *Media and Symbols : The Forms of Expression, Communication and Education.* Chicago: University Press. 1974.

Dennis, Everette E. *Of Media and People.* Newbury Park, Calif: Sage, 1992.

Dertouzos, Michael, and Joel Moses. *The Computer Age.* Cambridge: Massachusetts Institute of Technology Press, 1979.

DeSonne, Marcia. *Spectrum of New Broadcast/Media Technologies.* National Association of Broadcasters, Washington, D.C., March 1990.

Dizard, Wilson Jr. *Old Media New Media*, 2nd Ed., New York: Longman Publishers, 1997.

Dizard, Wilson P. *Television : A World View.* Syracuse, NY : Syracuse University Press, 1966.

Dizard. *The Coming Information Age.* 3rd ed., New York: Longman, 1989.

Dobb, A. and G.E Macdonald. "Television Viewing and fear of victimization – Is the relationship casual". *Journal of Personality and Social Psychology*, 37, 1979.

Dominick, Joseph; Barry Sherman; and Gary Copeland. *Broadcasting/Cable and Beyond,* 3rd ed., New York : McGraw Hill, 1996.

Dorr, A. "Television and effective development and functioning : May be this decade". *Journal of Broadcasting*, 25, 1981: 335-345.

Drew, D. G. and T. Grimes."Audio-Visual redundancy and TV news recall". *Communication Research*, 14, 4, 1978 : 17-26.

Dublin, J. and T. Hedley (1969). "Interactivity in Instructional Television, in *The SITE Experience No. (9). The Reports and Papers on Mass Communication.* Paris: UNESCO, 1983.

Dwyer, M.F. "Colour as an Instructional Variable". *AV Communications Review*. 18, 1971: 399-416.

E. L. Palmer and A. Darr (Eds.). *Children and Three Faces of Television — Teaching, Violence and Selling.* New York: Academic Press, 1980

Edwardson, M.; D. Grooms; and S. Proadlove. "Talking news information gain from interesting video *vs.* talking heads". *Journal of Broadcasting*, 25, 17, 1981: 367-378.

Edwardson, M.; K. Kent; & M. McConnel. "Television new information gain : Video text *versus* a talking head". *Journal of Broadcasting.* 29, 4, 1985 : 367-378

Ellery, J.B. *A Pilot Study of the Nature of Aesthetic Experience Associated with Television and its Place in Education.* Detroit: Wayne State University, 1959.

Emery, E.; P.E. Ault; and W.K. Ager. *Introduction to Mass Communication.* Bombay: Vakils, Feffer and Simons Pvt. Ltd., 1955.

Fidler, Roger, *Mediamorphosis : Understanding New Media*, California : Pine Forge Press, 1997.

Findahl, O. and B. Hoijer. *Fragments of Reality : An Experiment with News and TV News.* Stockholm : Swedish Broadcasting Corporation, 1976.

Fiske, John and Hartley John. *Reading Television.* New York : Methuen & Co., 1978.

Flood, J. and D. Lapp. "Television and Reading : Refocusing the Debate". *The Reading Teacher*, 49, 2, 1995 : 160-164.

Ford Foundation. *Attitudes Towards Instructional Television*, New York : International Research Associates, Inc., 1965.

Fowles, Jib. *Why Viewers Watch.* Newbury Park, Calif : Sage, 1992.

Friedman, Thomas L. *The World is Flat: A Brief History of The Twenty-first Century.* Farrar: Straus Giroux, 2005.

Furu, T. *The Functions of Television for Children and Adolescents.* Tokyo: Sophia University Press, 1971.

Gagne, R. M. *The Conditions of Learning.* NewYork : Holt Rhinehart and Winston, 1965.

Gandhi, V.P. *Media and Communications Today: Policy, Training and Development.* 2, New Delhi : Kanishka Publishers Distributors, 1995.

Gates, Bill. *The Road Ahead.* New York: Viking, 1995.

Gerhard Tulodziecki, "Educational Television in Federal Republic of Germany", *Programmed Learning and Educational Technology,* 14, May 1977.

Gilbert Seldes. "ETV's Community Job" *Educational Television : The Next Ten Years.* Standford : The Institution for Communication Research, 1962.

Gilder, George. *Life after Television.* New York : W. W. Norton, 1992.

Gordon, G. N. *Classroom Television : New Frontiers in ITV.* New York: Hastings House Publication, 1970.

Gordon, G. N. *Educational Television.* New York : The Centre for Applied Research in Education, 1960.

Gordon, George N. *Classroom Television : New Frontiers in ITV.* New York : Communication Art Books, 1970.

Govindaraju, P. *Educational Television (ETV) in Higher Education : An Evaluation of UGC Countrywide Classroom.* Madras : Audio Visual Research Centre, Anna University, 1996.

Govindaraju, P. *Research Report* : 6, *Programme Evaluation Series II,* Madras : Audio Visual Research Centre, Anna University, 1993.

Gowds, H. and H. Anniah. *The Idiot Box.* New Delhi : Sterling Publishers, 1987.

Grant, T.S. and I. R. Merill, "Camera Placement for Recognition of Complex Behaviours". *Television in Health Science Education.* Washington: US Office of Education, 1963.

Greenhill, L.P. *TV in University Science Instruction.* Pennsylvania : State University of Pennsylvania, 1959.

Gunter, B. "Recall of brief television news items : Effects of presentation mode, picture content and serial position". *Journal of Educational Television,* 5, 2, 1979: 57-61.

Hartley, G. and P. Burnhill. "Fifty guidelines for improving instructional text". *Programmed Learning and Educational Technology.* 14, 1 1977, 65-73.

Herminghaus, E.G. "Large Group Instruction Television by Television and Experiment", *School Review.* 1957. 119-133

Himmelweit, H.; A. N. Oppenheim; and P. Vince. *The Television and the Child –An Empirical Study of the Effects of Television on the Young.* London: Oxford University Press, 1958.

Husain, M. *Distance Education through Television.* New Delhi : Anmol Publications Pvt. Ltd., 2004.

Idrus, R. "Collaborative learning through teletutorials". *British Journal of Educational Technology,* 24, 3, 1993 : 179-184.

Jan, Salima. *Regional Report on VYAS Channel.* Srinagar: Educational Multimedia Research Centre, University of Kashmir, 2007.

John Cary. "Plato at keyboard: Telecommunication technology and education policy". *Electronic Links for Learning.* 514 ed. Vivian M. Horner & Linda G. Roberts, 1991.

Johnson, G.N. and F. Harty. *The Norfolk City Experiment in Instructional Television: The Big Picture, September, 1957, June 1960,* Norfolk, Va: *Vision Project*, 1960.

Joshi, S. R. and B. Trivedi. *Engineering Education through Satellite: an Evaluation Study of ISRO-IETE Experiment.* Ahmedabad : Applications Centre, Indian Space Research Organization, 1992.

Kalam, A.P.J. Abdul and Y.S. Rajan. *India 2020: A Vision for the New Millennium.* New Delhi: Penguin, 2003.

Kellner, Douglas. *Television and the Crisis of Democracy.* Boulder, Colo: Westview, 1990.

Khan, M.I. and S.R. Sharma. *Instructional Technology : Media and Theory*. New Delhi: Kanishka Publishers and Distributors, 1993

Kinder, James S. *Audio Visual Materials : Television.* New York : American Book Company, 1959.

Kipper, P. "Television camera movement as a source of perceptual information". *Journal of Broadcasting and Electronic Media.* 30, 1986 : 295-307.

Kirkwood, A. "Into the Video Age : Open University Television in the 1990s", *Journal of Educational Television,* 16, 2, 1990, 77-85.

Kozma, R.B. "Learning with Media". *Review of Educational Research..* 61, 2, 1991: 179-211.

Kubey, Robert, and Mihaly Csikszentmihalyi, *Television and the Quality of Life.* Hillsdale, NJ: Lawrence Erlbaum, 1990.

Kumar, Usha. *Postproduction Feedback Report, on Fibonacci Numbers Part 1,* Roorkee: Audio Visual Research Centre, University of Roorkee, 1990.

Kumari, Abhilasha and Athar Ali. *Monitoring Report -1,* New Delhi : Mass Communication Research Centre, Jamia Millia Islamia, July 1991.

Kumari, Abhilasha and Athar Ali. *Programme Evaluation Series Report-1* New Delhi: Mass Communication Research Centre, Jamia Millia Islamia, Jan 1991.

Levin, H.M. "Cost effectiveness and educational policy". *Educational Evaluation and Policy Analysis,* 10, 1, Spring 1988 : 51-69.

Levy, Mark, and Barrie Gunter. *Home Video and the Changing Nature of the Television Audience.* IBA Television research monograph. London: John Libbey, 1988.

Liebert, Robert M. and Joyce Sprafkin. *The Early Window : Effects of Television on Children and Youth*, 3rd ed., New York: Pergamon Press, 1988.

Lifebert, Robert M.; John Neale; and Family Davidson. *The Early Window : Effects of Television on Children and Youth.* New York : Pergamon Press, 1988.

Livingstone, Sonia M. *Making Sense of Television.* Oxford : Pergamon Press, 1990.

Lombard, M.; R. Reich; M. Grabe; M. C. Bracken; and T. Ditton. "Presence and television : The role of screen size". *Journal of Broadcasting,* 26, 1, 2000:75-98

Madhu, K.P. "Use of Satellites for Education". *A Report.* Kuala Lumpur: Asia-Pacific Institute for Broadcasting Development, 2007.

Mandell, L.M. and D. L. Shaw. "Judging people in news – Unconsciously : Effect of camera angle and bodily activity", *Journal of Broadcasting,* 17, 1973 : 353-362.

Masterman, Len. *Teaching about Television.* London : The McMillan Press Ltd., 1980.

McLuhan, M.C. Understanding Media : The extension of man. London : Routledge and Kegan Paul, 1964.

McQuail, Denis. *Media Performance : Mass Communication and the Public Interest.* Newbury Park, Calif : Sage, 1992.

Metallinos, N. "Children's Perception, Retention and Preference of Asymmetrical Composition in Pictures". *Canadian Journal of Communications.* 13, 1984 : 10-15.

Metallinos, N. and R. K. Tiemens. "Asymmetry of the screen : The effect of left *versus* right placement on television images", *Journal of Broadcasting,* 21, 1, 1977: 21-33.

Millerson, G. *The Technique of Television Production.* New York : Hasting House Publication, 1972.

Minow, Newton. *How Vast the Wasteland Now ?* Columbia : Freedom Forum Media Studies Center, Columbia University, 1991.

Mishra, Rajendra. *Countrywide Classroom : Feedback Study from Himachal Pradesh.* New Delhi: UGC, INSAT TV Project, Teachers Training College, Jamia Milia Islamia, 1990.

Mohanty J. *Educational Broadcasting : Radio and Television in Education.* New Delhi : Sterling Publishers, 1984.

Moody, Kate. *Growing up on Television.* New York : Times Book Co., 1988.

Moris, J.D. "Florida Study : Improving achievements through the use of more dynamics in TV production.", *Technological Horizons in Education*, 12, 3, 1984 : 104-107.

Mosco, Vincent. *The Pay-Per Society : Computers and Communication in the Information Age.* Norwood, N.J.: Ablex, 1989.

Murray, Janet. *Hamlet on the Holodeck: The Future of Narrative in Cyberspace*, Massachusetts: MIT Press, 1997.

Narayanan, Andal. *Impact of Television on its Viewers.* Bombay: Somiaya Publications, 1987.

Neilson, J. "Does the background affect televised message reception"? *Educational and Instructional Television*, 11, 2, 1979 : 61-64.

Neuman, W. Russell. *The Future of the Mass Audience.* New York : Cambridge University Press, 1992.

Neurath, P. "School Television in Delhi". New Delhi: All-India Radio, 1966.

New Comb, Horace, (ed.). *Television : The Critical View.* New York : Oxford University Press, 1982.

Noam, Eli. *Television in Europe.* New York: Oxford University Press, 1991.

Ogawa, T. *Learning from Educational Television.* Nagano City, Japan: Institute for Educational Research, 1963.

Oskamp, Stuart. *Television as a Social Issue.* California : Sage Publications, 1988.

Pendharkar, Sushama. *Profile of the UGC's Countrywide Classroom : A Feedback Survey of Universities in the State of Maharashtra.* Pune : EMRC, University of Pune, 1988.

Pezdek, K. and E. Stevens. "Children's memory for auditory and visual information on television". *Developmental Psychology*, 20, 1-3, 1984 : 212-218.

Phutela, R.L. *A Study into Utilization and Comprehensibility of School Television Programmes in Delhi.* Mimeographed. New Delhi : CIET, NCERT, 1984.

Picciano, A.G. *Educational Leadership and Planning for Technology.* Third edition. Columbus, OH: Upper Saddle River, 2002.

Rani, Usha N. *Educational Television in India–Challenges and Issues* New Delhi: Discovery Publishing House, 2006.

Rao, Jagadeeshwar. *Needs and Expectations of Primary Target Viewers of Countrywide Classroom Programmes : A Research Report.* Hyderabad : Audio Visual Research Centre, Osmania University, 2004.

Rao, Jagadeeshwar. *Needs Assessment and Reasons for Non-viewing of Countrywide Classroom Programmes, A Research Report.* Hyderabad : Audio Visual Research Centre. Osmania University 1998.

Rasool, Shahid. "Television Violence and its effects on children and teenagers – The global perspective" *INSIGHT Journal of Applied Research in Education*, 9, 1. Srinagar: Faculty of Education, University of Kashmir, 2004 : 125-140.

Razel, Micha "The complex model of television viewing and educational achievement". *The Journal of Educational Research*, 94, 6, 2001: 371-379

Reddi, Usha Vyasulu., "*Educational Broadcasting in the Commonwealth*", New Delhi: COL-CEMCA 2003

Reddi, U. Television in higher education : The Indian experience, *Media in Education and Development,* 1987, 128-133.

Reddi, Usha V. and others. *Final Report, CEC-IGNOU-ISRO National Talkback Experiment, New Information and Communication Technologies.* New Delhi: UGC Media Centre and the Consortium for Educational Communication, 1995.

Rheingold, Howard. *Virtual Reality.* New York: Summit Books, 1991.

Robert Coonrad. Television goes to school : The impact of video on students learning in formal education. *A Report.* New York: EDC's centre for children and technology, 2004.

Rosengren, K.E., & S. Windahl. *Media Matter: TV Use in Childhood and Adolescence.* Norwood, NJ: Ablex, 1989.

Russell, T.L. Interactivity in television-based learning : Is it necessary ? *Open Learning,* 4, 3, 1984, 56-7.

Sakornia, H.J. *Television and Society.* New York: McGraw Hill Publications, 1965.

Salomon, G. & A. A. Cohen. "Television formats, mastery of mental skills and the acquisition of knowledge". *Journal of Educational Psychology,* 69, 1977: 612-619.

Scarborough, H.S. "Prediction of reading disability from familial and individual differences". *Journal of Educational Psychology,* 81, 1989 :101-108.

Schlater, R. "Effect of speed of presentation on recall of television messages". *Journal of Broadcasting* 14. 1970 : 207-214.

Schneider, Cy. *Children's Television.* Lincolnwood : NTC Publishing, 1991.

Schramm, W. *What we know about learning from Instructional Television, Educational Television: The Next 10 Years.* Stanford, CA: Institute of Communication Research, 1982.

Schramm, W.; J. Lyle; and E.B Parker. *Television in the Lives of Our Children.* Stanford: Stanford University Press, 1961.

Schramm, Wilbur. *Big Media, Little Media.* California: Sage Publications, 1977.

Schramm,Wilbur. *The Impact of Educational Television.* Urbana Ill: University of Illinois Press, 1960.

Scott, L.F. "Television and School Achievement". *Phi Delta Kappan* 38, 1956: 25-28.

Shapio and Varian. *Information Rules : A Strategic Guide to the Network Economy*, Harvard : Business School Press, 1999.

Shukla, S. and K. Kumar. *Satellite Instructional Television Experiment : Impact of SITE on Primary School Children.* Bangalore : Indian Space Research Organisation, August, 1977.

Singh J. and A.K. Singh. *A Study of the Impact of ETV Programmes on the Children of Classes IV-V in Sambalpur District (Orissa).* INSAT Evaluation Series-3. Mimeographed, New Delhi: CIET, NCERT, July 1983.

Singh, J. *A Report on ETV Utilization with Special Reference to TV Maintenance in Sumbalpur.* INSAT Evaluation Series-2. Mimeographed, New Delhi: CIET, NCERT, 1983.

Singh, J. and A.K Singh. *Reports of the ETV Utilization in Orissa* (Period ending December 1983). Evaluation series-4, Mimeographed, New Delhi: CIET, NCERT, 1984.

Singh, J. and A.K Singh. *A Study of the Impact ETC Programmes on Children of Classes IV to V, in Sambalpur District Orrisa.* INSAT Evaluation series-3, Mimeographed. New Delhi, CIET, NCERT, 1983.

Singh, J.; S. Prasad; A. Bajpai; and R. J. Kuar. *Pre-telecast Testing of the ETV Programmes : Some Observations.* INSAT Evaluation Series, Mimeographed. New Delhi: CIET, NCERT, 1984.

Singletary, Michael. *Mass Communication Research..* New York: Longman, 1994.

Skinner, B.F. "The Teaching Machine." *Science*, 128, 3330, October 24.

Skornia, Harry J. *Television and Society.* New York: McGraw Hill Publication, 1965.

Smith, Leslie. *Perspectives on Radio and Television.* New York : Harper & Row, 1990

Son, J., S. Reese, & W. Davie. "Effects of visual-verbal redundancy and recaps on television news learning". *Journal of Broadcasting and Electronic Media*, 31, 2, 1987: 207-216.

St. Peters, M.; M. Fitch; A.C. Huston; J.C. Wright; and D.J. Eakins, "Television and families : What do young children watch with their parents". *Child Development,* 62, 1991, 1409-1423.

Sterling Christopher H., *Electronic Media.* New York: Praeger; 1984.

Stoll, Clifford. *Silicon Snake Oil : Second Thoughts on the Information Highway.* New York: Doubleday, 1995.

Straubhaar, Joseph, and Robert LaRose. *Communications Media in the Information Society.* Belmont, Calif.: Wadsworth, 1996.

Thompson, F.T. & W. P. Austin. "Television viewing and academic achievements revisited". Education. *Chula Vista,* CA 124, 1, 194-202. Fall, 2003.

Tiemen, R.K. "Some relationships of camera angle to communicator credibility". *Journal of Broadcasting.* 14, 1970: 483-490.

Toffler, Alvin. *The Third Wave : The Classic Study of Tomorrow.* New York : William Morrow, 1980.

Trivedi, Harshad R. *Mass Media and New Horizons.* New Delhi: Concept Publishing Company, 1991.

Turow, Joseph, *Breaking Up America : Advertisers and the New Media World.* Chicago: University of Chicago Press, 1997.

Turow, Joseph. *Media Systems in Society.* New York: Longman, 1992.

Underwood, Doug. *When MBAs Rule the Newsroom: How Marketers and Managers are Reshaping Today's Media.* New York: Columbia University Press, 1993.

Van Evra, Judith. *Television and Child Development.* Hillsdale, N.J. Lawrence Erlbaum, 1990.

Vittal, N. and S. Mahalingam. *Information Technology–India's Tomorrow.* New Delhi: Manas Publications, 2001.

Wagmare, S.K. *Audio Visual Education.* New Delhi: Metropolitan Book Co. Pvt. Ltd., 1992.

Walsh, J., and Reese, B. "Distance learning's growing reach", *Technological Horizons in Education,* 22, 11, 1995, 58-62.

Wasko, Janet. *Hollywood in the Information Age.* Texas : University of Texas Press, 1994.

Wildman, S.S. and S.E. Siwek. *International Trade in Films and Television Programs.* Cambridge, Mass.: Ballinger Books, 1988.

Williams, P.A.; E.H. Haertel; G.D. Haertel; & H.J. Walberg. "The impact of leisure time television on school learning : A research synthesis". *American Educational Research Journal*, 19, 1982 : 19-50.

Williams, T. M. *The Impact of Television: A Natural Experiment in Three Communities.* New York : Academic Press, 1986.

Willis, Edgar, and Henry Aldridge. *Television, Cable and Radio.* Englewood Cliffs, NJ: Prentice-Hall, 1992.

Wimmer, Roger and Joseph Doinick, *Mass Media Research : An Introduction.* Belmont, Calif: Wadsworth, 1994.

Wittich, W.A. and C.F. Schullar. *Audio Visual Material : Their Nature and Use.* New York: Harper and Row Publishers, 1968.

Wriston, Walter B. *The Twilight of Sovereignty: How the Information Revolution is Transforming Our World.* New York: Scribner, 1992.

Wurtzel, A.H. and J. R. Dominic. "An evaluation of television Drama: Interaction of acting styles and shot selection". *Journal of Broadcasting*, 16, 1972 : 103-110.

Zettl, H. "The rare case of television aesthetics", *Journal of the University Film Association,* Montreal, 3, 1978.

Zettl, H. *Sight, Sound, Motion : Applied Media aesthetics,* Bellmont, Calif: Wadsworth Publishing, 1973.

Index